A Dame Abroad

A Dame Abroad

by

DAME SHEILA QUINN

The Memoir Club

First published in 2004 by
The Memoir Club
Stanhope Old Hall
Stanhope
Weardale
County Durham

British Library Cataloguing in
Publication Data.
A catalogue record for this book
is available from the
British Library.

ISBN: 1 84104 077 0

Typeset by George Wishart & Associates, Whitley Bay.
Printed by CPI, Bath.

*To the nurses of the world with whom
it has been my privilege to work*

Acknowledgements

To Sue Russell, my partner in Europe, for reading the whole text, and particularly for checking the accuracy of accounts of the work we did together and the many formal documents involved. Shelagh Murphy followed in my footsteps on the ICN board, and searched their records at times when my memory failed me, and both gave their continual encouragement. Betty Knox, my successor as Chief Nursing Officer of the Southampton University Hospitals, filled me in on dates and places in eventful years for the NHS in the early eighties. Ron Staker of the Brendoncare Foundation and Brian Stevens of SCA Community Care helped me to condense the task we shared in helping to bring those two organisations from infancy to maturity into a few pages. The Royal College of Nursing has been generous in allowing the use of photographs from its archives, and those of my earlier life were taken by the late G.J. France of Blackpool, who was a friend as well as photographer.

Bega Hood has been my 'family' for many decades and has given unswerving encouragement throughout my professional life, and particularly during these twelve months of writing. Lastly, for Mary who was always persuading me to write this account and who, although she didn't live to read it, has been in my thoughts so much during the writing.

After resisting requests to write a book for a number of years and viewing the task with some horror at the start, I found that the years gone by came to life again and I thoroughly enjoyed re-living my journey. This is largely due to Eileen Finlayson, my editor, and the staff of The Memoir Club, who made the whole process appear simple and were encouraging in their suggested amendments.

Perhaps the last word belongs to the profession which I love and the hundreds of friends I have made around the world who have passed through these pages.

Contents

Illustrations

Foreword

TWENTY YEARS AGO I was invited by the British Council to join four other British nurses for a lecture tour of China. The leader of our group was Sheila Quinn, then the President of the Royal College of Nursing whom I had seen from afar and admired for her ability, particularly her speeches to the RCN Congresses which she delivered fluently without notes. The visit to China was special: few English people had made such a journey, there were few cars, tall buildings or tourists although you could feel the country changing. It was an exciting tour learning a great deal about China's nurses and their health care.

I was impressed by Sheila Quinn's ambassadorial talents: she always knew how to address the people we met; she understood that nurses in China would be more excited by a photo of a Community nurse with her own car than by our carefully prepared lecture notes; and she managed to look gracious when given a delicacy to eat that came from a part of an animal that we never eat!

When I became General Secretary of the Royal College of Nursing five years later, Sheila Quinn was one of the College's Past Presidents whose wisdom was invaluable to me. *A Dame Abroad* has shown me many other occasions when her skills have been so important to nurses in the UK and in many other countries. It was fun to read of her early days training as a nurse, before the university education which she helped to achieve. Sixty years after those early nursing days Sheila Quinn is still inspiring nurses in countries as different as China, Indonesia, Romania and Zambia.

Christine Hancock
International Council of Nurses President, 2001-2005
Royal College of Nursing General Secretary, 1989-2001

CHAPTER 1

The Sheltered Years

HOME WAS A simple three-bedroom house in a quiet cul-de-sac in Blackpool, well away from the bustling town centre and the brash lights and pleasures of the central promenade. Throughout the summer and the series of brief holidays from the mill towns of Lancashire, the town was full of people and nightlife was noisy. On the whole, residents kept away from the beach and entertainment centres during the summer, although, of course, a very large number of local people were engaged in the tourist industry. One spot we did visit in summer, however, was a new Italian ice-cream outlet, Pablos, which opened in a back street behind large guesthouses, and quickly attracted crowds and queues. It not only sold delicious ice-cream with lots of new varieties, but it was also much cheaper than the well-established sellers who operated on the beach. I'm sure it made a fortune, but I do not know if the firm is still in business today. If it is, I doubt it would be in the same back street!

Autumn and darker nights welcomed the Illuminations, which transformed some ten miles of promenade and the central square into a magical fairyland, extending the season and employment to inhabitants of a town where a high percentage of the dwellers relied on seasonal work. It was one of the highlights of the year to go down to the southern end of the promenade at dusk and join the queue to board one of the trams which went all the ten miles of promenade as far as Cleveleys. At the terminus we just turned the seats of the tram round for the journey back, because, if you got off, it was a very long wait to get back on again. Even when relatives who had a car came to visit, we still went on the tram, because it used the track on the beach side of the road and was the way to get a perfect view. We also watched for new moving tableaux, and were very critical about our favourites.

When the crowds had withdrawn, through winter and early spring, the inhabitants claimed their town and it was a pleasant and friendly place in which to live, with plenty of amusements and a relaxed atmosphere. It had always been a town which was proud of its theatres and cinemas and had many pre-London productions. It was also a town full of 'show biz' personalities, which encouraged amateur clubs and shows. After mass on Sunday mornings we often went for a walk on the vast promenade. It was easy to avoid the ugliness of the Golden Mile, and walk the length of either one of the piers or the five-mile stretch of promenade going north. It was, I suppose, a man-made, concrete and uninteresting stretch of walkway, and when comparing it to that of its neighbour, Lytham St Annes, with broad greens bordering the sea, it must have seemed ugly. It definitely had its own austere beauty, and there was nothing like the bracing winds which raced across it. In winter wild storms made it dangerous just to go on the seafront. We considered Blackpool a very good town for shopping, with one or two large stores just behind the seafront. One of my vivid memories was of standing with Mother near Central Station, and watching one of the big stores burn to the ground.

Of course, the most famous building in the town was the Tower. On the one side of it was the Tower Circus, which lasted all summer, and then the animals which took part retired to their winter residence in the Fylde countryside, while the arena was used for a number of shows during the winter. On the other side was the access to the famous Blackpool Tower, though I'm sure that I am one of many Blackpool residents who have neither been up the tower, nor have any desire to do so. Below it was a small indoor zoo and aquarium, which was much more interesting to me as a child. On the ground floor was the great Tower Ballroom, then full of holidaymakers enjoying the most beautiful dance floor I have ever experienced, and the Wonder Wurlitzer organ, as it was called, with our own Reginald Dixon at the keys. For us, there was no one else who could compete with his playing. In the town centre, opposite the elegant church of St John set in a pleasant grass surround, was the Winter Garden. It was without the rather brash amusements of the Tower, but had an equally beautiful dance floor, which was the venue off-season for the Musical Festival and the Dance Festival. I was entered a few times at both festivals, owing to my attendance at a local Scottish dancing school. We obtained a second prize one year for a group display, and I took a third in the solo class with a highland fling – a triumph for a mere English child among Scottish competitors. Scottish dancing must have been very popular at that time, because we had many engagements during the year. One memory was of participation in a carnival at Morecambe, when the procession had a very long promenade to traverse.

My mother, Ada Quinn.

We were asked to stop at intervals and entertain the watching crowd, which we did a considerable number of times, at the cost of blistered feet in our thin dancing pumps. For singing, I studied with a very well-known singing teacher, who also ran a choir. Again, we won a prize with the choir, but not in the solo section. Now we read a great deal about the political conferences held in the Winter Garden. It also housed a large and very comfortable Opera House, which belied its name in putting on every other kind of show, but not much opera. The other well-known leisure feature in Blackpool was the Pleasure Beach, which I cannot describe because it was out of bounds to us as children, even as schoolgirls, and as it was at one end of the town it was not difficult to avoid.

I was born in September 1920, not long after my father had been demobilised from the army after the end of the four-year-long Great War. As a post office official, he had been fortunate enough to have had his wages paid to his wife throughout his army service, so there was less financial strain on the home than in many where only the army allowance was received. Nevertheless, I was conscious even as a child that money was short, especially towards the end of the month. My immediate family consisted of five members, mother, father and three daughters, of which I was the youngest. Grandmother on my mother's side lived with us, and I remember her as a quiet and gentle old lady, always dressed in black with an apron, either helping with the housework or sitting quietly in a corner. I never heard her raise her voice, but she often acted as a buffer between my eldest sister, Stella, a telephonist at the Blackpool Post Office, and my rather fiery-tempered mother. The most vulnerable family member was my middle sister, Laila, seven years my senior, a fragile and delicate girl who had developed kidney disease during the war years, and was a constant invalid. She was often confined to bed and unable to join with the rest of us children in our pursuits, but incredibly patient with her illness.

My father was a quiet, scholarly man, a lover of books, his pipe and home life, and was without doubt my favourite adult, both within the family and among our close neighbours. I remember him carrying me round on his shoulder as a child, and taking tremendous interest in me, and helping with lessons. He was a quiet humorist, and after his death I found a number of letters he had written, the odd poem, and one or two really amusing short stories. His colleagues often told me, after his death, how greatly he was liked among the post office workers, always willing to help both at work and with home problems, and of very even temper. He was a fount of stories to me as a child, and it must be from him that my love of books and writing has been inherited. In some ways mother was a rather remote figure to me, as she was constantly occupied with nursing my sister, and relied on my grandmother to look after me, which she did, quietly and unobtrusively, and certainly gave stability to the home.

The character of our street invited close relationships between neighbours and the children of some four families who lived within the street. It was a very safe environment, and I do not think that any family living there at that time had a car. Most of the inhabitants had lived there for many years, and we were a small group of children. In the opposite corner were two brothers, the younger of whom, Phil, was near my own

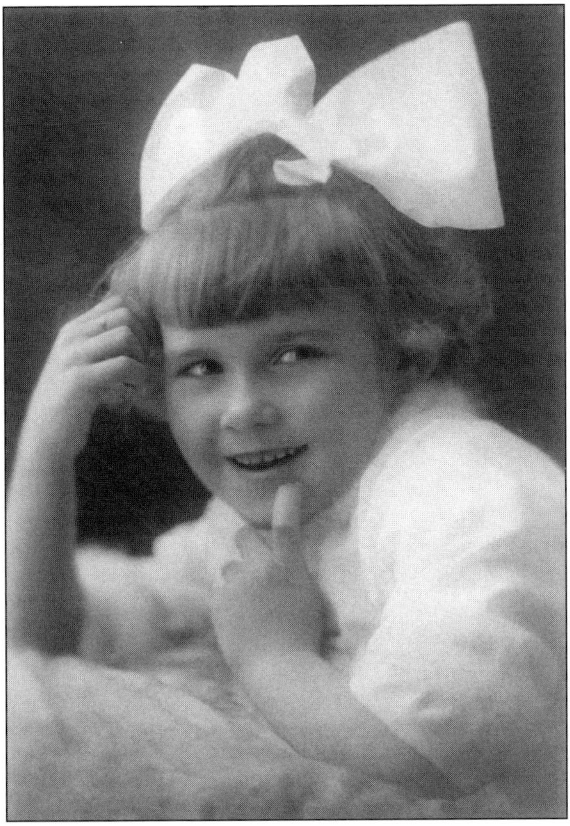

My sister Laila.

age; some years after we left the area he had a most unusual accident on Guy Fawkes night. A rocket stick fell into his eye, while he was looking up watching the display, and blinded him in that eye. He was a very clever boy, and I do not know how it affected him afterwards. His brother Tom was a few years older, and quite aloof, so I hardly knew him. Imagine my surprise, some sixty years later, when I had the most friendly letter of congratulations from Tom when the Queen granted me the Order of Commander of the British Empire (CBE). Although I replied, he never wrote again. After being made a Dame, I looked for a possible letter from Tom among the many received, but by then he must have died. At the other end of the street were a boy and a girl, but we were not encouraged to play with them, whatever the reason. There were another two next door but one, whose names escape me, but my best friend was Marion,

My father, Wilfred, escorting my sister Stella to her wedding, 1932.

an only child who lived a few doors away. It seems curious now that all our activities appeared to have been within the street, or going to the small shop at the end, and, very occasionally, to a Saturday matinée if we had the required threepence available. Mother's great standby was a family across the road, who were especially good when Laila was ill, as she generally was. The husband, who was a large rather burly man with an incredibly warm heart, was an expert at lifting her. There were two daughters, one a friend of my older sister, Stella, and the younger Laila's age and her close friend.

The local Roman Catholic Church and School was less than five minutes' walk from home and formed the boundaries of school and family life for the first few years. The school had separate infant and junior schools on the same site, each with its own playground, and with the church nearby. My earliest recollection was of being very irritated by the simple children's books for reading, because my father had taught me to read long before I started school, and he brought me a constant supply of storybooks from the public library. That was in the centre of the town and it was a few years before I was allowed to go there by myself on the tram. Once I was self-sufficient, books were my delight, although I was constantly interrupted by Mother telling me to put my book down and help her with the dusting. I enjoyed lessons in a small class where the teachers knew every child well.

The main event in my infant school was my first communion, celebrated with the entire class and wearing a brand new white dress with matching veil. New clothes were a rarity and they were kept for Sundays and special occasions and had to be worn with great care. We had a special breakfast after the ceremony with a great treat of boiled eggs. We were asked to supply our own eggcup and spoon, and I managed to lose mine and incurred mother's wrath. We knew the local priests well, as they were frequent visitors to school and knew each child by name. After three years we moved up into the junior school, which was the 'big school' to us and the children there seemed almost grown up. It was a very important occasion and also very frightening for the first few weeks but we soon settled down.

Two school events stand out, both in my final year before what was then the eleven-plus examination. The first was the news broken by Mother that I had been chosen for the ceremony of crowning the statue of Our Lady at the evening service on the first Sunday in May. This was a great privilege and rather overwhelming. There were dressmaker fittings for the dress, which was of white satin and very plain, but it was also my first long dress, and complete with veil and even a train. Mother decided that we had to have a professional photograph, and that was another first experience. When the actual date arrived, I had to change in a classroom, standing on a white sheet, with Mother and Stella fussing round me. Then there was a wait without moving, while Sister Pauline, who was the headmistress, and various other teachers came in to have a look. Finally, the two small boys to carry my train, and six small girls to accompany us, all in matching dresses and suits, arrived. We walked to the church through interested spectators and into the strong lights, the warmth and the small of incense and I was conscious of a mass of people and a very loud organ. When the moment came, I was worried that I would leave

Ready for the May ceremony, 1930, aged 10.

the crown crooked, but a sign from Sister Pauline reassured me, and I concentrated on backing down the flight of steps without catching my heel. Throughout the whole ceremony I was aware of Mother's open disappointment that it wasn't Laila in my place. I was looking forward to wearing the dress for parties and other special occasions, but mother gave it to the school to be used by girls who could not afford the expense of a new one. It was a very nice thought and was used for a number of years, but at ten years old I was in tears at the loss.

Sadly, Laila died in 1929 at the age of sixteen years, as quietly and uncomplainingly as she had lived. Only a few months later my grandmother followed her after a stroke. These two sad events were a watershed in our family life, and, as mother could not bear to be in the house alone with her sad memories, it was decided to move. The new house was only three miles away, but in a completely different part of the town. It was quite easy for me to get to school by tramcar, but I had lost the close friendship of the children in the street where we had lived, and there were none around our new home to produce the same kind of relationships. By this time I had moved out of the primary school and was working hard to prepare for the exam on which our further education depended.

Looking back, it is easy to see that my mother was in a deep depression following Laila's death; there was no such thing as grief counselling services in those days, and mother never fully recovered. Apart from her sorrow, most of her time had been taken up with nursing Laila. Now she could not bear to be alone in the house, and spent most of her time with one or two close friends, or around the town. She and my father became remote from each other, and it was not the happiest home.

Blackpool was a town where young talent was encouraged. The Blackpool Children's Pantomime, a very 'professional', though amateur, company was quite famous, and usually had one or two talent spotters in the audience. It occupied a week every year in the Grand Theatre, one of the two main theatres in the town. It was a very beautiful building, now listed, and had a special atmosphere backstage. As I was successful at audition, I soon began playing principal roles. Mother obtained a much-prized permit to accompany me to rehearsals and be my dresser for the week in the Grand Theatre just after Christmas. It was something very special to walk through the stage door in the footsteps of so many great stars. Robert Donat had been playing there just before us one year.

It was not easy to get into the Pantomime, and in my first years, the principal parts were played by the talented pupils of a well-known teacher in the town. Then a professional producer took over and auditions were organised. I was thrilled to be successful and, in full pierrot costume, speaking the prologue, a real tear jerker of a speech with emotive language about 'aiding our waifs and strays'. I can recite it to this day. The following week the part of the Genie of the Lamp in *Aladdin* became vacant and it was offered to me. It was non-speaking and depended on movement, but it was a great thrill. Succeeding years found me in ever-increasing roles and enjoying every moment. Participation was not approved of at school, as it was thought to interfere with work. At seventeen we had to retire, and it was a sad day when, as Fairy Godmother, I saw Cinderella off in her gold coach, pulled by real white ponies, for the last time. Later on I graduated to the Amateur Dramatic Society, which played well-known musicals, but it wasn't the same. And later still, with some friends, we started another dramatic society, The Astral Players, which survived for very many years, directed by a very close friend of mine, Bega Hood. From September until January, the Pantomime dominated our lives for some seven or eight years. Together with singing and dancing lessons, life was busy and my friends were from those engaged in the same pursuits. I certainly gained the ability to speak, move and be confident before large audiences, a lesson that has stood me in good stead through the years. The actual week of the show was an exhilarating experience. Many of my fellow artistes went into professional shows and careers, but, although the possibility went through my mind briefly, it was never realistic for me. Broadcasting was still in its infancy, television yet to come, and, although one or two friends had auditions with major companies, and one even in Hollywood, openings were for the few with outstanding talent. I had the sense to realise – not without some envy, and a bit of heartache – that it was not for me.

Family holidays didn't exist – there was no money to spare, and education had to come first. During childhood and my early teens, part of school holidays were spent each year with my aunt and uncle in the small town of Hebden Bridge in the West Riding of Yorkshire. It was not the mecca for artists that it has now become, but to me it was always a town of beauty, and set in glorious countryside. My cousin Joyce was of Laila's age, and as she had already left school and had her own interests, I found it rather lonely. The main excursions were to the shops in Halifax, Bradford or Leeds, though, at that stage of life, clothes were of little interest.

The scholarship examination came and went, and to my delight I was successful and started school life at the Convent of the Holy Child Jesus, run by an order of the same name. It was both a boarding and a day school, with senior and junior sections, and had a good reputation for scholarship. It was a big change from the friendly elementary school where I was used to being top of the class, and now I had to work hard to keep in the upper third of my form. I was only mediocre in games, and less than that in music. Choir and church music I enjoyed, but my performance as a second violin in the school orchestra was painful in the extreme, and my stage skills were frowned upon. Outside activities to school life were not encouraged. Halfway through my first year at the convent, my elder sister, Stella, married a young man from the Yorkshire town of Brighouse, where another branch of our family lived. Because of the eleven-year gap in age we were not very close. Apart from my father, we were a catholic family, but my mother had ceased to practise, and so had Stella, who decided to marry in the local parish church. This shocked the Sisters at school and mother was asked to keep me away from the wedding. The rather insensitive request greatly annoyed the whole family, especially as my other relatives were not catholics. There were murmurs of taking me away from the convent, and I dissolved into tears at the thought of losing my new school friends and starting all over at a new school. We had very rigid views on other religions at that time! I did, of course, attend as my sister's bridesmaid, but feelings ran high for some time and I was kept off school, which didn't help relationships and progress at school when I returned and it was a fairly unhappy two or three years. Eventually, however, the episode faded into the background. Mother Xavier, our headmistress, was loved, and very able, but she had a long history of illness and retired from teaching soon after I left. We had news of her death during the war. My favourite teacher had just come down from university, and taught Latin, but she left after a couple of years to enter the order as a nun, and we met again some years later when she returned to Layton Hill, our school, as a professed sister. By that time I had left, but I kept in touch with her over the years. Another great character was a lay teacher, Miss McCappin, who taught sports and gym; she was a quite small, wiry woman with a large personality, who introduced herself at our first class with the words 'remember – a mac, a cap and a pin' with appropriate gestures. She became a good friend in later years. They were just a few of the teachers who dominated our schooldays and left a great impression on us.We were very fortunate in our teachers, whether religious sisters or lay.

I pursued my rather undistinguished school career and left at the age of seventeen in the summer of 1937 with a respectable matriculation result. Although I doubt that I left much of an impression at the convent, they had given me something very precious, and that was a lasting faith as a catholic, which has sustained me through many trials and difficulties over the years. I had also made many friends among the Sisters with whom I came into contact, and visited them from time to time. I was sad when the convent changed its character and became a large comprehensive school, but that was probably inevitable in view of the harsh economic

In pantomime, as Gretchen in Babes in the Wood *with partner, Grand Theatre, Blackpool, 1934, aged 14.*

climate and the major changes which have occurred in education over the years.

It would have been my ambition to go to college or university, but it was a costly venture in those days, and out of the question, and, having succeeded in a competition for a place in local government, I found myself as a junior in the Borough Treasurer's department. This lasted for a couple of years, but the work was extremely dull, by my standards anyway, and that type of routine work was not for me. Illness intervened by way of a bacterial infection, which kept me at home for some months, and gave me time and space to think about work. I was sure I did not wish to return to clerical work and was delighted when my uncle offered me an apprenticeship in his busy pharmacy in the middle of town where my cousin was already established. By this time the war clouds were gathering, though the geographical position of Blackpool, together with its lack of heavy industry, made it a comparatively safe area once hostilities commenced. The town filled with new recruits for their early training, including many Polish airmen who had escaped the occupation of Poland, often under tragic conditions. I met one of them at the house of Bega Hood, whose hospitality was always open to many young men away from home for the first time. Zvygniev, a Polish airman who had flown his plane over from Poland when defeat appeared inevitable, was stationed in Blackpool for a time and was a frequent visitor to her house. He often spoke of his mother, who unfortunately died before the end of the war, and he was posted to the Polish Air Squadron at Silloth in Cumberland. I saw him occasionally when I was working in Lancaster. He remained in England, married and had a family, dying of a heart attack while his children were still young. Like many of his countrymen, he had a very attractive personality. Most of my companions by this time were young military personnel whom we had met at Bega's home, but none of them stayed very long in Blackpool. Her brother also came home from time to time. Having been in the Cunard fleet, he transferred to the Royal Navy on the outbreak of war, and looked very dashing in his uniform of a naval officer and sporting a fearsome beard. After the war he married and lived in Cornwall where he was a volunteer with the local lifeboat, until his sudden death in the 1990s. Bega and I had become friends, partly through the Astral Players and partly through participation in an animal welfare society with which Mother had become involved. Bega was a vivacious and able young married woman a few years older than me and she became a life-long friend. Her friends and contacts were mainly among the medical and nursing staff of our local hospital and this was the point where my own desire to become a nurse grew and matured into an enduring commitment to the profession.

But major changes were taking place within the family. My father was too old for active service, obviously to his regret! My sister had never really settled in Yorkshire, and, when her husband, who was in the retail business, failed his medical, they decided to move to Blackpool, where my brother-in-law found work in a munitions factory. Stella was looking for a small retail shop, which she could manage until the end of hostilities, when her husband would join her. In the meantime they moved in to share our home. Mother found an outlet in voluntary work, especially connected with animals, and after helping with an outdoor show one cold, windy day, she returned feeling ill. Following some weeks of not being well, she took medical advice, was in bed for some days, but started to deteriorate. This coincided with my twenty-first birthday, for which we all tried to put on a brave face, but it was a very small party with friends at a local restaurant, and no one's heart was really into celebrating. Within a day or two Mother was in hospital with an acute infection and, in those days before penicillin and antibiotics, there seemed to be no effective treatment. We were completely unprepared for her death. Time seemed to stand still and we tried to carry on as usual, but I suppose I was in a state of shock. Stella did her best to bring us together and to look after the home. Bega Hood was an enormous source of strength at this point, opening her home to me, which was always busy with visitors, whether hospital friends or visiting servicemen; the home of her parents was also equally welcoming. I was officially in a reserved occupation, but all these events had completely unsettled me, and so I made application for transfer to nurse training. My sister was horrified, my father supportive, and eventually I was called for interview at the Royal Lancaster Infirmary, and joined the preliminary training school on 1 December 1943. Lancaster, only thirty miles from home, was accessible on days off, and again in a safe area, and so Stella became more reconciled to the situation. It was also a lovely small town set in beautiful countryside and within easy reach of the Lake District, and some of the happiest years of my life were spent there.

Chapter 2

It Took Over My Life

'GOOD EVENING, NURSE.' When I reported to the porter's lodge in the early evening of a dark November day, the unexpected greeting took me aback. After giving my name, I was escorted by the porter over the road to the nurses' home and left in the charge of a tall, severe-looking woman, who was dressed in a dark blue sister's uniform and who informed me that she was Home Sister. She showed me the sitting-room and my bedroom and left me to unpack. Memory can still take me back to the room which was to be my home for the next four years. It was quite large and well-equipped with easy chair, fitted cupboards, desk and washbasin, and overlooked the small garden and beyond to the busy main road through Lancaster. Throughout my various moves, I looked back to this room with nostalgia, as it was quite the nicest I met, even when I was a sister, and unusual for 1943 when many nurses' homes were very spartan.

There were six of us on that first evening, and as one had been a nursing auxiliary, she instructed the rest of us on how to transform what looked like a large white starched serviette into a respectable traditional butterfly cap. Within a couple of hours the home came to life with the noise of the day staff coming off day duty at 9p.m. We received a friendly and enthusiastic welcome from the older student nurses in getting us sorted out with uniform and offering to see us over to the dining-room at 7a.m. for breakfast the next morning. Part of the welcome was, as one nurse admitted, that it was nice to know she would no longer be the junior and dogsbody on her ward.

Sleep did not come easily, and in no time at all night sister was calling us. Dressing in the unaccustomed stiff striped dress with starched collars and cuffs took more time than usual, but we all got over to the dining-room and sat at the table reserved for the junior nurses. Many things about those first few months left clear memories, and certainly that first breakfast was one of them – cold pilchards which none of us touched and I dislike to this day, but then, it was wartime. The next discovery was my assignment – female surgical ward – and to find that we were thrown straight into a ward routine. Lectures were scattered across the week, usually in the middle of our 'off duty'. In fact, we were the last group to be so treated. Our successors in the next intake had the advantage of a six-week period in school before being introduced to the rigours of the ward. Later still, a block system of organising lectures was introduced, and the old-fashioned system of throwing the prospective nurse in at the deep end came to an end. It certainly made life easier. We might have been recruited as student nurses but, to the sisters and staff nurses, we were still probationers and more often referred to as 'the junior pro'. Our place was in the sluice or helping the ward maid to clean the ward. How we hated Thursdays when all the beds were pulled out, the floor buffed to a fine sheen, and lockers cleaned out and tidied, while the patients complained that they could never find anything. The ward maids were well experienced in the ups and downs of ward life and we soon learned to keep on their good side, as it made all the difference to a reasonable life on duty. Actually, they were mostly long-serving employees, passionately devoted to the hospital, their ward, and sister in particular, had hearts of gold, and could be extraordinarily kind to clumsy young nurses.

The patients also were great allies and saved us from many errors and sister's wrath. Treatment and care of patients was very different in those days before penicillin, modern drugs and medical advances. Most ward patients would be in for at least ten days and on bed rest, even with simple and straightforward surgery, so we got to know them well and they certainly knew the routine far better than we did. Customs were very different, too. It was difficult to get used to being addressed by surname, with or without the prefix 'nurse', depending on who was speaking. We mainly tried to keep out of sister's sight. The staff nurse was marginally more approachable, but generally it was the nurse immediately senior to oneself who gave instructions, explained, taught, criticised, and generally was a guardian angel. On duty we never spoke directly to a doctor, but passed any message through the more senior nurse. Curiously, the whole rather strange system worked and produced not only an efficient, but also a happy, ward team. Wards, of course, had differing reputations, but we soon settled down to the routine of a new ward after the three-monthly changeover of all student nurses at the same time, even if tempers were short and chaos appeared to reign for the first few days.

I recall my first interview with Matron, a cultured woman with a somewhat intimidating manner who rarely unbent, but appeared to know each one of her nurses and how they were developing. Unfortunately, she retired during my third year, and I realised just how much help she had given me at various times. The one instance which stands out in my mind was when she appeared to do a ward round early one evening, when, because of some minor crisis, I had been left alone on the ward. Matron's ward round was a state occasion, with the ward looking immaculate, and the sister or staff nurse accompanying her giving a brief but detailed and accurate report on each person. If anything was left out or the answer to a question not known, there was a frosty silence. On this particular occasion the patients had sized up the situation, pushed articles in lockers and under bedclothes, and became unusually polite and cheerful. On the way out Matron paused and looked at me. 'You have just come first in your anatomy examination, nurse; you'll do!' and in the next second she was berating the senior nurse who had just returned, for leaving an incompetent junior in charge. The home sister, Sister Chadwick, was our main point of reference, and turned out to be a very approachable and kindly person, in spite of her austere appearance. She ran an immaculate home, policed its rules, including lock-up time, which was 9p.m. on evenings off-duty and our one half-day a week, checked sickness and generally acted as the mother figure to all the nursing staff. Soon after I had started training, the Rushcliffe Committee, which then governed our national negotiations, increased our off-duty to one day a week, restricted our working week to forty-eight hours and gave us the large allowance of £40 a year. It was amazing how far the money was stretched!

As we started training on December 1, Christmas was soon upon us, and the first Christmas in hospital was quite an experience. Like most hospitals, all nursing staff lived in, and it was quite unusual for nurses to be accepted for training in their own town. Even senior staff lived in, and I remember the staff nurse of my first ward, a superb nurse and teacher whom we all liked and admired and who applied for the vacant post of sister on our ward, and was turned down because she was not resident. She had made an impression on me the very first day, when, at the end of a long shift and feeling exhausted and bewildered, she sent me off duty with the words, 'Not bad, Nurse, provided you can learn to be a bit quicker!' The hospital lost one of its best nurses, as she moved into the community as a district nurse. Hospital and community nursing were quite separate in those days. We had little contact with each other, and knew even less about each other's work, a very different situation from today. For Christmas and Boxing Day all days off were cancelled, as this was the patients' day and was all-important. Nor did we have any off-duty on Christmas Day, but the atmosphere on the wards was such fun that no one minded. Every patient had a present, the consultant of the ward appeared to carve the turkey, and visitors were invited for afternoon tea. We had worked for days on preparing the ward decorations, and they all looked magnificent. There was only a meagre lunch for staff in the dining-room – not that it mattered, because our lunch had been prepared on the ward, and we retired to the ward kitchen for our turkey and Christmas pudding, while the patients had a rest to recover from their lunch and to prepare for their visitors. After that first ward, having completed three months' training and being confirmed in our employment, my set all went on night duty together for three months.

Lancaster was, and still is, a delightful and very attractive county town, set in beautiful country with the Fylde to one side, the sea nearby at Morecambe, and the Lake District within an hour or so of travel. Originally I had been disappointed at not being able to train in London, but, in view of the wartime conditions, my family were not happy with the idea. I soon discovered that there were consolations in the historic town of Lancaster and its position. The Royal Infirmary, or the RLI as it was affectionately referred to, was mostly an old building, with some two hundred and fifty beds arranged in seven long traditional Nightingale wards, so it was a comparatively small training school. I suppose there were disadvantages compared with the large teaching hospitals, but they seemed to be well compensated by the friendliness, and by the way that the senior staff knew us as individuals and were aware of the progress and problems of all the students. It was a voluntary hospital and, in contrast to the formidable health authorities of today, we were governed by a general management committee composed of local people from various walks of life but all with an interest in health care. Most of the members were known to us by sight, and they visited the hospital frequently and took an interest in both patients and staff. As in most voluntary hospitals, money was tight but equipment, though not as plentiful as it might have been, was always of good quality and the committee members were always open to suggestions for improvement. The consultant medical staff were

'Honorary', some having a general practice in the town while giving freely of their time to the demands of the hospital. Others were specialists in their own particular branch of surgery and medicine. They all took a keen interest in the student nurses, taught both in the school and informally at the bedside, if we were about, and they knew most of us by name. One of the sad results of the NHS coming into being in April 1948 was that our part-time consultants were deemed not to be qualified as specialists and had to relinquish their part-time posts, although they continued in their general practices in the town and to visit patients. There was also the suggestion that all private beds would be removed from NHS Hospitals, and the British Medical Association lobbied the Minister of Health, then Aneurin Bevan. It was a fierce argument, and the doctors were accused of wanting to keep the private beds in NHS hospitals for their convenience and the income from those patients. From the point of view of a relatively small hospital, we had only a few private patients, two rooms attached to each ward, and a small group of individual rooms. However, the income which came to the hospital from the private patients was very welcome in those days of voluntary contributions.

My bicycle had been brought to the hospital, so that it was possible for me to ride home in good weather, along the shores of Pilling sands, a tidal estuary, across the ferry (which no longer runs) to Fleetwood, and on to Blackpool, some twenty-five miles. As it was quite a marathon, it was not carried out very often. The alternative was a two-hourly bus going via the pretty village of Garstang, taking two to three hours and costing the large sum of three shillings and sixpence, quite a consideration on a salary of £40. Another reason for the bicycle was that it became a great asset for off-duty excursions, although it was possible to visit home on most days off. By this time we had moved to Hardhorn on the outskirts of Blackpool and the village of Poulton-le-Fylde was our nearest stop. My father usually met me at the bus stop, with our lovely pointer dog, Beauty, who was technically mine, but had attached herself to my father, and they were well-known around the district. The local bus between Blackpool and Poulton stopped at our door, and it was fairly common to miss Beauty and then to see her calmly alight from one of the buses. She obviously enjoyed the rides and the conductors knew her.

Apart from the countryside, the nurses had one precious and quite unusual leisure facility. The hospital owned a boat, housed on the canal and, as the hospital backed onto the canal, it was a matter of minutes to cross the bridge and reach the boathouse. My immediate friends and I were some of the few who actually took advantage of it, and we used to pack a picnic and row the boat some miles up the canal to tie up and enjoy its peace and tranquillity. There were times when other people took the boat out and abandoned it somewhere, but it was always found and returned, and it provided many happy hours, especially with a book for study as exams loomed near.

The transition from day to night duty was an interesting experience. The hospital was fortunate in having quite large grounds near to the main building and opposite to the nurses' home. Within this park was a large old house, in good condition, which was used as the night nurses' home. It was a perfect situation, a few minutes' walk to the wards, and completely quiet. Again, all the student nurses moved at the same time and it was quite an operation. The porter brought one case per nurse on his trolley, but even by the end of the first three months we had each acquired more extra belongings that you can imagine. A constant stream of nurses could be seen walking back and forth between the night and day homes, laden with various bits and pieces, most of which were large and ungainly. Eventually, we were all established in our rooms which, like the house, were large, so we shared, two to a room with a friend of our choice, except for the staff nurses, who had their own rooms. The move had to be completed and all night nurses in bed by 12 noon, and the '12 o'clock rule' applied to each day, with home sister doing sporadic checks to make sure we were in bed. Fortunately, the large rooms had a good view across the park and of anyone approaching, so there was ample time to conform. In summer when weather was good, we would take blankets and pillows and sleep outside, although this was frowned upon. The one drawback of night duty was the timing of lectures, which tended to be 11a.m. or 3p.m. The morning lecture meant staying awake, which was not the easiest thing to do after a hectic night. For the junior nurse on the ward, work was pretty well nonstop, especially with a ward of thirty patients to wash and have tidy before the day staff came on duty at 7.30a.m. A ward sister would think nothing of sending a message to the dining-room for a nurse to return to complete an unfinished task. Even worse was getting out of bed at 2p.m. to attend a 3p.m. lecture, and all lectures had to be attended in uniform. Nights off were movable, and if other nursing staff went off sick, they were postponed. If lectures were in the middle of nights off, they had still to be attended, which meant that you could not get home on your off-duty. Annoyed though we might be, that was the rule, and we were quite philosophical about it. Although many training schools had adopted a preliminary training school and block system of lectures by then, it was some years before it was a general pattern.

Work during the night was very different from day duty. Some wards were busier than others, especially the surgical wards, and the two nurses on each thirty-bed ward had their work cut out after a busy theatre list. On other nights, the pace was quieter, patients were asleep, and the nurses had the opportunity to catch up with lecture notes, or even do knitting or sewing. The corridors could be eerie during the night when all was quiet, especially the very long corridor which led to the newly built orthopaedic ward, and nowhere else. As it was an old hospital, and the kitchens left a great deal to be desired in terms of health and safety, we left the light on in the kitchen all night. Night Sister would often turn it off on her rounds, and then, when we turned it on again, it was to find a black scurrying floor of cockroaches. My pet hate as an assignment was the maternity ward, where the staff on duty consisted of two midwives and one junior nurse. Quite apart from the fact that the junior was the general factotum, it was her job to change all the babies as soon as she came on duty. The sight and noise of the main nursery and thirty or more squalling babies, all needing changing, was quite daunting to a sleepy nurse, but somehow it was done. Meals at night were collected from the kitchen and were very variable, but the patients often saved something special brought in by their visitors to help us through the night.

We all dreaded our first encounter with death and mine is still clear today. The patient was in a side ward at the entrance to the ward, and my senior nurse sent me at intervals to check on her condition. I always stopped outside the door to listen for the noisy breathing, and then crept in, but was terrified to be alone when the patient actually died. The senior nurse carried out the care after death with great sensitivity, an example which has always remained with me. However, she had to ask me to accompany the patient to the mortuary, along with the night porter, who was quite a character but very thoughtful in looking after young student nurses for the first time. Night Sister joined us and again gave a model of care in seeing the patient carefully placed on the mortuary slab – we didn't have refrigerators in those days. It was a ghostly place at night, tucked away at the back of the hospital and near to the canal. There was the odd time when a luckless junior nurse forgot to replace the patient's dentures, and was sent down to remedy the incident, but fortunately it never happened to me. Later, the mortuary was rebuilt to conform with modern requirements – a relief for everybody concerned. Time went on, and we felt very senior receiving our second-year belt, and no longer being the lowest of the low – the ward junior. The maternity ward was different. The staff were all trained midwives, except for one solitary student nurse who was at everyone's beck and call. It nearly put me off midwifery training later.

War continued during most of my training, but again, with Lancaster being in a comparatively safe area, it did not affect us very much, apart from rations and difficulties in obtaining many things, especially stockings. We had a special privilege at the Infirmary, in that Matron had agreed we could go without stockings and wear sandals instead of the regulation lace up shoes for the duration of the war. She did not like it, and tried to persuade us to go back to correct uniform but, having won the privilege, we weren't prepared to part with it until the war was over. We also had many soldiers in the town, and struck up friendships. I was fortunate in meeting a young officer, and we spent a lot of time together but, as he moved on, the friendship waned, as did so many in wartime. We also experienced the very fierce winter with heavy snow towards the end of the war, and, although the country around Lancaster looked as if it was out of a fairytale, it was very uncomfortable when central heating was low because of a shortage of fuel. The other sign of war were prisoners of war on the wards, mainly Italian, who had been working on the surrounding farms and were good patients for the short time they were with us.

We had no male nurses, whether trained or students, and it was not until the end of the war and demobilisation that we had one or two in each year. Some had been carrying out nursing duties in the forces, and were on a shortened training, and others had seen it as a new career opening for men. It is a different situation today, where male students and trained nurses are about a stable ten per cent of the whole, but with a very high percentage applying for and occupying senior posts. There are a variety of reasons for the discrepancy, including the number of career breaks by married women, and the fact that, while most male nurses had trained in and were working in the psychiatric field, they are now mainly general trained in the first instance and then specialising, in the same way as female nurses. I certainly don't remember any prejudice against male nurses, who are as able and professional as their counterparts, and many have emerged as outstanding nurse leaders.

We had quite a few changes among senior staff, mainly our tutor, and I certainly had four different tutors in the course of my training, which was a bit unsettling as we relied considerably on the student/tutor relationship. However, hospital examinations came and went, and were passed fairly easily. The State Preliminary Examination was a real hurdle, but it had a very basic curriculum which was well covered in both classroom and ward experience. We took our 'Prelim' at Preston Royal Infirmary and I was completely overawed by the examining matron in a smart uniform and a curt manner. Attempting to carry out her instructions was disastrous. The result was two months of misery waiting to hear the worst. Even receiving the results was an ordeal. We collected in a solemn line outside Matron's office and were called in one at a time to open our envelope in front of her and Sister Tutor and inform them of the result. Why this ritual was observed I do not know, as Matron received the list direct. However, it was good news and I joined the telephone queue to phone home.

It was well into my second year when Matron announced that we had an officer from the Royal College of Nursing coming to talk to all nurses at the Infirmary, and the students were required to attend. The lady concerned seemed rather elderly to my eyes, and somewhat dowdy, but gave a very good, if dull, presentation on the advantages of the College, and in particular its Student Nurses' Association. The immediate outcome was to establish a branch of the RCN, and a few months later our tutor persuaded us to form a unit of the Student Nurses' Association. There was considerable interest, and we set up quite a solid organisation with most student nurses joining. Looking back, the enthusiasm was largely due to the fact that we had little social life at the hospital, and Matron wisely gave us a number of things to organise, particularly two successful hospital dances, and the sale of our own Christmas cards for student unit funds. I was elected chairman of the unit, and a few months later an exciting and unexpected invitation arrived from RCN headquarters in London. The Princess Elizabeth, as she then was, had become president of the Student Nurses' Association, and was to visit the RCN to open the new nursing library. Certain student nurse units had been invited to send a representative to be part of the guard of honour for the arrival of the Princess, and Lancaster was one of the fortunate ones. The nurses elected me, as their chairman, to go and Matron agreed for me to take two weeks' days-off for the event. I was given a brand new uniform and cloak for the day and told firmly that it had to be returned to the sewing room on my return. Accommodation was offered me at a hospital in Isleworth. It was a magical twenty-four hours, although I couldn't help comparing the hospital room rather unfavourably with mine in Lancaster. It was a hot sticky day in London. We were rehearsed for ages, stood in our guard positions for longer, and eventually the Princess arrived, in uniform and looking rather shy. She spoke to all the student nurses in the main hall, went on to open the Library, and then the members of the guard of honour were privileged to have tea with her. After it was all over, there was time for a tour of London by bus, and a meal at the Corner House Salad Bar before it was time to get the night train back to Lancaster. The next two weeks without a day off seemed a very long time, but it was worth it.

There was, as I soon discovered, a downside to being the student nurse representative, as the students expected me to put forward their grievances. The main point at issue was the 9p.m. curfew for all students, and they instructed me to approach Matron to negotiate this. It was a nerve-racking interview but I emerged triumphant with the concession that those who had taken their prelim could be out until 10p.m. A victory for democracy! I suspect that Matron had a quiet chuckle after my departure and that she enlivened the sisters' dining-room with the tale. Sister Chadwick, the home sister, was not impressed. This story was to emerge some forty years later, recounted by the public orator, when Southampton University conferred an honorary degree on me, mainly for my contribution to nursing. The many distinguished nurses in the audience were highly amused.

It was about this time, towards the end of my second year, that I was assigned as the senior student to the women's surgical ward on which I had originally started. This meant that whenever Sister or Staff Nurse had a day off, I was left in charge for the afternoon shift, which was usually quiet. But the best-laid schemes can go awry and first Sister and then Staff Nurse went off sick, leaving me in charge, and suddenly the ward became busy with emergency admissions and operations. There was nothing else to do except put my best foot forward, and the other students rallied round me. Two other student nurses were sent to help, and for three months I had my most exciting experience as a student nurse. After the initial shock, I thoroughly enjoyed the work and responsibility. My main recollection of the time was rushed mealtimes and rarely being off duty until after 10p.m. Amazingly, there was no catastrophe and I was quite disappointed when a new sister and a newly-qualified staff nurse were appointed.

Once into the third and final year of training, it was all eyes on the State Final. Our hospital final came first and was a good dress rehearsal, but it was just at the time our matron had left, we had an interim tutor, and the assistant matron had to take our hospital examination. She did it very ably, but it didn't seem quite the same. By this time I was in theatre, the experience being restricted to third year student nurses, and it was just like my first days on the ward again. It was such a different atmosphere. Everyone seemed quite at home, and completely confident in their complex work. We worked in close contact with the consultant surgeons, who all seemed to have a short fuse on their tempers, and each with his own idiosyncrasy. The nursing staff were all helpful, but Sister Roberts, the sister-in-charge, was brilliant at her job, a good teacher and an absolute perfectionist. Sadly, she had had a lot of illness, and very rarely took a case herself, but she knew exactly what was happening in each of her theatres, and her eagle eye spotted the slightest mistake. My saviour in the early days was the theatre technician, a very even-tempered and able man by the name of Coward. He had followed in the footsteps of his father who had been the theatre technician before him. He was expert in getting the patient into just the right position, something which I never achieved; he acted as buffer when we were working with an irritable anaesthetist, he was incredibly patient with new nurses and was a mine of information.

At about the same time, we had a new ward sister on the male surgical ward opposite to theatre. She was a trainee of the Infirmary, and came to us from running an operating theatre in another hospital. One of my friends was her ward staff nurse, so I came to know Maisie Hulme very well, and continued the friendship throughout my own career. She was often a good antidote to the strains and stresses of theatre. It was an assignment that nurses either loved or hated, and I soon fell into the former category, but many of my set complained bitterly about the lack of real contact with patients. Sister Roberts was very quick to notice when the stress was getting to staff, and to give some extra off-duty where needed. After some months it was my turn for night duty, and this was usually quite boring, doing extra cleaning or sterilising, but there were nights when work never stopped. It was towards the end of my night duty that an emergency occurred which made my theatre experience memorable. A message was phoned in by a general practitioner out in the country that he was bringing in a serious emergency, a young woman with a penetrating injury, and that he had alerted the senior surgeon, who was on his way. That left little time for preparation, but getting theatre ready for the emergency caused me to panic. I had only ever taken charge of straightforward list cases under supervision, and was anything but skilled and experienced. The Junior Night Sister came in to act as 'runner', but she was in the same state as me.

The patient arrived about the same time as the surgeon, desperately shocked, with a large penetrating wound through most of her body, through the abdomen and piercing the chest cavity. She had fallen on to the sharp handle of a farm instrument and was in a critical state. The surgeon was a brilliant man, with a very short temper and colourful language. He had not had much to do with me, and did not look particularly pleased when he realised that I was the only nurse available. He performed meticulous surgery, with the patient on the brink of survival, and eventually, some four to five hours later, was finishing and asked me for sutures. My fatigue took over; I gave the wrong suture and the surgeon exploded in wrath.

'How on earth,' he demanded, 'can you work perfectly with me right through this case, and then make a mess at the last minute?'

However, we got the patient back to the ward, where the day sister was waiting on duty to do all she could. Some few weeks later that young woman walked out little the worse for wear, perhaps never realising how much her own life had affected those of us who were there at her time of need. The morning after the surgery, the surgeon sought me out to tell me I hadn't done a bad job under the circumstances. For my part, it was a night never to be forgotten, and it confirmed my decision to remain in nursing.

The time for the results of our state final examination was near, and we again lined up before Matron's office to hear the results and, to our delight, to celebrate a one hundred per cent success rate. As we filed out, Matron called me back to inform me that I had been awarded the Gibson

Medal for the year. It was called after Dr Gibson, a former surgeon, greatly loved and respected, and it was presented to me at a meeting of the Management Committee, the only time I had seen that august body together. It was also decision time about my future, and I reluctantly decided that the time had come to move on, although I remained another six months to complete my postgraduate year. In those days it was usual to follow general training with midwifery training, and most posts advertising women's ward or department insisted on at least Part One midwifery. It did not qualify a nurse as a trained midwife, and a further six months for Part Two, which included district midwifery, was necessary to practise as a midwife. It must be said that midwifery education has changed considerably since that time. The Midwifery Directives of the European Union have increased both the length and content of training, and every country of the EU has to conform.

My application to the Halifax Royal Infirmary, which had a small midwifery unit, was accepted. There was a large municipal hospital with a bigger unit in the town, but, having started in a voluntary hospital, I decided to continue in the same system. Halifax was chosen, because it was in the West Riding among country I loved and wished to explore further. The other members of my set at Lancaster had either decided to stay, or to move in other directions, so I was alone to start a new era in my career. The Infirmary was an old building, but part of the unit was modern. Of the eight other pupil midwives who started at the same time, five were from the Infirmary, and we other three automatically became friends, although we were generally a happy and friendly set. It did not take long to be nostalgic for Lancaster. We had our own floor with very large and well-furnished rooms, but without heating, and it was winter, and a hard one at that. We also had a small sitting-room of our own, also without heating, so inevitably we bought forbidden small electric fires, which had to be hidden rapidly at the sound of footsteps. It was a strange experience those days, to be starting on a new training as students, and yet always being reminded, when it was convenient, that we were trained nurses. My short experience on the maternity ward at Lancaster now stood me in good stead, but nevertheless it was obvious to me that midwifery was not going to be one of my favourite occupations. The six months actually passed very quickly. Lectures were interesting, work was comparatively light, and I enjoyed my ante-natal patients and the supervised deliveries. We were cohesive as a group of students and had a few outings together, particularly enjoying Haworth and the Bronte moors. Very soon it was examination time, and we all passed and were on our way home. At this stage my mind was not made up as to whether to go on to Part Two training and become a qualified midwife. Eventually I decided to postpone it for a while, when an invitation was received from the matron of the Royal Victoria Hospital, Blackpool, to see her and discuss a junior sister's post.

The thought of being home for a while, even if having to live in hospital quarters, was quite appealing, but the national negotiating committee took a new line in its pay structure, giving the rate for the job, and stating separately the board and lodging charge if living in. Women's lives had changed during the war years, and recruitment also differed. Quite large numbers of men decided to come into nursing on leaving the forces; women no longer wished to be tied to living-in conditions and their expectations were to be able to choose their own place of residence and enjoy freedom when off duty. So I felt free to live at home and enjoy its comforts, especially as transport between the town and the hospital was good. The matron of the Victoria Hospital, Blackpool, was well-known in the town and was nearing retirement when she called me for interview. She was a formidable figure and kept firm control of her hospital. At interview she told me she was in need of a Junior Night Sister, experienced in theatre, to take emergency cases at night, and suggested a one-year contract, which we agreed. One day was allocated for me to become acquainted with the hospital before seeing it only at night. There were some qualms as to my ability to cope with a strange operating theatre and unknown surgeons, all of whom would have their own idiosyncrasies. Night duty itself and its supervisory duties were quite familiar. There were three of us as night sisters: the senior, Sister Murphy, who had been at the hospital for many years and was a superb nurse and manager, somewhat brusque in manner, and not easy to please, then another night sister and myself. Apart from theatre emergencies, and assisting with general ward rounds, one of my duties, and the one most disliked, was to call the maids, supervise them at breakfast, and make sure they were all on duty on time. They were not going to make it easy for me, as a completely new arrival, and had many ways of making sure that my register was wrong, and I never did get them all sorted out. We had few emergencies of any size, and no problems with theatre, but it was necessary to share with the other sister any deliveries on the maternity ward at night. Fortunately for all concerned they were quite straightforward. The worst of the problems during summer and the Illuminations were the casualties, of which we had many late at night. The hospital was on the edge of the town and casualties were brought in by ambulance. On busy nights there would be considerable waiting time, the last bus would have gone, and the only available transport was a taxi. That didn't go down well with the holidaymakers, who had often run out of money for the night, and might even have been on a day trip, with a bus to catch. It was therefore quite a job to empty casualty, and we tried to leave it to the porter, who was more than capable of parting with the loiterers.

As my sister and brother-in-law were both working, I used to go via Bega Hood's home in the morning for coffee before going on to bed. It was good to have a home and social life again with longstanding friends, and even to take part in the Dramatic Society's productions when nights off permitted. Night duty was always enjoyable for me; the constant mix of work, including casualty and theatres, both of which had the unexpected and the dramatic, was full of interest, and longer periods of nights off than we were used to allowed a social life. However, there was one part of work which worried me, and that was midwifery. When the one midwife scheduled for night duty was off, the night sisters had to be available for unexpected deliveries, and I was very conscious of not being fully qualified, although legally covered by supervision. So, as my year came to an end, rather than accept the ward sister's post offered, I resigned and applied for a vacancy to do Part Two training. On leaving the hospital and looking back over the year, I realised there were no personal regrets. It had been a good experience, especially to be living at home, but no close friendships had been made, and few lasting memories. It was strange to have been so involved with my local hospital, and yet it was the one in which I had never felt at home, and I had no regrets on leaving.

During the last months at Blackpool, I had been investigating Part Two training schools, wanting to try somewhere quite different from my current experience. Knowing that half the time would be spent on the district, my choice was Birmingham, in order to have the experience of a busy city. In 1950 the country was still recovering from war, still shabby, although the huge city areas of devastation were being restored with new building. Munition factories had turned over to peacetime production, but there were still many shortages and marks of the conflict, such as large areas of the city covered by the new pre-fabricated housing. Many of my patients lived in them, and they were remarkably cosy dwellings, quite a contrast to the tiny, and very poor, houses they had lived in until 'bombed out'. My experience with families showed children who were healthy on the whole, due to Government policies of free milk and orange juice for the children, but the parents were often undernourished, and it showed with the strain of pregnancy.

Part Two training was started in a large home run by the city in a pleasant district. Nearby was a convent of the order which ran my old school in Blackpool and, surprisingly, one of the young nuns who taught me was teaching there. It was an unexpected pleasure to be able to spend some of my half-days within its quiet atmosphere, and it was a real break from the hectic pace of the maternity hospital. We were housed in twos and threes in rooms nearby, as the home had no accommodation. Being mindful both of the cost of travel and transport of luggage, I decided to travel by long-distance bus, and so I arrived the afternoon before starting duty. I should have known better than to put myself in the situation to be placed on night duty the same evening. With hindsight it was obvious that the last set of pupils would have left, and the cheapest option was to put two of the incoming set on night duty on arrival. This practice did not take into account travel fatigue or newness, nor the fact that we didn't know the home, or anybody in it, but one didn't argue in those days!

Our room, just across the road, was large and comfortable, with a gas fire which ate shillings at a great rate. Our landlady was supposed to give us two shillings and sixpence each week for the fire, but she had a very poor memory. Most of my standards of comfort revolved around warm rooms, and very few rooms passed the test. My companion was a local girl, who was miserable from day one, and did not return from days off after a few weeks, so the room was my own, and the two and sixpence was scarcer than ever. The first night on duty was enough to make anyone turn round and go home. There was a rabbit warren of narrow corridors and small rooms, all badly lit, and we neither knew anyone nor what we were supposed to be doing. Daylight improved the situation, except that we had to stay up for introductions and formalities. The sister-in-charge was pleasant and well-organised, and the other eight pupils had varying backgrounds and most lived at a distance. Four of us had a religion in common, and were able to get to the same church together, which was a bond. The patients were mainly young, with husbands invariably working in the motor trade, and we each had a number of deliveries, about which we had to make very precise notes. Our book and notes would be scrutinised by our examiners later. I was able to make one or two visits to the convent in Edgbaston to see Sister Gerardine and spend a relaxing couple of hours. At my old school she had taught Latin, which was never one of my better subjects. She also introduced me to the Birmingham Oratory, a beautiful church with equally good liturgy, which I enjoyed visiting from time to time.

The time at Lordswood passed quickly, because we only had three months there, and arrangements were being made for our next three months on the district, living in the home of the district midwife, who was to supervise our essential ten deliveries and aftercare of her patients. My mentor was a previous hospital tutor, who had opted to work on the district and was a very good teacher, with a comfortable home to which she made me very welcome. The other pupils were placed in twos, but as my companion had left, I was the odd one. The next day we visited the patients who were expected to deliver within the next three months. The district was near the Lickey Hills and lovely country. We were also quite near to the Cadbury Village, where many of the husbands worked, and when we visited a patient and baby after a safe delivery, there was usually a large paper bag of chocolate misshapes waiting for us. As chocolate was still scarce, the gifts were very welcome. After the introductions, the mothers were my responsibility, and on answering the telephone call, usually at night, from the anxious father, I would ask him to come and collect the gas and air machine and accompany me on my bicycle to the house. I first informed the midwife of the relevant name and address. As there were no telephones in the houses, the husband had to go to the nearest kiosk and keep the midwife informed of progress or sometimes call the doctor for help. It all went remarkably smoothly, too smoothly in fact for my casebook, as the examiner was somewhat suspicious of my uneventful labours and deliveries. My tutor had another concern, and that was the fact that there was a low level of deliveries in my area, and there was a danger that the required number would not have been achieved before my examination was due. In order to avoid this happening, we liaised with a nearby teaching midwife whose area covered part of the Cadbury Village, but also a very poor area of the city. Inevitably, a call came late at night from a completely unknown address at the other side of the village, and precise instructions were given to me with a promise that the husband would be looking out for me to guide me to the right house. I had just finished washing my hair when the call came, so, getting quickly into uniform and pushing my hair under my cap, I set off on my bicycle. The first mile was fine, but then I lost my bearings completely going through the Garden Village, where streets and houses looked very much the same, and I was unable to find my way. It was after midnight and few people were about, the mother waiting for me had had other babies, and time was running out. So remembering our tutor's phrase, 'Your uniform will protect you, nurse', I risked asking directions from one or two dubious looking characters and, fortunately, my informants were right. In the distance was a worried husband with a flashlight. There was no time for wasted words. The tenement appeared and we both rushed up the steps with minutes to spare. My dishevelled appearance could not have given the distressed mother and her relatives in the room much confidence, but I hastily removed my coat and with nowhere to place it dumped it on some newspaper, tried to tuck my hair back under my cap and delivered the baby very rapidly. After I had made the mother and baby as comfortable as possible with the limited facilities, we all introduced ourselves and drank the baby's health in stone jam jars of scalding tea. I cheerfully made my way back to bed for what remained of the night, and after breakfast returned to the house to make sure all was well. The father and relatives greeted me like a long-lost friend. Mother and baby were fine, but the poverty and lack of belongings were only too obvious, as was the delight at the arrival of another member of the family. It gave me food for thought on the way home, and the memory of that scene is as clear today as it was half a century ago, when I was privileged to be a participant in a happy event.

Apart from the practical side of our work, we attended lectures given twice a week at the city office in Birmingham for all the students in the city on practical work, and the lectures were both very good and a great social opportunity, for we were able to meet up with our colleagues and exchange experiences. We took the tram into the city and, after our lecture, indulged in a cup of tea before returning to our respective houses. Our tram fare was also reimbursed on these occasions, as well as two pence per mile for the use of our bicycle visiting our patients on the district. At the end of our six months, our examinations were held at the Birmingham Maternity Hospital, and unfortunately one of our set was referred and had to take her district experience again. The rest of us were then qualified midwives with the pleasant responsibility to care for women throughout pregnancy and childbirth. The whole experience was very satisfying, and my immediate thought was to stay in midwifery, but it didn't last. I returned home for a few weeks' break, and have never practised midwifery since.

CHAPTER 3

Doors Begin to Open

HAVING DECIDED not to practise midwifery, I had to make up my mind about my next move, feeling that it was time to consider a sister's post. One of my friends at Lancaster had completed Part One training at Halifax in the set three months ahead of me. She had then taken a ward sister's post at Park Hospital, just outside Manchester, where she was able to live at home with her widowed father. We had kept in touch and she had alerted me to a vacancy at the hospital and suggested that I applied. It seemed a good idea to go to a new post where there was a friend. Manchester had a great deal to offer and was accessible to home for days off. I decided to take Joan's advice, applied to Park Hospital and was called for interview. The hospital was comparatively new and Matron was impressive. However, she felt that my experience was not sufficient for an immediate ward sister's post, but offered me a six-month trial as a staff nurse, after which she would consider promotion. It seemed a very fair proposition. I agreed and started work at the beginning of the following month.

I arrived at Park Hospital as planned, and was met by an assistant matron who showed me to my room where my uniform was ready, and gave me a quick tour of the hospital. I was somewhat puzzled by being addressed as Sister, and even more to be shown a ward and be told that the sister's post had been vacant for a while and my appointment would be warmly welcomed. When I returned to my room, it was obvious to me that it was indeed a sister's uniform on my bed. When I saw Matron before duty next morning, she explained that the ward had been without a sister too long and needed someone in charge to bring it up to standard. Her words were very true. It looked generally unloved, and the staff nurse in charge was leaving next day. A new consultant was expected, and a registrar was in charge. The only person who appeared stable was the cleaner, who was one of the old school, and proved to be of great assistance. Without thinking of my very recent arrival, I returned to Matron and said that the ward desperately needed a good staff nurse who knew the hospital and how to get things moving, and the next day a delightful, bright nurse appeared, loaned from another ward for six months. Between us we got to work and began to make a difference; the new consultant arrived and started to bring in his patients, and within three months it was a different place. A newly qualified and enthusiastic staff nurse was then appointed to the ward. The hospital was in a residential area with a good bus service from the gates into Manchester, and to the small shops nearby. Exploring in my off-duty was enjoyable but it was also very easy to go home for days off, either by bus or train, and I was often with Joan at the weekend, sometimes staying overnight. One thing did disappoint me and that was my room, which was smaller and less well furnished than the one at Lancaster in student days. However, for no apparently good reason, living out was not an option.

After a few months, Matron sent for me to tell me of forthcoming changes. The medical ward was to be moved down the corridor, and my ward emptied to be prepared for a new service. The consultant team was to be led by Mr Graham Bryce, a surgeon famous for his pioneering work in chest surgery. His service was currently in a former fever hospital on the outskirts of Manchester, and the patients were to be moved across. Staff Nurse and I were to go to the hospital for a few weeks to acclimatise ourselves and to become acquainted with the quite specific and demanding nursing care required. It all sounded very challenging and when we set off, it was with high expectations but also with some trepidation. Staff Nurse had temporarily become a junior sister so that we could both live in the Sisters' Home and use their lounge and dining-room, otherwise we would have been split up. The other sisters were polite, though not too friendly, and our living conditions were quite good. Like all old former infectious disease hospitals, it was set in very pleasant grounds and the ward blocks were all separate, as were the living quarters of the nursing staff. Fortunately, the weather was reasonably good, although it was the end of the year, but it was very cold and often wet at times. We both decided to be away for weekends in our off-duty, and I took the opportunity to go home.

On the first Monday morning we were introduced to the ward and the ward sister, but we were not prepared for the first sight of the chest ward and its patients. The wards were old hutments, which lent themselves to a Nightingale Ward pattern of two long lines of beds; a few, very basic, toilets and bathrooms were at one end, with a very small sister's office.

The only heating in the ward was from an old coke stove in the middle of the ward, around which the patients huddled, coughing endlessly. They were all men, gaunt and obviously very ill, but they remained up and about wherever possible because of the severity of their chest condition. Tuberculosis patients occupied some of the other wards. The next day we met Mr Graham Bryce and his team, all delightful and caring men, and very friendly. They were looking forward to moving to better conditions, and told me that most of the patients had cancer of the lung, and it was only too often inoperable. It was then a comparatively new field, patients were often referred too late, and results were not good. It was distressing to see patients struggling on their feet, obviously desperately ill, in the oppressive atmosphere of the ward. Sister, who had been at the hospital for a number of years, was obviously a very good nurse and only too aware of the difficulties. One patient, in particular, looked terribly ill; very breathless and coughing badly, he was still on his feet but, almost as I observed him, he collapsed and died in a few minutes.

After two weeks we returned to Park Hospital to get the ward ready for our new patients, and to move the medical patients to their new ward. Staff Nurse decided that she had had enough of the NHS and applied for a commission in the Army as a nursing sister. She was accepted and left quite suddenly, and was replaced by a bright young Irish nurse, who knew nothing about chest surgery, but set about learning and getting to know the ward very quickly. She was a very cheerful girl and a great asset as second-in-command. On the appointed day, some fifteen patients arrived from their former hospital, together with a handful of completely new admissions. The change in the character of the ward and its routine was very great, and, although one expected to find them pleased to be in better, lighter and cleaner surroundings, they weren't! The patients claimed that the ward was too clean and clinical. It didn't seem to have the camaraderie of the old situation. There was much more routine and nowhere to walk outside and it took a long time for them to settle. It was a week or two before any surgery was carried out, and the early results were not good. We still needed to get used to working as a team and were very grateful for an extremely good group of doctors who were real specialists in their field. They each moved on to head up their own teams in different parts of the country, and all acquired a well-deserved reputation for excellence. They worked extremely hard, and cared fiercely for their patients.

Presentation of certificates and badges to newly qualified nurses at the Prince of Wales's Hospital, London. The author end front row right.

From the day I became a ward sister I felt that it was a pity to have to learn how to run a ward by trial and error, and about two years after my appointment an interesting article in the *Nursing Mirror* caught my attention. It was written by a nurse who had been on a course for new ward sisters at the Royal College of Nursing in London. I wrote to the College, and had a reply inviting me for interview. The invitation was attractive, but London hotels were expensive, and it was necessary to stay overnight for interview the next day. However, a friend introduced me to a hostel for girls run by the Sisters of Charity, mainly for students attending college or university. The atmosphere was relaxed and other girls friendly, and the sister-in-charge offered me accommodation if my application to the college was accepted. My interview was also pleasant and constructive, and the short examination was easy and qualified me for a small bursary. The course was twelve weeks in length, and by NHS rules it was eligible for leave with pay. There was plenty to reflect about on the journey back to Manchester. In due course a letter arrived from the College to tell me that my application had been successful, and confirmed the bursary which would more or less cover my fees. It was really very exciting, but my interview with Matron was less encouraging. The matron who had interviewed me for my post had retired and been succeeded by her deputy, who was very able, but without the personality of her predecessor, and to me she seemed always to be looking for errors. She promised to take my application for paid study leave to the Board of Management, but appeared unenthusiastic about the usefulness of the course, so it was no surprise to find my application agreed for leave, but without pay. In addition, my superannuation payments were to be my responsibility. As living in London for three months without pay was just not possible, I wrote to withdraw my application. The reply unexpectedly offered me financial assistance from one of the College funds, which went a long way towards expenses, and I also wrote to an agency to ask if there was any possibility of weekend work in hospital. This resulted in my working on Saturdays at the Ear Nose and Throat Hospital in London's Golden Square, which was interesting and taught me a lot, as I was a complete novice in that speciality. The ward sister was delightful and interested in the course and one way and another I was almost solvent, as my father also helped with a useful gift of money. It was hard work having only Sunday free, but London was enjoyable. My fellow students were friendly and hard-working, but also ready to explore the capital, and we certainly did that.

Two students became particular friends, both obviously destined to be quite a force in the profession. One was Doreen Norton, a Londoner, and the other, Wyn Haworth, from the General Infirmary at Leeds. Both were to make their mark in nursing. Doreen had been off work for some time convalescing from a chest complaint and was using the course as a means of getting back into the profession. She had trained in one of the London hospitals which had a long-stay section, and she was quite passionate about the situation of elderly patients, especially those of very low income and in hospital for some time. When she returned to nursing she became one of the prime movers in the reform of elderly care. She obtained her doctorate with this as her thesis; her work was recognised by the College, which created her one of the first Fellows, and she was also awarded an OBE for her work. Today, her name is widely known as the nurse who made a real difference to the care of older people. Wyn was also marked as one of the future leaders of the profession, and was appointed a regional nurse in the NHS at an early age. Sadly, her promise was never to come to fruition. Returning home one night, she was run down in her car by a lorry, and was a paraplegic for the rest of her life. She was already married and had a baby girl. With incredible courage, she rebuilt her life from her bed and from a specially adapted wheelchair; she acted as a guinea pig for the first 'possum' machine, to allow paraplegics to communicate, and she provided herself as a model for district nurses and their pupils. Her husband was incredibly supportive and had a new house built to allow Wyn as much independence as possible. She was alone for most of the day and learned to cope in an amazing way. They travelled abroad on holiday, had an au pair to look after their daughter, and Wyn attended conferences, often as a speaker, and generally refused to be beaten by her situation. We kept in touch by letter, and by meetings at the Congresses of the Royal College of Nursing. It was a great sadness a few years ago to hear of her early death, but she certainly left her legacy behind and had lived long enough to see her daughter qualify in law.

We continued on our ward sisters' course, and two separate weeks were spent on observation at London hospitals. My first was St George's Hospital, then an old building at Hyde Park Corner, of which there are two major memories. The first was meeting Muriel Powell, later Dame Muriel, who had been appointed as matron of a London teaching hospital at the age of thirty-one. She was dynamic, very charismatic and was one of the leaders of the profession for many years. Our paths crossed frequently in the years ahead. The second was the fact that the ward sisters had a flat and actually lived on their ward. The sister who looked after me was in charge of a male ward, and she admitted with a laugh that it was a bit off-putting to return from a night out, in appropriate dress, to the comments of the patients. The second practical period was at the London Hospital, where one felt immersed in the history and traditions of the very old hospital, quite fascinating to a young nurse from a very provincial setting. My main recollection of the actual hospital was the length of the dark corridors on night duty.

One personality known and loved by many generations of RCN students was Nora Mackenzie, who taught us psychology. She was a fascinating figure, in an academic gown almost green with age and covered in chalk, and she had a very mobile face when speaking. This was my first acquaintance with her, and she became a familiar figure in my future work with the RCN. Examinations were also a feature of the course, and we all passed, most with at least one credit, mine being in Psychology and the Theory of Nursing, which was taught by Muriel

Powell. And then it was back to Park Hospital to try to put some of my theory into action. After being refused paid leave for the course, I didn't feel loyalty was owed, and while I was in London, Maisie Hulme, a friend from Lancaster, approached me. She had been working at the Prince of Wales's Hospital in North London, first as Night Superintendent and then as Ward Sister. Another sister from Lancaster was about to leave night duty at the Prince of Wales's and she said that the matron would be interested in an application from me. An interview was duly arranged. The matron, Dorothy Allin, made a lasting impression on me, and an offer as night superintendent was made and accepted. Returning to my ward in Manchester was quite sad, knowing it would be my last three months there. The medical team were a joy to work with, the ward had matured, and it was a wrench to leave, but one good point was that my staff nurse was appointed to succeed me. My friend Joan suggested that I lived with her and her father for the last few months, as it would help me to recoup some of the financial loss of my three months away. It was a pleasant time. Many years later when I was invited to give a major lecture, I discovered that the organiser was the Principal Tutor of the Group School of Park Hospital, and it was obviously greatly changed from my days.

Once more I had a few days' break at home, and then it was time to pack for London, more carefully this time because, although nights off were generous, the distance from home was greater and the rail fare was quite a consideration. The salary of even senior sisters was quite small compared with other professions, but then it has always been, and still is, an uphill struggle to obtain salary increases for nurses,

The Prince of Wales's Hospital was an interesting foundation, established by the deaconesses from the Kaiserworth Institute in Germany, where Florence Nightingale did some early training. They wore a distinctive brown uniform and cap, of which the brown cape was still worn by their successors, the modern nurses. One of the era of the deaconesses, an old lady called Sister Mabel, still lived at the hospital and shared the sisters' dining-room and sitting-room, as it was part of their contract to be cared for throughout their life. Sister Mabel died while I was still at the Prince of Wales's. The hospital itself consisted of some 240 beds, most being in the main and old block, but with a newly built private wing and a small, but very good, nursing school. Most of the senior staff were trainees of the hospital, but it had almost become a tradition that the

Night Superintendent came from Lancaster. The Preliminary Training School was some miles away in the country at Woodford Green. Miss Allin was a tall, friendly woman who ran the hospital quietly and efficiently, with two assistant matrons and a home sister, and was both respected and well loved. We had very pleasant grounds behind the hospital, with a very old and beautiful pink chestnut tree, and the home, with its comfortable accommodation, lay just behind. Sadly, some years later after my departure, the planners decided that the hospital was too small to be cost effective, and the grounds at the nearby St Ann's hospital were large and could accommodate more and newer ward blocks. The chestnut tree also fell victim to the buildings. We used to joke about the ghost of a deaconess reputed to walk the corridors at night, although as night sister it was never my misfortune to meet her, but surely those far gone deaconesses must mourn the demolition of their beloved hospital.

The hospital was part of a group for administrative purposes, and came under the North East Metropolitan Region. The night staff lived at St Ann's, one of the nearby hospitals in the group and a former infectious diseases hospital, and we occupied one block, in which I had a delightful bedsitting room, with a lovely fire, for off-duty. We also had two wards of patients under the care of the Prince of Wales's Hospital. The only drawback was the fact that we had to go by hospital bus and had our breakfast at our own hospital before going on duty. The same journey was made in the morning after night duty had finished, and there was always a long wait because some nurses were required for appointments with Matron, to see the doctor or sister tutor, and so on. It meant that we never returned to St Ann's for at least an hour after finishing our meal, and it was a great source of irritation after a twelve-hour spell of duty. Night duty was always enjoyable, full of interest and often extremely busy. There were two junior sisters with me, but with four nights off every fortnight, only two of us were on duty at any one time. The junior night sister post was often a first promotion and a very useful learning experience because of the entire range of patient care covered. Sometimes it was a definite training post for a staff nurse to assess her capabilities, and apart from the variety, the supervision and training of new sisters was very enjoyable. Tottenham was an interesting area, with many lovely old houses, and its population, which had changed dramatically since the war years, was predominantly West Indian. It was the era when we still had a management committee. One prominent member, who spent a lot of time at the hospital and took a great interest in the nursing staff, was Lady Morrison, the wife of a Labour peer who had grown up in the area and had a great love of the hospital. Her husband died suddenly while I was there, and she was determined to carry the torch for both of them. She was a very great lady, who made no secret of their early background.

The hospital was on the main road and extremely busy, especially, it seemed, at night. The operating theatre was often in use until well into the night, and the surgeon who used it most at that time was a very well-known London surgeon by the name of Mr Dickson Wright. If he came in during the day, he sometimes brought with him his young daughter Clarissa, who was to find television fame when she grew up. Going on night duty on the nights that 'Dickie' was operating was always unpredictable. His patients would be prepared during the day for his allotted time for surgery, but that time was movable, to say the least. Occasionally he might have finished his list, more often it was ongoing, and the worst scenario of all was when the patients were still waiting for him to appear when we arrived on duty. More often than not he would appear at two or three in the morning but sometimes not at all and his list had to be cancelled. The unfortunate night nurses on his ward had quite a time of it, to say nothing of the patients who had to wait, but idiosyncrasies were just accepted in those days, and although we grumbled, that was the way it was.

One of my never-to-be-forgotten experiences was the two or three nights of the great London 'smog' of the late1950s. In those days the smoke pollution was very great and, whereas London had been known for its fogs, one winter we were hit by a real 'pea souper' which lasted for two or three nights. My experience with it started when my telephone rang at 4.30p.m. and woke me out of a deep sleep. Our usual call time for night duty was 7p.m. but this call was Matron to alert me to the state of the weather. The bus was on its way to bring us in for duty, because the visibility was so bad that it would take the best part of an hour to cover what was usually a ten-minute journey. It was a bit hard to believe, and none of us appreciated having our sleep curtailed to that extent, but a grumbling collection of night nurses duly collected. It really did take time to get to the hospital at walking pace, and the choking atmosphere penetrated the bus. Matron was waiting to give me the report. She broke the bad news that the night nurses, who had just finished their nights off, were telephoning in to say that they could not get through to the hospital, and of course their counterparts, who had gone on nights off that morning, had left. We faced the prospect of a night with very sick people coming in as emergencies, but with little more that half the night staff on duty. Fortunately, one of the other two night sisters was available. It was not long before the ambulance called to say it was on its way in with great difficulty, bringing a desperately ill man, who turned out to have cut his throat in an attempted suicide. The nurses and doctors tried very hard to save him, but he was quite violent and died in spite of everything we could do. His wife told us that he was an asthmatic, and simply could not breathe in the thick fumes. Nor was he the last. We had another two in similar state, but we did manage to save them. Other patients who had come to casualty couldn't get home, and the corridors had more than a few sleeping forms wrapped in rugs. Halfway through the night, yet another ambulance arrived, this time with a young woman, in labour, with her husband. They were bound for the nearby maternity hospital, but had had such a bad journey that the driver was afraid he wouldn't make it in time. Unfortunately, we had no midwifery services, and I had to go out to the ambulance to talk to and examine the patient, who was understandably very frightened. I was able to reassure her and the driver that it would be safe to continue. My midwifery did come in useful after all. The driver was obviously afraid in case the baby did decide to put in an unexpected appearance, and one of our precious nurses had to be sent with her for assurance. But the last straw of the night occurred halfway through when, somehow, my junior night sister got a needle embedded in her arm, and it disappeared into the tissues. She had to be put in bed on one of the wards and immobilised until a surgeon could operate to remove it. It left me single-handed for the next two nights. Things couldn't get much worse, and mercifully they didn't.

Even without the high drama of 'Dickie's' erratic time-keeping, and the London smog, there was rarely time to sit down for more than the meal break. We had a high proportion of accidents as we were on the busy main road into central London and near to an underground station. One very unusual incident was a sudden halt on the escalator late in the evening, which filled our casualty department with many patients, fortunately none with major injuries. The main problem was how to get them home when public transport had stopped, and quite a few had to settle down in Casualty for the night.

It was part of my responsibility to support the ward nurses, especially if a comparatively junior nurse was in charge of a ward, and invariably the greater proportion of deaths took place at night. One very distressing experience was with a young girl of about sixteen who was dying and whose parents couldn't take the strain and had gone home for a rest after many nights' watching. She deteriorated quite suddenly and was crying for her parents when the young junior nurse, hardly any older, knelt on the bed and cradled the girl in her arms while she died, quietly and apparently peacefully. I was nearly moved to tears, when the junior nurse felt she had been unprofessional and needed my assurance that she was just being a wonderful nurse. Seriously ill children were always distressing, and their parents were devastated on a child's death, which often occurred at night. Fortunately, we had one of the most wonderful hospital chaplains I have ever met, and I have never met any who were not caring, hard-working and compassionate. This was an anglo-catholic vicar, who always wore a cassock on his rounds, and liked to be addressed as Father Clarke. He would come at a call any time of the day or night, and spend as long with the patients and relatives as they needed him. He was just as caring with staff. Many years later, I met one of his daughters at Southampton University, and she gave me the sad news of his death at a great age.

We had our amusing incidents, too, of course. Matron had a small flat near to the wards, and would occasionally appear during the night to see if all was well. She had a little white Scotty dog which was always with her and gave the nurses good warning that Matron was on her way. She also had a large black cat, which was not averse to making his presence felt with his claws, and sometimes Matron would 'bleep' me to ask me to come and let Peter out. After a few of these little outings, Peter decided to befriend me, and began to accompany me round the wards as my shadow, so the nurses also had early warning of my visits. They all knew of my off-duty, too, because Peter then retired to Matron's flat and did not reappear until my return.

Time passed and night duty came to an end. Matron talked with me about taking a ward on day duty, and I explained that I had always wanted to teach, and would like to be considered for a secondment to take the two-year Nurse Tutor's course at the Royal College of Nursing. An unqualified teacher at the hospital's preliminary training school had just been accepted on the course, but she said she would enquire if two students could be seconded. There was a national fund for secondment to this particular course because of a lack of qualified teachers, and it did not depend on hospital funding. To my delight the answer was positive, provided that the College accepted me. Once again, I went for interview, and was not only accepted but invited to sit for the Cowdray Scholarship, which gave me a substantial cash grant for the many extras, such as books and travel, and it was arranged for me to join the programme in the September. That was six months away but Matron offered me the post of relief sister on day duty, which I accepted with pleasure. Interesting though night duty was, it was nice to get back to a normal day routine, without the half-awake feeling which always accompanied the first hours of nights on duty. Another perk was the tickets to London theatres and other events which were frequently donated to the hospital, and we made good use of these on our days off. This was how we were able to see many musicals of that time, my favourite being the Ivor Novello shows and their foot-tapping music – probably due to nostalgia for my pantomime days. The best outing of all was to the Centre Court at Wimbledon, using tickets donated by one of our surgeons. I have seen Wimbledon since, but, instead of such luxury, it was after hours of waiting in the queue for standing room.

And so the time came to leave the Prince of Wales's Hospital, and start the Nurse Tutor's course, once more packing for the move. I had again decided to live in a student hostel, this time run by the Daughters of Mary, and they allowed me to leave a case there while I went home for a two-week break. It wasn't an entirely happy stay, due to tension between my sister and my father, who was obviously lonely since the death of my mother and my absence from home, even though he did assist my sister and husband in running the shop. He had become very friendly with an old colleague from his Post Office days who had lived next to us for some years with her elderly parents, both of whom had since died. Friendship had matured into something stronger and they decided to get married. To me it seemed a good solution for two lonely people who had a lot in common, but Stella thought otherwise and she and my father were completely estranged for a few years. It did not help when I was home from hospital and insisted on going to visit them, but my father and I were too close to break up, so it was a very uneasy time. Bega Hood was a great source of strength, and our friendship developed further, but it was a relief to return to London and a new phase of living in Kensington and studying at the Royal College of Nursing in Cavendish Square.

The other student from the Prince of Wales's Hospital, Muriel Bowman, introduced herself the first day, and we immediately became friends. She was a quiet, clever young woman who had spent some years as a missionary nurse in China, and had a very good command of Cantonese. She had had to leave China in the days of the cultural revolution, which had obviously been a very difficult time for the missionaries, and had suffered from tuberculosis, which had to be checked periodically. Another of her friends, by the name of Emma Walsh, or 'V' as we called her for some reason, was also on the course. They had both been at an orthopaedic hospital near Wakefield, Muriel as a nurse and Emma as a patient. Although recovered, she was not fit enough for heavy nursing, and so had applied for the Nurse Tutor's course. Even with the Cowdray grant, it was not easy to manage on my ward sister's salary, so it seemed a good idea to walk across Kensington Gardens and Hyde Park daily to the College at the other end of Oxford Street and economise on bus fares. On one of my first days I met another student from the Nurse Administrators' course, Catherine Mary Hall. She went to the Middlesex Hospital as assistant matron when her one-year course ended, and a few years later she became the general secretary of the Royal College of Nursing, and was one of the finest leaders of nursing we have had. Under her leadership the College grew in membership from around 30,000 to over 200,000. It became a registered trade union while keeping its professional status, and, when she retired in the mid 1980s, she left a very strong organisation which has continued to grow from strength to strength. She died in her seventies and was greatly mourned by a packed congregation at her memorial service in the crypt of St Paul's Cathedral. We had worked in partnership at the RCN for many years and, when the unenviable task of paying tribute to her fell to me, it was difficult to contain my emotions. Our early friendship had grown from those walks across the park, sharing the same religious faith, and generally putting the nursing world to rights. She finished her course while mine had another year to run, and my walks across the park became quite lonely.

We had a variety of tutors and lecturers at college, some extremely good, such as Dame Muriel Powell who taught us Administration, and others less memorable. It was delightful to come into contact again with Nora Mackenzie, who taught psychology, oversaw our assignments, and was particularly involved with our teaching practice. She really was the teacher whom many generations of students remember with gratitude and real affection. Many are the stories which abound about her lectures and conversations. Her husband was a well-known psychiatrist who died before her and she spent her final years in St Monica's Home in Bristol, where she was as loved by residents and staff as she was at the college.

There were two main periods of practical teaching, and mine were in two very different hospitals. Nurse education was not completely brought into the realm of higher education until almost the turn of the century. At the time of my course, in the late fifties, nursing schools were in the hospital setting, with their own teaching staff, but under the control of Matron and the general running of the hospital. We were funded for teacher training, and for all the equipment of the school of nursing, lecture fees and other related matters. The size of the schools and their equipment varied, relating to the size of the hospital and practical experience, although one or two group schools had been set up, and we saw the early emergence of university courses leading to a degree. Liverpool and Glasgow were two of the leaders in this respect. My first period of teaching practice was at the Hospital of St John and St Elizabeth in North London, a small but long-established hospital, which was run and owned by a religious order, and which had a small nursing school. In many ways it was akin to the Prince of Wales's Hospital Training School, and it provided an environment where slower learners could flourish, but it did not stretch the ability of the more able students. Practical experience was limited, and students had to be seconded to other hospitals to fill the gaps, a policy which was never popular with the students.

My second period of teaching practice was very different, at St Bartholomew's Hospital School of Nursing in the City of London, familiarly known as 'Barts'. Nurse Tutors from Barts could be found heading up other nursing schools, both in London and in other parts of the country. A lasting relationship was again set up here with the principal tutor, by the name of Winifred Hector, a tall, rather austere woman with a brilliant mind, and a very characteristic style of teaching, and I enjoyed her immensely. When she retired from Barts, she headed up the nursing degree course at Queen Elizabeth's College of London University. In her later years she lived in a delightful flat near the hospital, in a block where many of her colleagues also lived, and I was able to see her on a number of occasions before her death in the early years of the new century. She was a fascinating character, a brilliant teacher, and I owed her a great deal. The Nurse Tutor course had only recently been extended to two years and it was strange to be away from hospital for so long. We did keep in touch with the Prince of Wales's Hospital, as the hospital administrator insisted that we came to the hospital each month to collect our pay and to be sure that we were still on the course. It was quite a journey out of central London to the hospital.We were the only ones of our class who had to report in this way; however, though we felt it was only too typical of the attitude towards nurses, it was a minor irritation.

Inevitably, examinations arrived, and they were very testing. My teaching assessment was at St Bartholomew's, and we could choose our own topic. Mine was on international aspects of nursing and health. The student nurses were aware that it was my assessment and were doing their best to be bright and attentive and ask intelligent questions. After my comments about Albert Schweitzer and his work, one student asked me how he fitted into the United Nations, and, after a stunned silence, I had to admit that I didn't have the slightest idea. After the class the student concerned was more upset than I was, but we both thought the incident would be enough to fail me. Nora Mackenzie just laughed and said, 'Why on earth didn't you choose something nice and simple like an aspect of nursing?' However, the worst didn't happen and, after many weeks, the examination results came through and I was awarded the Diploma in Nursing of London University. Today, nurse teachers have similar degrees to their colleagues in general education.

We were not bound to return to our previous hospitals, but courtesy required us to ask. Muriel Bowman had already worked for some years as an unqualified tutor, and wanted to be nearer home, so Matron agreed to release her. She asked me to take the assistant tutor post at the Preliminary Training School, a separate building and residence in large grounds at Buckhurst Hill, north of Tottenham. It wasn't easy for transport, the nearest tube station being a good twenty minutes' walk, with unreliable buses at infrequent intervals, and so at this point it seemed sensible to obtain my first car. While at home I had driven my brother-in-law's car for a number of years and had passed my test, and the only problem was cost. This was solved by a two-year hire purchase agreement on a second-hand Morris Minor, bought in Blackpool and driven back to London with some trepidation. It stood me in good stead, as I had chosen to live out and had found rooms very near the underground station with a delightful elderly lady who lived alone. This made it easier for me to follow the friendships and interests already established in London. The Principal of the PTS, as we referred to the school, was an elderly woman near retirement who was a friend of Miss Allin, the Matron of the Prince of Wales's Hospital. She did not appear to make friendly relationships with her staff and colleagues, and, after taking the anatomy and physiology class in the morning, she repaired to her bungalow near to the classrooms for the rest of the day. However, it did not interfere with the smooth running of the school. The other unqualified tutor was a very quiet, likeable person who taught her classes well, was always available for help if required, but didn't interfere. The students were resident and wore uniform during classes, remaining at the school for twelve weeks, with a number of outside visits of observation and interest, and supervised half-days on the ward towards the end of the course. A home sister, Sister Brigham, was in charge of the home and the students' welfare. She was a real character, a disciplinarian where the students were concerned, but also somewhat old-fashioned in her views, and the students alternated between exasperation and working out how to get round her. She regarded the junior tutor as a somewhat grown-up student and very useful for all kinds of responsibilities in the evenings and at weekends. Muriel Bowman had warned me of this, and her advice played a large part in my decision to live out. We had intervals of snow that year and as it wasn't always possible to get the car out, it was a trudge up the hill in the snow to reach the school. One of my other duties was to teach Anatomy and Physiology to the senior class of the local high school who were going into medicine or nursing, so there was an escape to Tottenham and my friends at the hospital twice a week. Just after the first set of students at the preliminary training school had ended their course and departed to the main hospital, the senior tutor announced her retirement, and was replaced by a very pleasant lady who was a graduate of the Prince of Wales's training school. We had good communication and there was a much happier atmosphere all round.

No sooner had we settled down to that change than there was a request for me to see Matron. It was a great surprise to hear that the principal tutor at the hospital had given in her resignation as, very late in life, she was to be married, and Matron offered me the post, subject to approval by the committee. This really was unexpected, and, to my delight, my interview with the committee turned out well and my appointment was confirmed. That meant another move, and my landlady was given notice, and the question of where to live was on the agenda again. This was unexpectedly solved by Matron, who told me that the hospital had just taken over a large house in a nearby road and it was being redecorated and equipped for the sisters. It was very comfortable indeed, and I had a large sitting room to which were added some extra pieces of furniture. It was good to be so near to the hospital, and, with the car, London was easily accessible. The change to the senior training school was plain sailing, as there was a very good, young, married male tutor in post, who had hopes of promotion. His disappointment was understandable, and, although he decided to look for another post and was successful within the year, we were able to work together very amicably and kept in touch after he moved. However, his resignation caused a problem in the work situation as teaching staff were scarce and it was impossible to run the school single-handedly. Matron asked if I knew of anyone who could help temporarily. By a strange coincidence, Joan Roberts, who had married a man from Romford, was working as a staff nurse in the outpatients' department. We talked about the possibility, and she agreed that she could take the practical sessions at the school. Matron then suggested one of her former casualty sisters, Mary Niven, who had been working near home because her mother was nearly ninety years old and very frail, and who now wished to return to London. She arranged for Mary to come and see me. We had known each other at the hospital but not closely, and we both thought it was a good arrangement. Mary had taken the first year of her tutor's course, but failed her examination in anatomy and physiology, and hoped to re-sit and then recommence her second year. This was the start of an unexpected friendship which was to last until her death in 1994.

In the meantime it had become obvious to me that a degree would become essential for all nurse tutors, and I decided to attempt a London degree in Economics by correspondence with Wolsey Hall. Hard work though it was, the first year went well. However, the second year was much more difficult and I did want to finish my studies within the normal three years. One of my tutors, Professor Gordon Mackay, was particularly good, and we had added correspondence with the written tutorials. He offered to give me individual tutorial sessions and invited me over to his home in north Oxford to see how we got on together. After that, every other Saturday was spent travelling to Oxford for a three-hour session, and it was immensely valuable. Professor Mackay was quite a character, and we sat in his cluttered study at home, he wearing a big green eyeshade and a gown that almost matched in colour. We had a tea tray between us and I had instructions to fill his plate whenever it was empty. He was so pleased when I phoned him with the news of my second-class degree, and we kept in touch afterwards until his death some few years later.

Teaching the senior student nurses and carrying out the administration of the school took some getting used to, and my sets of lecture notes were gradually compiled late at night, but the students were delightful, and quite a mixture in nationality, making it very enjoyable hard work. The school itself was a big wooden hut of a building with one very large room and two small offices. All the equipment, including beds and models, were kept in the same room, and, if a second lecture coincided, we had to retreat to a small lecture room in the main hospital. The situation was obviously unsatisfactory, and we were delighted to be offered a brick-built extension with a grant from the King's Fund for London. This included a large hall, which was used both for lectures and social occasions such as the annual nurses' pantomime, produced by me for staff and friends. We also had a modern kitchen and a very good library with a generous allowance for new books. Unfortunately, there was another staff change. Joan had developed bad asthma and decided to give up nursing and live quietly with her husband in Romford. One of the ward sisters had been on the tutor's course and returned to us as the assistant tutor, while Mary Niven continued to remain in the school. Having decided to stay at the hospital, she proceeded to look for accommodation, and as our friendship had grown, we thought it was a good idea for me to live out and then we could share a home. As she had a great friend in the Woodford area, we decided to look there. One thing led to another and we felt we could try buying a flat. It was a struggle to raise the deposit and to equip the flat with essential furnishings, and, when we moved in halfway through the month, we sat down to assess our financial situation. Between us we had exactly thirty shillings for the rest of the month, but we were more amused than worried, and survived until the next pay day. We were fortunate in finding a new build in a small and delightful close very near to the station, and we shared my car for getting to and from the hospital. It was a very happy five years which passed very quickly, and then there was another major change of course.

Mary noticed an advertisement in the *Nursing Times* for a new position at the headquarters of the International Council of Nurses, then based in a delightful three-storey house in Dean Trench Street, Westminster. The main qualification required was a degree in Economics – which I had – and the remit was to advise nurses throughout the world on salaries and conditions of work. It sounded interesting, and I wrote to apply. I was more than a little surprised to find myself shortlisted, and even more so to be offered the job. Apart from myself no one seemed to realise that my knowledge of salary negotiation and related subjects was practically nil, and there was a real problem in making my decision. This was compounded when Matron sent for me to tell me that she was retiring, and the committee wanted me to apply for the post. It was a very hard decision to make. I had grown to love the Prince of Wales's Hospital, and to make such a drastic move was very much a step into the unknown but, after many days of arguing with myself and discussions with Mary, the economic welfare post with the International Council of Nurses (ICN) was accepted. Even then, I could not have known the major change it would make to my life.

It was only fair to give three months' notice of my departure from the Prince of Wales's, so that there would be ample time to advertise the vacancy and attract good candidates. In fact, the post was taken by a senior tutor from the London Hospital, who had conducted our hospital examination for us. It was very fortunate for me that there was a good period of time before the change, as bad news from home intervened. My brother-in-law telephoned to tell me that my sister was very ill and in hospital. As it was towards the end of a week, it was possible for me to go home for the weekend, with Matron's permission to stay longer if necessary. Mary drove me to the station and Sam picked me up at Preston, as we lived a few miles outside. It appeared that Stella had been having abdominal trouble for some time, but it had become acute, the doctor was called in and he made arrangements for her immediate admission to hospital. Sam was a quiet, unassuming man, rather helpless in an emergency, and had not thought to ask for an appointment with the hospital doctor. Fortunately, the breach between Stella and my father and his wife had been healed, but they lived some twenty miles away and my father was in poor health, so it was left to me to sort out the situation. We had an assistant in the shop who was very efficient and a great help at the time. On visiting the hospital, it was obvious to me that Stella was acutely ill and, when I saw the doctor, he explained that they wished to operate the following day. It took both explanation and persuasion for Sam to sign the consent form, and we returned home feeling very anxious. I then went to Blackpool to alert my father to the seriousness of the situation. All went well with the surgery, but when we visited in the afternoon and saw the surgeon, the news was bad. Stella had an inoperable ovarian cancer and, while she was able to come home, it was a matter of a few months. My father was shattered at the news, but Sam did not seem to take it in. The only point that registered was that it was cancer and, for some reason known only to himself, he refused to let anyone know and turned away all visitors, apart from my father and his wife and a cousin who had moved to Blackpool. It was a terrible dilemma – I had to return to London while Stella was still in hospital, and then I took a week's leave to bring her home and assess the situation.

We finally settled on my returning to work and coming home each weekend, which put a great strain on everyone, but it seemed the only solution. Stella began to deteriorate fast, and only a few weeks later it was obvious that she could not live much longer. Fortunately, I was at home when she lapsed into coma and died within a few hours. The local priest came in but, as our grave was in Blackpool, he arranged for a priest from that town to take the funeral service and burial. My father was devastated, and Sam was still holding to his position of not letting anyone know of the cause and discouraging visitors, so it was a very trying time in a number of ways. Finally, all was over and I was able to return to London. Sam asked his sister to come and live with him but, though he carried on with the shop, it was obvious that Stella had been the driving force, and the business went down until he decided to sell and return to Yorkshire to live with his sister. I saw him occasionally until his health deteriorated and he died in hospital some five years after Stella. It had all been very harrowing and it was a relief to return to London, face the forthcoming changes and turn my mind to other things.

Chapter 4

The International World

THE INTERNATIONAL COUNCIL OF NURSES (ICN) had been based in Geneva for many years until war broke out, when it was transferred in some haste to the USA, and returned to Europe in 1947, but to London and not Geneva. A brilliant nurse, Daisy Bridges, a graduate of the Nightingale School of Nursing at St Thomas's Hospital in London, was appointed as general secretary. She had a great personality, an insatiable appetite for work, and quickly became known and loved by nurses around the world in her considerable journeying to visit nurses' associations in many countries. She seemed oblivious of weather changes, and the many photographs of her show her in a neat dark suit and white blouse. Her deputy for many years once remarked to me that Daisy's idea of getting ready for one of her marathon tours was to buy a new blouse. By the time my nursing journey had brought me to London, ICN was well established at 1, Dean Trench Street, Smith Square, Westminster. My 'History of Nursing' lectures must have told me something about ICN, but if so, it didn't register; lectures at the RCN course on the same subject, however, did tell us about its history and that it was based in London. One or two members of my class made visits to ICN headquarters, but it was not part of my schedule. I remember frantically looking for information on the Council, and actually going for interview with only the scantiest knowledge of the organisation, and even less as to what would constitute an international economic welfare programme. Since the end of the Second World War, ICN had re-established itself. Meetings were first held in rented or 'borrowed' accommodation, then offices for the very small staff were acquired in Queens Gate, London, then in Gloucester Place, and finally a charming three-storey house with a lot of character was purchased in 1955. It was at this point that Daisy Bridges became general secretary.

The interview committee included Florence Udell, who had been doing work on the salaries and conditions of nurses throughout the world. She was the nurse working with the Government Overseas

Department, had first-hand knowledge of the work and conditions of nurses in very many countries and was my mentor for my first years. Daisy Bridges had just announced her retirement at the recent ICN Congress in Melbourne, Australia, and her successor was Helen Nussbaum, a Swiss nurse with a lot of international experience during the postwar years. About two weeks later Miss Bridges telephoned to ask me to visit her, and was able to tell me something of the background of the new post on economic welfare and, though the idea was still daunting, the post now had more substance to it. She assured me that, with Miss Udell's help and an international orientation programme, things would begin to fall into shape.

A month later I left the Prince of Wales's for the last time and felt it was the most colossal mistake. A tutor from The London Hospital had applied for and obtained my post, but Mary and I were still able to keep our home in Woodford Green, and it was quite easy to commute into London as we lived so near to the station. Mary had been offered a place on the course for senior nursing administrators run by the King's Fund College in London. The first weeks at ICN were spent in various visits around London relevant to my new position. It was a period of hard learning, much of it shared with another new staff member, Ingrid Hamelin, of Finland, who had been appointed assistant to Ellen Broe, of Denmark, an awe-inspiring figure, who was director of the Education Division. Ingrid and I got on well from the start, and were fast friends, not only throughout our ICN days, but later when Ingrid succeeded Ellen Broe, and later still when she returned to Finland to take up a major appointment. She was a board member of ICN for eight years but died soon after her retirement from work, and was greatly missed on the international field. Frances Beck, a rather remote, but very clever, British nurse, was director of the Nursing Service programme. The editorial department was run by Marjorie Wenger, an experienced journalist, who produced a very informative and interesting publication, *The International Nursing Review*, and also handled publicity. Gwen Buttery, the deputy general secretary, was a very experienced South African nurse, friendly and with a great deal of knowledge about the nursing world at large. Apart from secretarial staff, that was the sum total of ICN staff, and there was usually at least one person out on fieldwork at any one time.

It was only about six weeks after starting work with ICN that a telegram arrived from Jamaica from the president of the nurses' association, telling of a general strike in that country, and asking for help from the Director of the Economic Welfare Division – me! It was a wonderful title, but the nurses concerned had no idea of my complete inexperience. They explained that there was a general strike in their country, the major union with considerable nurse membership was taking action at the hospital and was putting pressure on the nurses who were members of the Jamaica Nurses' Association. The Nurses' Association, true to their constitution, held that nurses should not leave their patients even in a general strike, and feelings were running extremely high. Helen Nussbaum was by now the chief executive of ICN, and she called Florence Udell to meet and advise us. Miss Udell – I never called her anything else, even though we got to know each other very well and worked together a great deal – came to lunch and we talked over the situation and what we could do to help. We decided to cable and ask if they would welcome a visit from me and they replied to come as soon as possible. I was plunged into such a flurry of activity that there was no time to worry about it and an air ticket was booked via New York. As Mary was on her course at the King's Fund College, we could only speak on the phone, and she was quite scathing about my possible usefulness in the situation. In fact, there was a delay of a few days and Mary came home for the weekend and helped me to prepare for the journey. Except for short breaks in Europe, it was my first overseas trip and my wardrobe was certainly not adequate, but that was a minor problem and in any case there was no time for shopping. Mary and ICN staff saw me off from the Kensington air terminal. It was my first experience of long-haul flights and the hutted building, which was the long-haul departure terminal in those days, looked very dreary in the late evening. The plane was one of the early 707s and my first experience of a jet. Though it was less crowded and more comfortable than today's packed flights, I had grave misgivings as to its ability to get me across the Atlantic safely. It all seemed very strange and lonely. I was too stressed to sleep on the flight and we arrived at what is now Kennedy Airport at 6a.m. to a deserted terminal. With five hours to kill before the next leg of the flight to Kingston, Jamaica, I called the American Nurses' Association, and spoke to my counterpart, to arrange to spend a few days there on the way back. Then there was a long wait for the plane to take me on to Kingston, Jamaica and my first experience of tropical heat. A group of Jamaican nurses, led by the president, were waiting for me, and we went to the

Appointment to ICN staff as Director of the Social and Economic Division, London, 1961.

home of my hostess, Grace Marsh, a nursing tutor who lived with her sister and niece in a charming house and garden in a suburb of Kingston.

The nurses brought me up to date with the situation, which had become very heated, and we discussed a plan of action, but eventually decided to postpone any further activity until a meeting with the full council of the association the next day. My hosts suggested it would be a good idea for me to have an early night, so I thankfully retired to bed. The meeting on the following day was at the newly-built association headquarters, when it was decided to ask the Government officials to meet me so that I could express the nurses' concern. We also planned to travel to the main towns and centres on the island to meet as many nurses as possible. That was the beginning of a most hectic programme with hardly a minute free. The Premier and all governmental officials we met were happy to offer any facilities needed, and they thought that an outsider might be acceptable to both sides. In between, the matrons saw me as a useful visitor for nursing functions, such as the presentation of prizes and certificates, and these were a good way of getting the message across of the nurses' responsibility to the patient at all times. One of those functions was a graduation ceremony for midwives one afternoon. The morning was spent travelling to the other side of the island to meet nurses from a group of clinics. Driving on some of the roads across the hills was quite difficult and, on the top of one pass, the car skidded badly, left the road and landed on its side. Fortunately, though we were shaken, we were not otherwise injured. A passing boy came to our aid, and obtained a taxi for me to get back quickly to Kingston, while my driver waited for help. From the nearest place with a telephone, I phoned through to the hospital explaining the situation and asking for someone to bring my outfit to the hospital so that I could change and then I hurried on to the hospital alone. Reaction set in when I got to my feet and my legs didn't support me too well, but the function appeared to go smoothly.

The strike gradually subsided after my departure, and I suspect it would have done so of its own accord, as my efforts could not have made any impression on what was so clearly national discontent. The government hospitals were very crowded and in many respects there were legitimate grievances. One hospital visit remains very clear in my memory, and that was to the main psychiatric hospital, with conditions more prison-like than those of a hospital. The nurses invited me to see it, and I was accompanied throughout a full round of the various sections, my escorts remaining very close to me, for which I was grateful. Although there were many hard feelings left, they eventually healed and on my next visit many of the nurses active in the dispute had become strong members of the Jamaica Nurses' Association. The University Hospital was much newer and had many advantages over the government hospitals and was therefore mostly clear of the problems. One thing that this trip did for me was to give me a lasting feeling for the Jamaican nurses, many of whom still number among my friends. This was when I first met the then Chief Nursing Officer of Jamaica, Nita Barrow of Barbados, who became a figure renowned worldwide. She had a great warmth and infectious laugh, was truly hospitable and very helpful to me. Her invitations to dinner were always memorable, with distinguished people as fellow guests, and her rum punch was positively lethal. Our paths were to cross many times. A year or two later she was in London and invited me to dinner at the Hilton Hotel. She asked if we might wait a while for 'the boys' to return. Only then did I remember that her brother was the Prime Minister of Barbados, in London to carry out the final negotiations for independence. It was quite a night! A few years later Nita moved to Geneva to the World Council of Churches and we spent happy evenings over rum punch, reminiscing about Jamaica. Nita became her country's governor-general, and also carried out many international diplomatic functions. She was tremendously popular, and there was very great sadness both in the country and among all her international friends, when she collapsed and died at a major government function. A memorial service was held in Central Hall, London, which was packed to the doors in memory of a strong Christian, a very great lady and nurse, and in thanksgiving for her life and work. Another Jamaican friend who served on the ICN Board of Directors with me was Syringa Marshall Burnett, a large lady with an even larger sense of fun, who became the head of Senate, and one year sent me the most gorgeous photograph of herself in a great tricorne hat and majestic robes.

My week in Jamaica had been extended more than once due to the situation and difficult negotiations, but after some three weeks it was time to leave. The sadness of leave-taking was softened by the fact that many of the nurses would be at various ICN meetings, and there is often a Jamaican nurse on the board or a committee of ICN, so it was not really a farewell. Mary had been more than irritated by the calls from ICN announcing yet another delay, but was delighted to see me back home. At ICN headquarters another invitation was waiting, this time from the Northern Nurses' Federation, composed of the nurses' associations of Denmark, Finland, Iceland, Norway and Sweden. All these countries had good salaries and conditions of work for nurses, and the leaders of each of the associations were formidable negotiators. They had led the demand for ICN to have a strong economic welfare programme and still do. At the time, the president of the federation was Gerda Hoyer, a legendary figure to me, read about in my history of nursing and a former ICN president. She was very critical about my hurried departure to Jamaica so soon after appointment, complaining that I was completely inexperienced, knew nothing about the volatile situation and could only make things worse. She could have been right, of course. However, the Federation invited me – summoned would have been a better way of putting it – to their council meeting, which consisted of the presidents of each country. Talk about being thrown to the lions! It was a question of

Early field work. With a WHO nurse on a small island off Singapore.

turning round quickly and setting off for Stockholm, where the meeting was to be held. After it ended, my orientation programme was to continue with a visit to Denmark.

One might have expected me to be better organised in matters of travel, but this became one of my nightmare journeys, and a telegram from Stockholm to ICN headquarters asking 'Where is Sheila Quinn?' more or less caused an international manhunt. There was a perfectly simple answer to it all, and my lack of awareness of how easily a journey can go awry was to blame. First there was a delay on the flight to Stockholm, which increased at every announcement and ended up with a night in a hotel near Heathrow. My main luggage, which contained all my documentation, including phone numbers and addresses, was kept at the airport and I learned never to pack like that again. It was also a weekend when the ICN office was closed, and individual home numbers were not known. As I was not expected until the meeting started on the Monday, no one was worried, and my hope was to arrive before anyone realised I was missing. But the morning flight was delayed, and then the direct flight to Stockholm was cancelled, and the only way was through Germany, which involved another hotel night. Again there was a cancellation, but a plane finally went via Copenhagen, with a long wait before the Stockholm flight. Eventually I arrived and took a taxi to the small hotel used by the association, where the proprietor was waiting anxiously. She phoned the meeting place for me, and got a taxi, while I rushed to my room, swept up my papers and departed in haste. There was relief all round when ICN was informed of my safe arrival, some thirty-six hours late, but I felt a distinctly frosty atmosphere when I arrived. I was given a chair and a small table on the opposite side of the room, while the meeting continued in what seemed to be abnormally loud Swedish, the common language among the country representatives. The inevitable happened and my eyes simply would not stay open, except when the coffee appeared, and a small box of chocolates was also put in front of me. There was obviously far too much business to attempt translation, and the president felt that the atmosphere of the meeting would be enough! There was a respite during lunch and the members introduced themselves to me, and were clearly both sympathetic and friendly. Three of the members were immediately obvious. One was Margarethe Kruse, of Denmark, who was internationally known for her work with the International Labour Organization on nurses' salaries and conditions of work, the resulting findings having led to the decision of ICN to appoint an expert in the subject. She became a great friend and colleague and a very fine ICN president later. The youngest member of the group was Toini Nousianen, of Finland, who had succeeded the great Kyllikki Pohjala as president of the Finnish Nurses' Association, and the host of the meeting was Gerd Zetterström of Sweden. The meeting drew to a close at 4p.m. and we retired to our hotels to meet at Gerda Hoyer's flat later that evening. There were about two hours to spare and I was feeling very weary but, although I tried to rest, I was completely awake at that point and so, after a shower and change, I went by taxi to the appointed address.

Gerda Hoyer was no less intimidating in her own home, but greeted me in a kindly way. After supper she wasted no time. 'Now, Miss Quinn, please tell us what you have been doing in Jamaica. Did you solve their problems?' I remember feeling that things couldn't get much worse and then, annoyed, deciding to make a good story of it. A lot of questions followed and I had the feeling that the crisis had passed. Miss Hoyer then proceeded to show us some of her slides, which went on and on, and, between four days of travel and lack of sleep, I was practically moribund.

Somehow, though, the evening was weathered and, with murmurs of thanks to my host, I staggered out and to my bed. The next day I left for Copenhagen, somewhat apprehensive as to what awaited me there.

In Copenhagen, arrangements had been made for me to stay at the 'Nurses' House', owned by the association, and attached to the building housing their headquarters. My room was old-fashioned comfort, but bath and toilet were down the corridor, and the first night of getting into a very tall bath, on legs, which rocked like a ship at sea, was quite an experience. The room was beautifully warm to cope with the harsh Danish winters, there was a tall coffee pot with the most delicious coffee, and the bed was heaven under a great fluffy duvet. After breakfast the Danish president, Maria Madsen, came to meet me and take me to the association. She was a tall, imposing figure, rather short on words. She did tell me about her love for England, and how every time she came over, she visited Edith Cavell's statue, and always bought packs of multi-coloured crystal sugar to take home. She was soon to retire from the association, and the members would be voting for a new president. Margarethe Kruse was the secretary to the association, and a real expert on negotiation, although the president led the delegation. They were in the midst of some bargaining at the time, and a similar scenario was repeated as for Sweden, except that one group was the Nurses' Association, and the other was the Municipal Employers. At least it did not go on as long, there was ample coffee, and every now and then Margarethe would give me an idea of the situation. Danish seemed quite a noisy language, and the arguments back and forth sounded as if they were hurling insults at each other. Later, I was shown a small restaurant used by guests of the association, so ventured there alone. There was absolutely no common language between us, and my choice of food turned out to be an odd mixture.

The next day was spent outside of Copenhagen seeing something of the work of community nurses, and Miss Madsen accompanied me. We went by train some distance, got out as the train stopped at a small station, and then, without a word, Miss Madsen got back into the train and it left! There was nothing else for me to do but wait, and in a few minutes a young, and very smart, nurse appeared to look after me. She did not seem surprised to find me alone, took me to a restaurant for a quick lunch and then to her office. She showed me a map with the area she covered, told me about the conditions and work of a community nurse in Denmark, and then we went to a children's clinic where we passed an interesting afternoon. It must have seemed rather strange that I did not know the time of the return trains to Copenhagen, but my hostess looked up the most likely and drove me to the station. The train arrived in a few minutes and, to my amazement, out stepped Miss Madsen, swept me up rather like a forgotten parcel, and we rattled back to Copenhagen and the Nurses' House. All was forgiven when Miss Madsen invited me to a lovely smorgasbord supper. The next few days passed without incident, and I learned a great deal from Margarethe Kruse concerning the work of the International Labour Organisation on nurses' salaries and conditions of work and of the resulting report, of which she was the consultant. Things began to fall into place, and we established a rapport, which led to a good working relationship over the next ten years. Margarethe was then elected ICN president, and was one of the most vital and innovative.

I also managed to see quite a lot of the Danish Health Service, including their hospitals, and then it was back to headquarters in London where the pace of work slowed down and there was time to get to know the range of work carried out by the other staff in the field of nursing service and education. However, the peace did not last long. I had written an article about my work in Jamaica for *The International Nursing Review*, and within a few weeks a letter was received from Miss T.K. Adranvala, ICN second vice-president, and chief nurse to the Ministry of Health in Delhi. She wrote of her interest in my work, and outlined some of the problems of nurses in India. She then issued an invitation for me to attend the national conference of the Trained Nurses' Association of India (TNAI), which was to be held in Madras, and to give a presentation on the ICN economic welfare programme. About the same time we had a visitor to headquarters in the person of Jane Muntz, president of the Australian Nurses' Federation (RANF), and chief nurse of the State of Victoria. Her federation was going through a difficult time in salary negotiations, and she also issued an invitation to visit Australia. She argued that India was halfway, and by combining the two countries in one journey, it would save money. It was difficult to refute this, but the size of the project, in two very large countries, filled me with more than a little trepidation. But the decision was made to go ahead with the visit, so another round of packing began.

Having regard to the timing of the nursing congress in India, my first stop was Australia, and the long flight was quite a bit longer in those days than it is now. The plane was not full, so there was a possibility of some rest and two stops en route before arriving in Sydney. There I changed planes for Melbourne where the headquarters of the federation was situated. Officials from the New South Wales's branch, together with a reporter from the State newspaper, met me at the stopover in Sydney. To this day I have no idea of my comments, probably quite innocuous, but found myself clutching a small gift, which the reporter had given me. It was then time for breakfast, Australian style, and my hosts whisked me into the restaurant and introduced me to a large steak which was quite beyond me after the long flight. In an hour or so I was back in the plane for the short trip to Melbourne, and another reception committee in the familiar form of Jane Muntz and the RANF secretary. My lodging was a residential club in whose building the headquarters was situated, and my hosts left me to settle in and to sleep off the journey. It was still summer in England, but a very cold winter down under, and central heating was not as general as it is today, so the first weeks seemed very cold. Jane soon suggested I moved into the flat she shared with a friend, Jill Morey, and it was both more convenient and very friendly. Each state was largely autonomous, and had its own state nursing association, with the presidents and one other member forming the Federal Council, for country representation for ICN and other purposes. This principle applied to the separate structure set up for negotiating purposes, and although the individual nurses were strong negotiators, the organisations were not unions, and the size of the membership varied considerably. This had an effect on their ability to improve salaries and conditions, with one exception, and that was in New South Wales, which had a separate association, not part of the RANF, which was far ahead in bargaining and obtaining recognition. The RANF member association in that state was not as strong, indicating that membership and strength tend to go with the organisation which has bargaining rights. Legislation can enter the equation, and quite often government legislation restricts the activities of a professional association, so the situation can be complex. My programme was set out for me to visit each state for a few days, which mainly included a state gathering, Annual General Meeting or similar, and finally to speak at the national conference of the federation, and to make suggestions for their consideration.

The Australian nurses were great company, and the country fascinating

Welcome tea party in Enugu, Nigeria, 1963.

and at each stop the president or secretary of each association went out of their way to show me something of their huge country. As with every visitor, the great interior and outback filled me with awe. Darwin was delightfully hospitable, much smaller and more isolated than it is today, forty years later. I treasure the nurses' gift of the book '*I, The Aboriginal*', signed by the author Douglas Lockwood, but with a handwritten message on the flyleaf to me 'from my people of the Northern Territory' and signed 'Waipuldanya of the Alawa tribe of Australian Aborigines', whose life story it was. In Perth I fell in love with the beauty of the city and its surroundings, and the particular friendliness of the nurses there. Olive Anstey, the president, and also chief nurse of the hospital, was a delightful person with a great sense of humour. She became ICN president from 1977 to 1981, and was very popular, but died at quite an early age soon after she retired from work.

My return to Melbourne brought a few days of welcome rest and opportunity to put my thoughts together and offer some recommendations to the federal council, as well as speaking at the congress. These were all highly professional and gifted nurses, and I felt it almost impertinent to make recommendations. I was only telling them what they already knew, and hopefully providing the impetus to make the necessary changes. Overall, my suggestions were to make the RANF one body, and not have a separate mirror organisation responsible for bargaining; to appoint an industrial advisor, and replicate this in the states where the actual negotiations were carried out. A great deal of change has occurred since my visit and the success of today's negotiations can be seen in the excellent salaries and conditions of work achieved by the Australian nurses. I had made many friends and it was a sad leave-taking, but many of us would meet again at ICN congresses. Jane Muntz came to Europe a couple of times and we spent happy days touring together, but she died quite suddenly and was greatly mourned both in Australia and by her friends around the world. Jill Morey spent some months in England after Jane's death and we saw a lot of her. She continued to be a world traveller, but one Christmas her card was missing, and we heard of her death later from her relatives.

New Zealand was my next port of call, flying from Melbourne via Sydney to Christchurch. Looking down as we banked for landing, the vista of fields below us was so like England that I began to feel homesick. There was no time for anything like that, and I was swept quickly into a full programme, centred almost entirely on Wellington, because it was only of a few days' duration. It was good to meet Margaret Pickard, the executive secretary of the New Zealand Nurses' Association, a very likeable person and an able administrator, who organised meetings and discussions. As New Zealand is a smaller country, the nurses' association did not have the problems of Australia and were able to be more cohesive. The organisation was well-respected by government and negotiations were handled well, so the visit was largely social and served to bring ICN close to the New Zealand nurses. There was only time to see a little of the North Island, but it was obviously a beautiful country. Margaret's first husband died at a young age, and she decided to get away from home for a while, and joined ICN staff after we had moved to Geneva. After a few years, she returned home and married her second husband. I was able to visit them while on holiday in 2000, but Ian died early the following year, and Margaret has since lived in a delightful retirement village. She was one of my closest international friends and we still correspond. It was soon time to make my farewells, and as the plane left Wellington, I was wishing it could head straight for London, but I was booked to Madras with changes at Sydney and Delhi. As we stopped at Darwin, a telegram was handed to me with the farewell and thanks of the Australian nurses. And so to India.

The stop in Delhi was brief and a small plane took me on to Madras and the Congress of the Trained Nurses' Association of India (TNAI). A delegation was awaiting me at the airport, with Edith Paul, a cultured Anglo-Indian, who was president of the association, and Lakshmi Devi, the general secretary. The congress was large and fascinating and its organisation unlike anything I was used to. India had quite a number of World Health Organisation (WHO) and US AID nurses working in various parts and with different remits, and it was a delight to meet them, and we had one or two meals together.One of the American nurses was responsible for setting up central sterile supply services across the country. She lived in Hyderabad, which I was to visit later, and she promised to meet me there. Many of the Indian nurses were fluent in English, but it took me a while to get used to their delightful lilt and to their head movement which indicated yes and no opposite to our own gestures. That was very confusing for a while. The heat was difficult to adjust to, particularly when I was in accommodation without air conditioning.

It was at the congress that I met Miss Adranvala, a stately lady, slim and erect with slightly greying hair, and an air of quiet authority. She was another person whom no one addressed other than 'Miss' and she obviously carried much respect and admiration from the nurses. As the congress drew to an end, Lakshmi Devi went through the programme with me. I had grave doubts about trying to do anything about salaries and conditions in the huge subcontinent where there was so much poverty. It was obvious that the programme was more to show me the nurses' problems and the wide variety of situations in India, and to bring me into contact with as many of the nurses as possible. Meetings with relevant ministers in Delhi were planned for later in my itinerary. I stayed on for a few days in Madras at the Catholic Centre, where I had two friends, one from England and the other from Belgium, who were both working at the Centre. Visits were made to local hospitals and clinics, but it was a great pleasure to return at night and have the company of friends, and become acquainted with some members of the Catholic Nurses' Association while staying there. One evening we went out for a picnic with the local priest, who took us up to St Thomas's Mount, where we picnicked outside in the cool and dark, with nuns from the local convent who came to join us. The church was unfortunately closed.

Next I moved on to Vellore, seat of a very famous, and long-established, Christian Medical Mission and Training School, travelling by train, which was quite an experience. One of the consultant medical staff travelled with me and was able to give an account of its history and growth. My hosts at the hospital were a small group of senior sisters from America, who welcomed me to their bungalow. A meeting with the students had been arranged for me after the evening meal, and they explained the way to the meeting room. However, I was given a warning for my return in the dark to watch my step carefully, as there was a nest of cobras near the balcony. I did not need telling twice and reached my bed without mishap. The Indian student nurses were a delightful group, shy and difficult to persuade to talk, but with a strong sense of vocation. There was one non-Indian girl among them and she explained that she was an American college student on a one-year exchange programme. She admitted that she was having culture shock (actually the first time I had heard the phrase) and that it was difficult to adapt, especially to the living quarters. From Vellore I visited a village where three auxiliary nurse/midwives were based on the upper floor of a very small dwelling with a leaking roof, which did not help sleeping. They explained that they covered a few villages, all on foot and carrying their equipment, and often walked up to twelve miles a day. It seemed as if the lower floor was occupied by noisy card players, which again didn't help sleep. The nurses themselves seemed quite resigned to the conditions, and didn't expect anything better. Lakshmi Devi agreed with me that such conditions were unacceptable, but there were many more equally poor and the money was just not available to improve things.

From Vellore my next journey was by four-wheel drive to Nagercoil, a settlement with a small Salvation Army hospital. A very warm welcome awaited me from the New Zealand doctor and head nurse, and I stayed in their bungalow, simple but clean and comfortable, where I felt completely at home. The doctor's speciality was reconstructive surgery, particularly hands, for patients affected by leprosy, and, watching his outpatient surgery, it was obvious that his skill was very great and that it was making normal life possible for many badly crippled patients. An assistant nurse training school was attached to the hospital, and the sister asked me if I would mind presenting badges to the nurses graduating the next day, and speaking to them. It is one of the occasions I enjoy, as it is always happy, brings me into close contact with the young and eager nurses, and no two occasions are alike. There is always the unknown element of surprise. On this occasion my concern was about dress, because the poverty was such that I did not want to look too affluent. The matron had different ideas. She asked me to wear the best dress I had with me, which was a long blue-and-silver creation. So on request the finery was donned, and completed by silver slippers and long white gloves. Matron said it was just what was needed. But man proposes, and the weather thought otherwise. It was the monsoon season and a vicious rainstorm swept the compound, turning it into a quagmire. As the show obviously had to go on, we processed across the muddy compound in the driving rain and into the auditorium, feeling distinctly damp. The students looked immaculate in spite of the weather, and the ceremony commenced. The sight of about forty young men and women in spotless white, holding small candles and solemnly repeating the 'Nightingale Pledge for Nurses', was very moving. As we finished, an announcement was made to the effect that we were to process to the other end of the compound to inaugurate a new incinerator. Again a wet and muddy journey for the small ceremony and then back for dinner on my last evening.

In many small hospitals in the country, the nurse training was not accredited. This was partly because of the lack of education to the required entry standard, and also because so many hospitals were too small. They may not have had enough variety of experience, sufficient trained staff or adequate equipment to come up to the standards of the Nursing Council of India. The hospitals, therefore, put on their own training schemes; they were often Mission Hospitals with expatriate staff, and provided an adequate training for their students to give care, and, hopefully, to be able to transfer to a larger hospital with a recognised training course later. The administrators and teachers were very proud of their students, who were equally serious and committed to their patients. They were a delightful group of people and I was sad to say goodbye, after an enjoyable and laughter-filled visit. The silver slippers were beyond repair, but the dress was cleaned and packed for the next stop. This proved to be a small village caring for leprosy patients whose disease was burnt out but the effects remained. Most had disfigurements, which rendered them incapable of making a living in their former communities, and they were still regarded as untouchables. Some were indeed a pathetic sight and often in need of reconstructive surgery. My visit was

With nurses and students in Freetown, Sierra Leone.

greeted with delight from the small group of nurses caring for the residents, as it was a long way from habitation and there were very few visitors. I began to have some idea of the sense of isolation of nurses in so many small villages in this huge country. I stayed overnight in a small but spotless cabin with its own tiny open-air yard for ablutions. As I was leaving the next morning, Sister stopped on one of the paths leading out of the village to talk to a very old man, who was searching the undergrowth. In reply to her he said that he had seen a large snake lying dead nearby, and he was looking for its mate. I said goodbye, feeling quite sure that I had no vocation for this type of work!

Another short stop was made at a nearby convent with a large nurse training programme, both for girls who were entering the order, and an equal number of student nurses seeking a career in nursing. Reverend Mother was a delightful European, who entertained me for the evening, and gave me a lot of insight into the problems of nurses and hospitals. The following day was Sunday, and I was touched to find one of the sisters patiently waiting outside my room in the morning until I was ready to go to mass with her in the chapel. There was a delightful air of hospitality here. By this time I was in the state of Kerala, famed for both its beautiful women and its high degree of education. My next visit was to Trivandrum, a large town with its own university, where I was staying for a few days in the nurses' home. The university was one of the first to have a degree course for nurses, and the Dean was an imposing figure, who was also a major influence in the trained nurses' association. My room was large, with little else but a bed, and with windows without panes but with iron bars to discourage intruders. It was on the ground floor near to the entrance, and I was fascinated to see the cows brought to the front door and the nurses buying their own milk directly from source. It was very hot in this southern state of India and the nights seemed endless. It was also an area noted for its hot cuisine. The nurses thoughtfully took me for evening meals to a local restaurant which was noted for its special, very mild, cuisine. It was just possible for me to eat it without showing that I felt almost on fire, for it was so very hot. They were also very concerned as to what I could eat for breakfast, and we settled on a boiled banana and coffee with milk but no sugar. The breakfast arrived in the morning, coffee heavy with sugar and separate milk without. Next day I tried again to explain that I preferred coffee with milk. There was a great deal of shaking of heads, meaning yes, they understood. Breakfast arrived with coffee, milk and lots of sugar, all in the same container, so after that I just got used to the sugar. I was able to visit the university and talk with the teachers about the nursing courses, which were very advanced, and I also went round the hospital, which was badly overcrowded, and indeed typical of hospitals across India in the early 1960s. The nurses had an incredibly difficult job, and it was not surprising that it was very hard to keep nursing staff, working under such conditions and with very low pay. I was told that the Kerala girls were in high demand because of their beauty, and it was also possible for them to move overseas to work because of their standard of education.

It was very interesting to visit Trivandrum almost forty years later, this time to work as a facilitator to nursing MSc students on project-based workshops run for the university. The workshop participants were beautiful girls, obviously in competition with each other in the daily choice of very beautiful saris, and all highly educated. They all intended to go overseas as soon as their theses were complete, and they had no difficulty in obtaining well-paid posts in the USA, the UK or the Middle East. The hospital appeared little changed from my original visit, as regards the pressure of both in-patients and out-patients, and the nursing staff were still carrying out overwhelming levels of work with the same devotion. One thing had changed and that was our accommodation, in a charming small hotel a few minutes away, where the food was still as hot and spicy as I remembered.

After Trivandrum I returned briefly to Madras, again staying in the Catholic Centre by the cathedral. Winifred, my English friend, accompanied me to the airport. That was the last time I saw her, because she continued to live and work in the centre until her death. She was buried in the nearby cemetery and her grave is tended by her Indian friends and co-workers. Then I travelled on to Hyderabad, a lovely city, perhaps my favourite, but, after meetings with the nurses, I fell victim to an ailment common to visitors to India. Joel Bishop, the American AID nurse, who was working in India setting up central sterile departments in hospitals, collected me and took me to her home to recover. She was a highly-organised person, with a great sense of humour, and a love of India and its peoples. She gave me a great deal of information, showed me Hyderabad, and looked after me until I recovered and was able to proceed to Delhi. We became lifelong friends, and I was a yearly visitor to her home in New Orleans, after she had completed her work in India and returned home. Her death in the mid 1990s was a great sadness and left a large gap in my life.

On my return to Delhi I was again met by Edith Paul and Lakshmi Devi. Lakshmi was a highly intelligent and very good-looking woman of New Zealand descent. Some years after my visit she returned to her native New Zealand, where she was employed by the New Zealand Nursing Association as editor of their journal and public relations officer, and reverted to her old name. She died while still in post. The few days in Delhi were spent in visits to relevant Ministry officials, usually accompanied by the stately T. K. Adranvala, who was the chief nurse. At the office she wore European dress, and I remember her in white blouse and navy skirt, which strangely diminished her presence and serene beauty. It was clear that she was held in high regard by Government officials. A farewell dinner was held for me at the headquarters of the TNAI with the president and some members of the board. I was able to give them my impressions, but had to acknowledge the real difficulty in increasing salaries and conditions of work in the face of the general economic problems and huge population of India. The one aspect which was improving was nursing education and the status which went with it, but so often it is a passport to work opportunities in another country. The weeks I had spent in India had given me a real understanding of the nurses' problems and an insight into the difficulties of low economies and overpopulated countries.

It was time to return to London, and a final stop was made in Bombay. This was also a very short visit, and only gave me time to meet with TNAI leaders from the State, and to talk to the nurses while visiting one of the main hospitals. Next day I visited another nursing school run by a religious order. They offered to send a sister with a car to bring me to mass in their chapel beforehand, and only when I had accepted with pleasure did the Superior mention the time. I was to be picked up at 4.30a.m. That visit was my last experience of India, and I headed for the airport late that night for an overnight flight home, which again had problems. We were held up in Tel Aviv for a few hours, owing to a technical fault, but eventually we re-boarded the plane for home. It was winter, and a very cold one in England. We landed just after 5a.m. to a snow-covered scene, with Mary waiting for me in her small car, accompanied by Ingrid Hamelin of ICN staff, and a large rug, and we headed home at a very cautious pace. It was wonderful to be back and I felt I could sleep for a week. The time change intervened, however, and night turned into day for quite a time, but home never did seem so good.

After a couple of days' rest I returned to headquarters, which seemed very organised and peaceful after the last hectic months. We had a staff meeting for me to report back and to catch up with events in my absence. Then another home situation intervened. When I had left for the tour, it was obvious that my father was becoming increasingly frail, and he was very concerned that I would be so far away, but equally he did not want me to refuse on his account. There was not then the ease and cheapness of today's telecommunications, but I wrote every few days, and telephoned once or twice to be sure all was well. However, now there was an SOS from my father's wife to say that he was not at all well, so I took a few days to go home to assess the situation. While I was there we saw the family doctor, and examinations revealed a prostate malignancy, for which there was only palliative treatment. Father was very philosophical, and as he seemed to rally, I returned to London. One night about a week later, I received a phone call from my cousin in Blackpool to say that my father had died suddenly in the street and that he had been notified and had identified the body, because my father's wife was in a state of collapse. It was a great shock and I was only thankful that I had been home and seen Father so recently. After notifying our general secretary, and checking train times, I packed and set off for home the following morning. The weather had continued to be very wintry, and, having left the car overnight, I found it completely snowed up and had to dig it out before driving to the station. Arriving in Blackpool, I discovered that Nellie, my father's wife, was completely confused and apparently unaware of what had happened. My cousin, Stowell, was a great help and we made all the arrangements for the funeral and notified relatives and friends. He also told me that, on the day of his death, my father had been to the library a few minutes' walk away, and on the way back had stopped to speak with friends, left them and, only minutes later, died instantly as the result of a massive heart attack. It was some comfort to know what had happened, but it was a great blow, for my father and I had always been very close and there was to be a great vacuum in my life. It was also very difficult to leave Nellie in her state of confusion, but she had a nephew and his wife who lived some miles away and they undertook to keep in close touch with her and to see that all was well. After my father's affairs were settled, I returned to London and work, and managed to visit Blackpool every few weeks.

Back at the office, we had been preparing for a short first meeting of the Social and Economic Welfare Committee, with members from America and the Philippines, who were surprised at the speed at which the programme had started and seemed to have its own volition. Work was also going ahead for the next meeting of the ICN Board of Directors and Council of National Representatives (CNR) to be held in Geneva in the summer of 1963. These were held in between the large meetings of the CNR combined with the Congress, which are held every four years. At the interim meetings the officers and board had a preliminary meeting, and were then joined by the presidents and secretaries of ICN member associations. Forty years have elapsed and the interim meetings have changed considerably in that they are much larger, and have some associated activity, such as a major conference, which individual members of the various associations can attend. They can also sit as observers at the actual CNR meetings.

A great deal of preparation and paper work was involved for the interim meeting to be held in Geneva in 1963. My part was to prepare the first report of the Social and Economic Welfare Division for my chairman, Miss Udell, to present. At least there was plenty to write about.

The meeting itself was quite low-key and our first report was well received. It brought a number of requests from country representatives asking for a visit, and the coming year looked like being extremely busy. I was able to make contact with the relevant officials from the International Labour Office, staying for a couple of days to visit various departments and to get to know people and whom to contact when back in London. The Chief Nurse of the WHO, who had a wealth of knowledge of countries around the world, was also an important contact. She was Lyle Creelman, a Canadian, who was in post for much of my time with ICN, and she was a great point of reference, as well as being a delightful companion. She had a beautiful chalet in the lovely alpine village of Champery, some two to three hours' drive from Geneva, and I spent many happy hours there as her guest.

The other important matter which had arisen from discussion at the meeting was a possible move of headquarters from London to Geneva. This had apparently been discussed at the main CNR meeting in Australia just before I joined ICN, and of which I was unaware. The subject had been put to the following meeting for further consideration, and there was pressure at the Geneva meeting to take the idea further. The rationale was that Geneva was the place where most international organisations were based, and it would be beneficial for ICN to be there. We left Geneva with two ad hoc committees set up to look into the possibility and to report conclusions to the CNR meeting in Frankfurt in two years' time.

I returned home feeling distinctly worried. Had this been made clear to me at interview, I would not have accepted the post. Various considerations came up: first, the flat shared and jointly owned with Mary in London, and then the situation of my stepmother who needed frequent visits. I was, therefore, seriously considering whether it would be possible for me to continue with ICN should the organisation move to Geneva. Mary had completed a year's course in nursing administration at the King's Fund College in London, and had recently taken a post as deputy matron at the Mile End Hospital in London, so we had to think very seriously about the future. However, discussions about Geneva were vague at this point, and so the only sensible course seemed to be to carry on and wait for the conclusions of the two committees. In the meantime, there was a collection of invitations for country visits, and the need to set out a programme.

CHAPTER 5

London or Geneva?

AT HEADQUARTERS work had begun by the two committees looking at various aspects of a possible move to Geneva, one group working on the economic consequences and the other on the 'political and professional advantages'. The members, from different countries, included consultants from the business world. Staff attended some sessions, but apart from the general secretary, the committees worked alone. One consultant was responsible for visiting relevant international organisations in Geneva and the Swiss Nurses' Association. I did not have much input because I was starting another round of travel, but I was content to leave it until recommendations were made and then to consider my position. The secretarial staff and two of the professional staff had decided to retire or to take redundancy, and Ingrid Hamelin was almost certain to be returning home to an important post, so the availability of staff for a move was quite small. However, my immediate priority was to draw up an itinerary and timetable for the Far East. Following correspondence with the associations, it was agreed that I would visit Singapore, Malaya, Hong Kong and Japan, in that order.

Singapore had a small nurses' association and a very strong General Workers' Union, with a well-known national union leader. Many of the nurses belonged to the latter. The salaries and conditions of work of the nurses were, in fact, quite good at that time and are even better today. The main problem of the association was lack of membership, because most of the nurses, who were members of the union, were quite satisfied with the situation and saw no reason to belong to another association and pay two subscriptions. At that time ICN had a firm membership policy of one association per country and this led to difficulties, depending on the tradition, background and history of the country. There were many countries where nursing was still an emerging profession, and the professional association was often new and small in comparison with the trades unions, and both groups competed for members. In Scandinavia the numerical strength and expertise of the nursing organisations have been such that they are the obvious bodies for negotiations of salaries and conditions, but it is not an easy pattern to achieve. In those countries which had gained independence around the 1950s and 1960s the trades unions were very strong and nurses' associations small. Often the latter were only a few years old, perhaps started by one of the country's leading nurses who had been to the UK on a scholarship. They had seen the strong professional position of nurses in the UK, with a voice at government level in the form of a Chief Nurse at the Ministry of Health. Nurses returned home and tried to set up a national association, often supporting it with their own money. When WHO nurses were working in a country, they did their utmost to help the nurses to become a professional group, and where an association was established they gave it support, but they had a distinct role of their own. There could be real hostility between the professional organisation and the union. The atmosphere was quite hostile to my arrival in Singapore, and I accepted an invitation to meet members of the union and their leader over a meal. After what could be described as a free and frank exchange of views, the atmosphere cooled. It was interesting to return in the mid-1990s on an invitation to speak at a nursing conference covering a number of countries in Asia, and to meet the same union leader as a main speaker at the conference, on good terms with the profession, and we had very friendly meetings.

In Singapore I had the pleasure of staying with a British nurse who was the team leader for a group of WHO nurses working as leaders and counterparts to the local senior nurses in different sectors of the profession. Kay Fowler had previously been the Principal Nurse Tutor at the Middlesex Hospital in London, and led a very successful programme in Singapore for over ten years. Nurses in many countries have cause to be grateful to the WHO nursing teams for setting good foundations for the excellent nursing services seen today. When the international nurses withdrew, they left good leaders who continued their work. At the time of my visit I was impressed by the quality of the service, both in hospital and community. I made many visits to see the nurses in action, including one to the out islands to see the conditions and the nursing care available. It was delightful to be able to relax in Kay's very comfortable home and be looked after by her amah, and it also provided an opportunity to talk over my impressions and get a view of the whole. The local nurses were very hospitable and we shared some pleasant meals together. On the last night

I was invited to a dinner at Government House, and when they realised I was concerned about my lack of a formal dress, the nurses put their heads together and altered a beautiful dinner dress, which belonged to one of them. They assured me that no lasting damage had been done to the dress and it would be able to be worn again by its rightful owner. My one free day before moving on to Malaya was spent travelling up-country to visit the War Cemeteries in the Johore Straits. It was a moving experience for me, because some of my friends of schooldays were buried there.

In spite of initial difficulties I enjoyed my stay in Singapore and was sorry to leave. (I pass through, or spend the odd night there these days, and it is interesting to see the amazing development which has taken place, although the sight of the renovated Raffles Hotel does not give me quite the same feeling as before.) The flight to Kuala Lumpur was short and the usual hospitable reception committee was waiting. My stay was in a hotel quite near the famous station and the cricket ground. The general atmosphere and way of life were much quieter and more relaxed than in Singapore. My visit was quite short and the nurses wanted to discuss both the structure and the activities of their association. Apart from visiting hospitals, they took me into the countryside to see their community services and the homes of the people, and one evening was spent at a fish restaurant on the edge of the Indian Ocean with some of the union officials. Another pleasant interlude was as the lunch guest of one of the senior British diplomats. Soon it was time to move on to Hong Kong, but although my plane took off for Singapore to change flights, schedules were affected because of the failure of the second British Airways Comet and we were sent to hotels for the night. My luck was in and my overnight stop was Raffles, where I simply had to visit the Long Bar and have a Singapore Sling before retiring to bed and a very early call for a 6a.m. flight to Hong Kong.

It was Good Friday when I arrived in Hong Kong and my hosts had the forethought to take me to the cathedral for the main 3p.m. service. After going to the house of one of the nurses to have tea and freshen up, I awaited the arrival of the nurse with whom I would be staying. There were no tunnels under the harbour in those days, the airport was in Kowloon and the only way to reach Hong Kong Island was by the Star Ferry. It is only a journey of about seven minutes during which one has the best view of the entire harbour, and the operation moves very smoothly, with docking and changing passenger load carried out in a very few minutes. It is still one of the bargains in Hong Kong, compared with the cost of negotiating the tunnels by taxi. The underground is new, spotless and efficient, but there are many returning travellers who head with nostalgia for the Star Ferry and a breath of sea air. My host was Grace Chan, then Matron of the Nethersole Hospital, a Christian Mission hospital with a very high reputation for its work. Today, Nethersole is a small hospital on Hong Kong Island, but a large, new hospital has risen in Kowloon, and together they form the United Christian Hospitals, still with the same high reputation. Grace Chan married and left for Canada, and Paula Chow was the Chief Nurse of UCH, now also retired but still active in Hong Kong. At the time of my first visit the Chief Nurse of the Health Service was a British nurse, and so were the matrons of the large hospitals. On retirement they were replaced by very able Chinese successors, but the Government Health Service was very centralised until a few years ago when a major change took place affecting all government hospitals and those run by charities.

It was good to reach the hospital which was to be my home for the next ten days, and I was introduced to the problem of water shortage. Relations with mainland China were not good at that time, and there was a major difficulty about water, most of which was brought by boat from China. It was vital not to waste it, and baths or showers were restricted to one day a week. I soon learnt that it is possible to keep fresh with a very small amount of water, but it does take a lot more time. Grace Chan was a delightful host, and the Chinese nurses looked upon her as the Florence Nightingale and leader of the profession in Hong Kong. They had started a small association which grew quite quickly and for a time provided most of the professional updating for Chinese nurses. Grace Chan was the leader in a project starting a ward sisters' course for staff nurses, using the facilities of the Nethersole Hospital. A small headquarters in the central area was bought and established for meetings, lectures and other professional activities.

Grace organised a very hectic programme, and seemed determined that we should visit every hospital and community project. The government hospitals were very large and both wards and clinics heavily overcrowded. The community nursing service was not very well-developed at that time but nurses did visit in the huge blocks of flats with tiny apartments and no lifts, and after I had spent a day following a nurse to her patients, the stairs seemed an insuperable obstacle. It was also a time when there was not enough housing and shanty towns had grown up in many places in Kowloon. The boat people at Aberdeen were also in very substandard and unhygienic conditions, and it took a number of years to catch up with the ever-growing population. It is a different picture today, of course, but those young nurses were quite heroic in their work. One day a nurse took me into what was then the walled city in the centre of Kowloon, more like an enclave, in which a crowded population lived with what appeared to be minimum sewage and general hygienic conditions. It was not the sort of place where one would find Europeans. The nurse was obviously well loved and my presence was tolerated because I was her friend. My main recollection is of the small school children dressed in spotless school uniform in spite of coming from the very poorest of habitations.

Not only did Grace Chan act as a perfect host and escort for my programme, but she knew all the hospitals and their matrons, and they all seemed to have their nurses' graduation ceremonies in the few days I was there – just by chance! The opportunity was obviously too good to miss when a visitor arrived. We had a busy but delightful time and, of all the hospitals which we visited and where we presented certificates and badges, one remains firmly in my memory. It was a very small hospital called the Haven of Hope – a missionary hospital with a tall, angular, Scandinavian nurse as matron. I believe that at the time it was largely for children and tuberculosis patients. It was situated a long way from habitation, and we took about an hour, in a very sturdy car, along a path across the tops of the peaks to reach it. The nurses had been preparing the hall all day for the occasion and all was well polished, including the platform. Matron had shown us the children's wards, and it was obvious that they had the most loving care and that she was extremely proud of her hospital. We assembled on the platform, but as Grace stood to make the introduction, I noticed she seemed a little uneasy. When I also rose, the reason became obvious. The combination of high humidity and rather more polish than was needed produced a sticky skating rink. Had it not been for Grace's restraining hand, my feet would have shot from under me. We decided to stand very still but the first two young male nurses approaching were skidding dangerously. The situation had every possibility of degenerating into farce, but by standing very still, and steadying each nurse carefully as they approached us, we somehow got through without incident. On the homeward drive, however, we collapsed into fits of laughter, and I remember it so clearly today.

My week's visit ended with a dinner on one of the floating palace restaurants at Aberdeen and it was a very regretful leave-taking, but I carried happy memories away with me. I have made many professional visits to Hong Kong during the intervening years, and I have nothing but admiration for the way the Health Services have been developed in hospitals and communities. The nurses have a high standard of professionalism and are well qualified, and the four universities enable nurses to achieve higher degrees. Some years ago the Hong Kong Hospital Authority had the enormous task of bringing all but the private hospitals under one management, and I was privileged to be a member of the multi-professional Expert Group appointed by the authority to visit and assist them over a number of years. It was a learning experience for all of us, and we were amazed at the drive and initiative which have brought about such a change.

The flight to Tokyo lasted several hours and I felt some apprehension about the visit, as there was not a great deal of interaction between ICN and the Japanese nurses at that time. It is a very different situation today, when the nurses come to ICN congresses in large numbers, with their own interpreters, and more than one distinguished Japanese nurse has served on the ICN board. On the occasion of my visit the very large national congress was taking place. The association had its own headquarters and a very able board of directors. The president of that time was also a member of the diet. A delightful girl had been allocated to me, not just as interpreter but also as a companion for my journeys throughout Japan. The culture and history of the country, the way of life and size of the population were all so different that it took time for me to adjust mentally. It was much colder than Hong Kong, and I appreciated the restaurants with a brazier under the table, or even a rug tucked round the knees. My hotel in Tokyo was huge, and the room tiny and compact with everything to hand. It was possible to have European food at the hotel but it was a different matter when visiting hospitals and schools of nursing. Etiquette on changing shoes entering a building caused me some problems, mainly because my feet were too big for the slippers offered. In one multi-storey hospital the problem was solved by giving me men's slippers, but as I climbed the many steps to the top floor, the large slippers became increasingly difficult to retain. To my embarrassment one escaped and fell down the stairwell to the ground floor, and someone had to bring it all the way back to me.

Apart from the hospitals and talks with the nurses through my interpreter, I was shown much of the culture of that beautiful land, including Kyoto and its temples, and the even lovelier site in Nara. One of the monks spent time not only showing me the shrines, but also explaining the Buddhist philosophy. In Kyoto I was the guest of a delightful lady who spoke perfect English, and I had the experience of living with her, Japanese style. During my travels we stayed in Japanese guest houses, and I was introduced to the refreshing Japanese-style baths, and the beautifully presented cuisine. On one occasion my stay was in a hospital and the nurses offered to leave their communal bath available for my sole use. Obviously, this was the height of hospitality, but there was much delight and laughter when I asked to share it with them and it was a fun-filled evening.

The congress was well attended and the nurses made me very welcome. My presentation and discussion were more on the International Council itself than on salaries and conditions of work, which at the time did not seem to fit in with the congress. We had lively discussion, and lots of questions, but they were mainly on nurses and nursing in the west, as if the delegates longed to have a window on the wider world. Senior professionals were highly educated, many of them with doctoral degrees from American Universities, and we spent many hours in various hospitals and centres discussing all possible aspects of the profession. My programme gave me time in the north of the country in smaller and less busy situations, and the nurses could not do enough to make me feel at home. They realised that I found large quantities of rice difficult, and insisted on providing an egg with my breakfast rice, but I was somewhat surprised to find a large, raw egg sitting on top of the bowl. One thing international travel does teach, and that is never to be surprised at the unexpected, and more important, to take it happily in one's stride. Nothing was too much trouble. The nurses were so keen to know as much as they could about me that their questions touched on religion and the kind of church I attended. Having ascertained my religion was Roman Catholic, they assured me there was a church nearby and they would take me on Sunday. So we set out, getting lost on the way, but eventually discovered the church and our little party entered for the service. It was conducted in Japanese and the service seemed strange, but no matter, they had demonstrated the lengths they would go to for hospitality, and we had a happy and noisy journey back to the dormitory. I found the tatami mats very comfortable for sleeping, but I did have the luxury of a soft pillow. It seemed as if the whole nursing staff of the hospital escorted me to the train next morning, and it was quite a sad farewell from my seat laden with tiny gifts, all beautifully wrapped. I was to visit Tokyo again some years later after my return to the UK and the Health Service, and it was as fascinating and hospitable as ever. My former interpreter found me and persuaded me to do a television interview, which she interpreted. It was a delightful reunion.

The journey home was long and in a full plane, although we did seem to have more room than we do in today's planes, but we also had more stops en route, and it was good to get home. After a couple of days' rest, I was in the office to unload the tapes made during my journey, in order to prepare my report, when the Executive Director, Helen Nussbaum, asked to see me. She broke the news that we were both going to Naples three days later to attend the Congress of the Italian Nurses' Association. There was a lot of unrest about the nurses' conditions, and the invitation specifically asked for me. One of Helen's mother tongues was Italian and she decided to accompany me. We arrived in Naples to attend the congress held in the old castle, and we were hosted by one of the foremost schools of nursing, of which the directress, Marina Caruana, was a member of an ICN committee. It was obvious that work was hard, the students paid for their training and took their practical experience in hospital, but, even after qualifying, the salaries were very poor. After listening to the presentations and visiting the main hospitals, I decided to return to do a survey in the main cities of the country, accompanied by a teacher who was working to help improve the conditions. Then it was back to London to try to catch up with my work and hear how the committees were getting on with their task of recommending the future location of headquarters. As the work in Italy seemed impossible without any knowledge of Italian, I embarked on a crash course of six weeks. Having little facility for languages, progress was slow and painful, but by the time of my departure I could understand quite well and get by in everyday talk. My itinerary was to start in the school at Naples for overall briefing and thence to Rome. One or two other cities, including Bologna and Milan, were to be visited before I returned to Rome to meet with the board of directors and give them an interim report.

By this time Mary had finished her course in hospital administration, and was established as assistant matron at the Mile End Hospital in the

East End of London. The matron, Noreen Compton, with whom Mary became very friendly and who later became Matron of the Prince of Wales's Hospital, was an able administrator. Mary was not very happy about my leaving again for another six-week journey, but at least she was enjoying her work and her colleagues. From my point of view, although it was tiring to be on the road again so soon, at least it was not a long journey and all the work was in one country. The short stay in Naples was mainly to meet my colleague and companion for the next few weeks and to be briefed on the journey, timetable and personalities I was to meet. Then it was off on the first stop, Rome, a city which I knew from earlier holidays. My home for the first two weeks was the Red Cross Nursing School in the city centre. The school was well organised and the students were delightful. Two hospitals were used for their practical work. They were all very proud of the reputation of the school and the status of their graduates, and the principal, Anna Platter, a very tall lady with a commanding presence, was extremely hospitable and friendly, as indeed were all the teachers. Here I obtained a thorough knowledge of the Italian nurse education system at its best and, on my visits, one of the teachers accompanied me, often speaking better English than my laboured Italian. The principal had obviously given me her suite of rooms in a building next to the school and her maid looked after me. And there was my first language disaster. The maid spoke only Italian, and, after showing me the rooms, she then asked my wishes for breakfast. I carefully explained that I would like coffee with milk and just bread with butter and jam. So far so good. We seemed to get along very well together, and, after supper at the school, I settled down for the night. My wake-up call next morning was accompanied by the breakfast tray, which I greeted with pleasure, only to find a large jug of black coffee and bread but no butter or jam. I made the best of it and thought I'd sort it out for the next day. Not a bit of it – that was my breakfast for the rest of my visit, and on every other return to Rome. In fact, I'm quite sure that if another visit were made today, they would remember that this particular English visitor had a most peculiar breakfast!

We visited ministers, hospital administrators and other relevant persons, attended many meetings with groups of nurses, and also met Red Cross officials who were responsible for some of the best schools of nursing. While I was there, the President was ill and when one of the national newspapers carried a photo of two nurses leaving the Presidential

Palace, there was great delight among my colleagues that the nurses were graduates of the school where I was staying. While the nurses with whom I was working enjoyed the siesta hours, my relaxation was to visit my favourite spots in Rome, and my companions showed me yet more and improved my knowledge of Roman history. Another national nurses' association existed. It was not a union but the National Catholic Nurses' Association, with a very large membership, much greater than the association in membership with ICN. It was also affiliated to the International Catholic Association, a counterpart of ICN. There had been many misunderstandings and antagonism in the history of the development of both international associations, and I was determined not to become embroiled in argument, and therefore made courtesy visits to keep all nurses aware of my work in Italy. I also visited other cities to get a general picture outside the capital. The nurses were always welcoming, insisted on showing me their beautiful cities and often included a concert. My main recollection outside Rome was of Milan and of being spellbound at the sight of the original *Last Supper*. A journey was made to a large sanatorium in the mountains outside Milan. It was winter and, in spite of the temperature being well below zero, I stood on my balcony before retiring to bed, quite captivated by the awe-inspiring view of the huge, snow-covered peaks rearing up before me, and seemingly near enough to touch. My final visit before returning to Rome was to the magical city of Venice. Again, I was staying in a school of nursing, overlooking the lagoon, and after visiting hospitals, I had free time during the siesta to go out and walk around Venice, absorbing the sights. One evening I did this after supper and got completely lost among the back streets and small alleyways of the city. It was then that I discovered that my knowledge of the Italian language was not as good as I thought it was, and the responses to my request for directions confused me even more. Panic was beginning to set in and it was a dark night, but suddenly a corner was turned and the welcome sight of the school building reassured me.

On the last evening the teachers and director took me out for a drink in a bar just off the great piazza. It is often said that we all remember exactly where we were when we heard of the assassination of President Kennedy. I learned of it that evening when a man rushed excitedly in with loud comments and wild gesticulations. It was a few minutes before I caught up with what he was saying and when I did I was sure I had misunderstood the Italian, but his gestures left no room for doubt. We returned home quietly pondering on the impact for the USA and the world. My room looked straight on to the lagoon, and next day, looking across to the Island of St Michele, the burying ground of Venice, I saw a funeral procession of gondolas making their way across, all draped in black, with the leading one piled with wreaths. It seemed a very relevant sight.

Back in Rome there was a press conference for me to explain my findings, which were the poor situation for girls going into nursing and the need to improve both the very small salaries and the long hours and poor conditions in which they worked. These certainly have improved over the years, but there is still a long way to go to make it an attractive career. In spite of all the problems, the nurses loved their work and were held in high esteem. After the conference there were a few days left for me to write my report and have final discussions with the association. It was at this point that the president revealed her closely kept secret. She had been able to arrange for a private audience with the Holy Father, Pope Paul VI, which, needless to say, was the most enormous surprise but also more than a little daunting. Anna Platter then took me in hand. 'First of all,' she said, 'do you have a long black dress and veil?' The Vatican had not then relaxed its protocol on dress, and of course I hadn't included such finery in my packing. Not to be outdone, she then proceeded to produce a dress and veil of her own. The result was rather interesting, as she was quite a lot larger than me both in height and width, but the dress did come down to my ankles and, with a belt round the middle, was passable. In any event, the veil was so large that it covered the lot! Next day, soon after 9a.m., a senior Red Cross nurse, who was a teacher at the school, accompanied me to the waiting Red Cross car which negotiated the heavy Rome traffic, entered the Vatican City and drew up at a long flight of steps, to be received by officials and also, to my relief, by an English priest. My borrowed fur coat was whisked away and we were escorted to one of the small audience rooms. The wait seemed endless, but it was made interesting by a gentleman and his wife at the other end of the room. He came across carrying a huge square box, which he uncovered and then reverently lifted out a wide-brimmed, white hat. He explained that his family had the honour of presenting the popes with their hats, and this was the latest. Then a tall, spare figure in white appeared and first spoke with the gentleman with the hat, after which photos were taken. Finally, he came across to us and my companion presented me. I knelt to kiss his ring and looked up into the most compelling gaze and a slight smile as he asked me, in Italian, about my work in Italy. Having been well rehearsed in Italian the night before, I managed to explain briefly, and he responded in perfect English, saying that it was good to hear me speaking Italian. Then he gave me a rosary and a blessing before moving along to the next room. I must have said my goodbyes and thanks but I have no recollection of anything until I arrived back at the school of nursing, where all the students were gathered to wish me goodbye and a safe journey. I have made a couple of return visits over the years, but those were weeks full of travel, meeting delightful people and ending with that magical visit. It is one of my most precious memories.

Back in England, I was at home for a few months, and in the office to complete reports and hear of the work of the location committees. Christmas was not far off and our 1965 quadrennial congress was booked for the following June in Frankfurt, Germany. The Economic Welfare report, as well as a special interest programme for participants, had to be prepared. In addition there remained one more round of country visits in the New Year, before I had to be back for the final preparations for Frankfurt. The staff were taking lessons in German at the office, so I joined them and quickly forgot my Italian. Mary and I spent Christmas at home together with some happy social occasions, and it was good not to have to think about planning more travel for a while. Nevertheless, the time came only too soon. The countries to be visited this time were in West Africa, starting in Nigeria and working back through Ghana, Sierra Leone, Liberia and The Gambia. It was to be another completely different cultural experience in a climate very different from the English winter.

Two prominent African nurses were already known to me, from the interim meeting in Geneva and visits they had both made at different times to ICN headquarters. Koforola Pratt of Nigeria and Docia Kissieh of Ghana had both trained at the Nightingale School of Nursing at St Thomas's Hospital, London, and then returned to their countries to follow distinguished careers, each becoming the Chief Nurse of her country. They were delightful people whom I was happy to call close friends, and they were respected in international circles as well as in their own country. Rola, as Mrs Pratt was known, was waiting for me as the plane touched down in Lagos, and I stayed with her at her delightful home where she lived with her husband, a well-known local doctor, and the younger of her two sons, who was still at school. She gave me a wide-ranging tour of hospitals and schools of nursing throughout the country, and organised a general meeting of the association. It was obvious that Rola was the driving force behind the association, but she had willing assistants in some of her very able nursing leaders. When she had returned from qualifying in England, she became a ward sister at the teaching hospital of Ibadan University. This was quite an achievement, as she was the first African nurse to be so promoted. She was promoted assistant matron some years later, and when the last British matron of Ibadan retired, Rola was appointed matron, the post that she held at the time of my visit. As Ibadan was about a hundred miles from her home in Lagos, it was obvious that Rola, and so many nurses like her, both held down very important jobs and ran comfortable and organised homes at a distance. The first journey we made outside Lagos was to Ibadan, a beautiful university and an extremely well-run hospital. Rola herself had a great sense of fun and an infectious laugh. She had to be away for one night, but the maid was sleeping in the house, while I was out for dinner as guest of one of the university professors and his wife. They returned me by car to the bungalow about 11p.m., saw me to the door and then made their farewells. In a few minutes it was obvious that no one was going to answer the doorbell, and the African night suddenly seemed hostile and intimidating. Each bungalow was fairly isolated and some distance from the hospital, so I had to pluck up courage to venture round the back to see if any light was available. One was showing so, after a lot of hammering on the door and shouting, the door opened a crack and the frightened little face of the young maid appeared. She was terrified of being alone and was quite sure I was a burglar, but I was too thankful to be safe indoors to be cross.

Generally, it was a very happy visit to Nigeria, and it gave me an insight into the hard work of British professionals and civil servants who had helped to build schools, hospitals and other vital services so far from home. Most of them had a real love of their adopted country and its people. The local nurses were now taking over the management of hospitals and the training of nurses. The time passed only too quickly for me and my final journey was to the town of Port Harcourt, with its thriving oil industry, where I met a British nurse in charge of the occupational health services there, and spent the night in her home.

Some years later I returned to Nigeria again, when Rola had retired from nursing and had been appointed Minister of Health of Lagos State. Again, after a year or two, I made another visit, this time to a big nursing conference and university graduation ceremony at Ibadan, which our new ICN president, Alice Girard of Canada, and Lyle Creelman and other WHO nurses attended. A famous American nurse, Virginia Arnold, who had worked with the Rockefeller Foundation, was inaugurated as a chief in recognition of her work in Nigeria. She was great fun, and introduced me to my first gin and tonic, which, she told me, 'is the only possible drink in this heat.' Rola was president of the Nigerian Nurses' Association, in addition to being a former matron of Ibadan, and was a prominent guest at the Conference. She presented to the library a locally-carved wooden statue of Florence Nightingale, which manages to contain both the face and image of Miss Nightingale and, at the same time, look very African. But in spite of the celebrations, the atmosphere was tense, following considerable unrest across the country and a change in government. Nigeria is a beautiful country and it is easy to understand why so many expatriates loved it.

Following my visit to Nigeria, I took a short flight to Accra, capital of Ghana. The country was in the midst of a very difficult period, during the final years of Kwame Nkruma's presidency. Suspicion was rife and I was only too aware of the atmosphere, the shortages in the country, and the efforts that were made to make my stay comfortable. Even then, it was a difficult stay and once again the WHO nurses were incredibly kind and protective, inviting me to stay with them and keeping me informed of the situation. A senior English nurse was Martha (Biddy) Shout, who had spent some years as Senior Tutor at Korle Bu hospital and was largely responsible for the setting up of the Ghanaian Nursing Council, acting as its registrar along with her full-time work. She welcomed me into her home and travelled with me on much of my journey, which was not too comfortable and fraught with political overtones. A senior sister accompanied me in a journey up-country to see rural services and the work of the dresser dispensers in remote areas. Hospitality had been arranged in the guest house of one of the few remaining district commissioners, an older, distinguished man, near retirement, who had spent many years in Africa. The local Catholic priest joined us for dinner, and I was amazed to find in that isolated setting a most beautiful table arrangement with lace cloth and fragile, matching Doulton dinner service. My escort had relatives in the village nearby, as had the driver, and my overnight accommodation was the guest-house some fifty yards away from the main house. When they bade me goodnight, I was warned to be careful going along to the bath-house in the night because of the possibility of snakes. That was a journey that nothing would have induced me to make! Apart from bed and chair there was little in my room and, as a board at the window blocked both light and air, it had to come down for the night. The only thing to do then was to get into bed and make sure the mosquito net was well tucked in. Sleep did not come easily. The African night was full of sound. I heard the priest's car leave, and tried to sleep, but the heat was sticky and then animal calls began. I'm sure they were only hyenas, or so I told myself, but they sounded as if there was a collection of lions and tigers lined up outside the unprotected window, to say nothing of the chance of an odd snake slithering in. My last waking thought was that there must be an easier way of making a living, but I woke to another hot day, took breakfast and then joined my companions and the jeep to head back to Accra.

A very interesting outing was arranged for me to accompany a health worker on his village inspection, which he was to assess as part of a survey to encourage the villages to clean and tidy their area. The reward was a radio for the village centre. As we stopped the jeep and walked towards the village, I could hear the drums and, turning to my guide, I asked him what they were saying. He was obviously amused and said that the man approaching was their friend. He has a woman with him who must be important because she walks beside him. I was somewhat embarrassed and couldn't help thinking – 'Ask a silly question.' We continued on to meet the Chief and were invited to sit with him. He welcomed me and asked how were my husband and children. Thoroughly embarrassed by this time, I explained that I had no husband and therefore no children. With great politeness, he changed the topic and then escorted us round the village. We ended drinking Coca-Cola and congratulated the village on its appearance, before returning to the jeep. I often chuckled at the memories of that visit.

Docia Kissieh was at the other end of the country on work and we did not meet until the last part of my stay, which ended in a formal dinner in the presence of a minister and journalists, during which I was invited to express my views on nursing in the country. That was a difficult moment and it was necessary for me to choose my words with great care. The next morning was time for departure, and, though Ghana is a beautiful country and I was among friends, it was with a sense of relief that I boarded the plane for my next stop in Sierra Leone.

The flight to Freetown was also short, but the airport was some distance from the capital and required a ferry journey and quite a long drive. A group of nurses and a British doctor, who was a senior paediatrician at the local children's hospital, formed the welcome party and the programme was relaxed and confined to Freetown itself. The atmosphere was a welcome change from the strain of Ghana and a local doctor and his wife, who was a nurse, were my hosts for the few days of my stay. The health services were smaller and less advanced than those of Nigeria and Ghana, and the itinerary less packed. Generally, it was a low-key programme, and the small group of nurses who accompanied me were delightful and made it an enjoyable stay. There was little hint on the surface of the fighting and unrest which was to engulf the country, and on one evening I accompanied my hosts to the ceremony of 'Beating the Retreat' on Independence Day. Apart from the weather, I could easily have been back at home watching the superb drill of the soldiers.

With the exception of general news about the sad warring situation, I had little further contact with anyone from Sierra Leone until I met one of the nurses in Copenhagen at the 2001 Congress of the International Council of Nurses. She told me that she and her husband were living and working in America and the family were very happy, but she had little news of her homeland and did not know if their home was still standing. A sad story.

And so it was on to Liberia, a country differing from the others as it was not a part of the Commonwealth but a small independent country, formed by slaves returning to their home country. My first memory was of a funeral procession down the central street of the capital city, with the head of state, President Tubman, leading the mourners on foot, which I was told was a frequent custom. My stay was at the only sizeable hotel in Monrovia, the capital, and I soon learnt of the shortages. The nurses would telephone me and then appear in a couple of minutes and I discovered that, as phones were few and far between, the surest way to contact me was from the internal phone in the hotel lobby. In spite of the poverty, citizens had their own piece of land and house outside the capital, and we went out to one for the weekend. The economy was dominated by the American-owned rubber industry and I was taken on a hot but interesting tour of the factory and rubber plantations. An audience had been arranged with the President and the waiting-room was full of ordinary citizens also waiting to see him. I was told that he was accessible to any of his subjects, and this certainly seemed to be the case. He obviously knew the names of all the nurses who were with me, what they were doing and all about their families. It was a completely different visit from any of the others, and quite delightful and interesting. When we moved into the interior of the country I shared a room with one of the older nurses, who had been instrumental in setting up the association years ago and negotiating membership with ICN. She gave me a fascinating insight into the life of the ordinary person. I was seen off at the airport with the gift of a length of African cloth wrapped in newspaper. During the flight, however, I became aware that it housed a number of unwelcome insects and it was sadly abandoned at the next airport. One other legacy of my stay accompanied me and that was the attentions of a Lebanese hairdresser. Being fairly tired, I had been dozing during my hair drying, and, although my hair did not look its usual colour, it was not until it was dry and I was being driven to the airport that I realised it was a distinct purple. As there was no chance of doing anything about it, it had to stay that way. Once the ice was broken at my next stop, the nurses admired it and found it quite amusing – more than I did!

And so to the last stop on my itinerary – Bathurst, capital of The Gambia, a thin snake-like country curled along both sides of the main river. *Roots* was still some years in the future, so the country was comparatively unknown. At that time the majority of nurses were men. There was one WHO nurse, British, with whom I stayed and was obviously welcome, as visitors were infrequent. The British Governor was very courteous and invited me to dinner. He was just embarking on a tour of the country to explain independence, and gave me an idea of the journey, arranging for me to have one of the small launches for my return to the capital. A new ambulance had to be taken up country, so that was to be my means of outward travel. The road ended a few miles outside Bathurst and the rest was pure jungle track. Even now I can remember the discomfort of that journey, wedged between the driver and my escort, a rather large nurse, on a seat meant for two. The heat from the engine was intense, and so was the discomfort. We seemed to travel for days, although actually it was only six or seven hours, broken by a welcome stop for a drink from the provisions we carried. We eventually arrived at the clinic for which the ambulance was intended, and then visited one or two other small clinics, each with a few beds – the extent of the provision of health care up-country. In one of the villages, the Governor had stopped to meet the people on his tour of the country. It was interesting to see the reaction of the people. One old man near us explained to the nurse that he had brought his bowl to receive his independence!

We stayed overnight at one of the clinics and then set off on the return journey. We had left the ambulance behind, and the small boat was waiting to take us on the long slow journey back by river. It had two crew and a very small cabin, which soon became stiflingly hot, so I left my companion to sleep and went up on the tiny, cluttered deck. It was fascinating to see the life on and beside the river as we made our way along it. Eventually we came in sight of land and I was surprised to see the British nurse with her car at the landing stage. She explained that traffic was scarce and it was easy for the lookouts to recognise the launch and alert her to our approach. It was good to have a shower and a night in a comfortable bed before leaving for the airport and home the next morning. The nurses saw me off with a huge, round, lidded, wicker basket full of oranges. No one worried about transporting fruit between countries in those days, but it was difficult to fit the basket into the cramped space. It was a long flight on a Viscount aircraft with an overnight stop in Palma in the Canaries, and the coast of England was a welcome sight. Even then there were problems. Fog prevented us landing at Gatwick and we were diverted to Bournemouth. After a two-hour wait, we were loaded into buses, and wended a slow journey to London and home. I had been able to alert Mary, and she was at the bus terminal to meet me. It was amazingly good to get into my own bed.

Back at the office, there was a hive of activity in preparation for the congress, which was being organised with great efficiency by the German nurses. The report of the Economic Welfare Division had to be prepared, and the new assistant director of the division, Mary Patten of Australia, had done much of the background work. She brought me up to date with congress planning, and the outcome of deliberations of the two committees. The recommendations had come down strongly on the advantages of ICN moving to Geneva, and it seemed inevitable. Ingrid Hamelin had been offered a major post at home. It was particularly hard for Mary Patten, as her move from Australia to London had been of such magnitude, but she was offered, and accepted, a post of matron at one of the major hospitals in the State of Victoria, and continued a very successful career. We met a couple of times on her later visits to London, and she was obviously happy to be back in her own country. Like all staff she had had to decide whether to relocate to Geneva or leave ICN and return home. It became obvious that only Helen Nussbaum was definitely moving with the organisation and for her it was a welcome move, although her home was in another part of the country. That meant it was necessary to advertise for Nurse Advisors. Mary and I started to discuss the pros and cons of the situation, but nothing could be settled until the Council of National Representatives made a decision at the forthcoming congress in Frankfurt. A few weeks later the staff moved to Frankfurt to work with the German Nurses' Federation on the final details. They were extremely efficient, as expected, and it was a matter of familiarising ourselves with the site and its facilities. We were housed in the post-graduate school of the Agnes Karl Verband, which was very comfortable and homely. Helen Nussbaum and her deputy were the only two in the congress hotel.

The 1965 Frankfurt Congress was the first large ICN meeting I had attended, as the Geneva Conference was the much smaller meeting of the presidents and secretaries of the member associations. About 5,000 nurses gathered in Frankfurt, the first two days being official meetings and the rest of the week the congress programme, with most of the presentations in four languages. It was quite a feat of organisation, but extremely well thought through, and it was a very successful meeting. Voting had taken place for a new president and board. Alice Girard of Canada became president, with the former president, Alice Clamergeran, as the first of her vice-presidents, supported by Ruth Elster of Germany and Rola Pratt of Nigeria as second and third, and nine board members from various countries, including Nicole Exchaquet of Switzerland.

The recommendations of the committees were accepted unanimously and the move to Geneva, which was to be made as soon as possible, was endorsed. As soon as the congress was ended Helen Nussbaum and I continued to Geneva with Nicole Exchaquet, while the rest of the ICN staff returned to London to organise the sale of the London headquarters and start the many tasks required to close down in London and open a headquarters in Geneva. The week in Switzerland was spent visiting agents about possible headquarters and the Swiss Bank about transfer of assets, appointing financial advisors and interviewing for the small number of clerical staff we would need in the initial period. We returned to London, feeling somewhat worn, to an office buzzing with activity but also with an atmosphere of sadness, as many long-serving staff would be making their farewells. Fortunately, those who were leaving our employ were able to remain to clear all remaining business and to deal with the closure of the office. We had had some applications for the posts of nurse advisors, one of which was from Biddy Shout, who had been so good to me in Ghana. She was in England looking for a new post, and so, after her interview, she joined us immediately and was a very great help in the last frantic weeks of preparations. Another American nurse currently on the mission field was also appointed to join us later in Geneva, but unfortunately her family circumstances forced her to leave ICN after only a few months' employment.

When I returned home, Mary and I carefully talked through the pros and cons of the situation. Once again the position of matron of the Prince of Wales's was offered to me, but, after long consideration, I decided to move to Geneva with the organisation for at least a two-year period. Mary then dropped a bombshell. She said she had always wanted to work abroad and so she would apply to the Cantonal Hospital in Switzerland for the same period of time. We had friends who were looking for a home in the outer London area and we agreed on an unfurnished let for the two years, so that we both felt we had our roots in England to return to. Only a few lines are needed to express our final decision, but it was done after much heart-searching and knowing there would be many problems ahead. Mary had an elderly mother in the north of England, who was quite well at the time, but she judged that she would probably need to return when the two years had elapsed. And so, with the minimum of luggage we felt we needed, we boarded the train at Victoria for the overnight journey to Geneva. If we each had qualms, we kept them to ourselves.

Chapter 6

Life on the Run

At dawn the following day the train stopped at the Swiss frontier, and we were surprised to see Helen Nussbaum on the platform. She had brought our entry permits with her and joined us in the carriage for the rest of the journey. As our agents had told us that it was very difficult to obtain a flat at a reasonable price in Geneva, we had opted to take one in the small town of Nyon on the lakeside, a fifteen-minute train journey and twenty-minute drive on the convenient motorway from Geneva. It was a delightful, picturesque, small town with everything we required, but it was in the canton of Vaux as opposed to the neighbouring canton of Geneva. That was to produce problems later, but at the time it seemed ideal. We had secured a large flat on the eighth storey of a new building, still under construction when we agreed the lease. The agent assured us that it would be ready on time and they were never late. Given the reputation of the Swiss, we believed them. For the first night we were booked into a small hotel in the centre of Nyon, and after a shower and unpacking of bare necessities, we went to see the apartment. Then came the first shock. It was ready as promised, but it was the only one, apart from that of the concierge, in the huge, twelve-storey building; the rest was full of workmen by day and deathly quiet at night. The concierge and his wife were delightful and helpful, although communication was difficult because they had no English, Mary's French was extremely limited, mine was only adequate and it was very hard to understand the thick Swiss accent. However, the concierge explained with pride that the inside of the flat was absolutely complete, the lift worked specially for us to the eighth floor only, and he had organised a light just outside our door – the only one in the half-finished building. We could leave our car in the courtyard until the underground car park was ready. Apparently the removers had already been and deposited larger kitchen items on the ground floor near the lift, and were to start unpacking the next morning. We returned to the hotel feeling a bit bewildered and decided to stay there for another two nights and get the flat sorted out before we moved in. Mary had an interview with the small local hospital in Nyon the same afternoon. We had an early night, and woke to the arrival of breakfast, together with a message from Yvonne Hentsch, Chief Nurse of the League of Red Cross Societies, the international organisation based in Geneva, telling us that she was arriving at 10a.m. to take us to the local garage to obtain a car. Yvonne, a very experienced Swiss nurse, well-known throughout the world, was a mine of information in those early weeks, both to us and to ICN generally. The other person who was to be our local guide and adviser for many months, and who became a real friend, was Verena (Vreny) Wutrich, the head of the Swiss Nurses' Association in Geneva. We were invited to lunch with her the following day.

Buying a car was not simple, but Yvonne steered us through the preliminaries. As foreigners, we had special number plates, and insurance was more complicated. After completing the formalities, we visited the police station in Geneva to obtain our permits to live in the canton, and these had to be produced both for the car and to obtain the keys for the apartment. Soon we became used to visiting the police for a number of things, including change of address or canton. It seemed quite strange at first, but we soon discovered the police to be extremely helpful on any occasion we visited them. Mary then went over to the hospital and returned to say she was going to start work on the Monday. By now it was Saturday, and we said goodbye to Yvonne after lunch, promising to contact her if needed, and drove the car carefully back to the hotel, realising that the rules of the road were somewhat different from those in the UK. The year was 1966, and it was the Saturday of the World Cup match between England and Germany, so back at the hotel we asked if there was anywhere to watch television. We were directed to the bar, full of customers with the same goal, found a table and settled down to watch the match with a French commentary. We soon realised that the room was entirely partisan for Germany, and we were a very small voice in support of England. As the game ended with England taking the Cup, the rest of the bar suddenly realised our nationality and crowded round us, congratulating us, and insisted on buying us drinks so that we could all toast our victory. It was a good end to an exciting but tiring and somewhat worrying day.

We left the car, went for a walk along the lakeside, gazed at Mont Blanc sparkling in the evening sun and then retired for the night. The next day

With a group of international nurses and Alice Girard, ICN President at the ICN Congress, Montreal, Canada, 1969.

we found the small Catholic church very near the hotel and then went to the flat, where carpets had been laid, curtains and lights fitted, and kitchen equipment installed. After our last night at the hotel, I was at the flat early next morning to supervise the arrival of our furniture and main cases. By the time Mary returned from the hospital, it looked more like home. We had a perfect view over the lake and the Mont Blanc chain, with the great mountain itself in full view. We used the one bedroom that night as we were not completely unpacked, but awoke very early while it was still dark to a rhythmic sound of bells, which seemed just like cow bells. As we were in a town, curiosity drove me to the window, and there below me was a solemn file of cows walking up towards the mountains. All this suddenly seemed quite comforting, for it had felt very isolated and quite scary when we retired to bed knowing we were the only inhabitants of the building, as the concierge lived in a small cottage in the grounds. We really were in Switzerland, home seemed a long way off, but we were determined to settle down and enjoy the experience.

Finance figured largely in the move, as the price we received for ICN House in London did not equate to the cost of buying property in

Geneva. Eventually we rented space in a new building on the side of the lake where most of the large international organisations were situated, and gave our requirements to an architect to organise the rooms within the shell of the office. The shape was such that we had to have a large internal boardroom, which did not have adequate ventilation and was a trial for the whole eighteen years the office was occupied by ICN. As soon as finance was available, a new headquarters was bought, although there were many legislative problems to overcome before ICN was allowed to sign the purchase of a new headquarters. We had many regulations to contend with in the early stages of setting up in Geneva, and one was the restriction on employing non-Swiss personnel. We were allowed eight, but five of these were executive staff and it was difficult to obtain Swiss personnel who were fluent in English, as they were in great demand by all the international organisations. We used French in everyday life and the operation of headquarters, but our main language of communication with most of our member organisations was English. We were fortunate in acquiring three recently retired secretaries from the International Red Cross, and one in particular, Madame Mermoud, stayed with us for a number of years and was absolutely invaluable in guiding us in the early days. There was a real problem with written work in English, and I had to get round it by writing all the letters by hand, and asking one of our Swiss ladies to type them. By the end of the first month Biddy Shout had joined ICN as a Nurse Advisor, and later Lella Raymond from England, as Editor of the *International Nursing Review*, and Susan Moore of USA, as another Nurse Advisor, joined us. Sadly, both the latter had to leave ICN and return home within the first year, so those of us remaining were very overstretched. Gwen Buttery, our long-serving Deputy Executive Director, had taken retirement rather than have the upheaval of moving to Switzerland for the last two years of her career, and I had been appointed in her place, while still holding the remit for Economic Welfare. The latter had to take a back seat while we were in the seemingly endless process of settling in.

It was time to pursue the agreed WHO consultancy, taking about twenty chief nurses from various countries on a 'Travelling Seminar' in the USSR. My fellow consultant, Dr Helen Mussallem, a very distinguished Canadian nurse, who was the Executive Director of the Canadian Nurses' Association, had come to Geneva and was spending a week with the World Health Association for briefing. I joined when it was possible to leave ICN work, and Helen was responsible for writing the report of the seminar. We barely knew each other, as we had only met briefly at an ICN Meeting, but we enjoyed each other's company and became firm friends. We also had a secretary and a delightful Russian WHO colleague, who was our interpreter and very much more during the month of our travels. It was not a good time for me to go, with neither the office nor our home completely settled and Mary working in a strange environment without English friends near. Biddy Shout was a great support and kept in close contact with Mary while I was away. In fact, on my return, I found Mary established at the Cantonal Hospital in Geneva and much preferring the busy environment of the spinal unit, especially as she had a number of English colleagues there. Helen and I set off for Moscow with the team at the beginning of October, and I remember we were sitting rather silently at Vienna airport waiting for the Moscow plane when Helen suddenly said, 'We had better get some more newspapers as this will be our last chance for a month' and we all went into uneasy laughter, unsure of what was ahead of us, in spite of our careful briefing. The flight seemed endless and we touched down at Moscow Airport in the dark. Going through immigration, I was horrified to find myself stopped, until one of the Russians meeting me came to see what was wrong. Apparently the stamp had obliterated part of my photograph on my brand new laissez-passer but on being identified I was allowed in. At the time, I would have gladly turned back.

Our temporary home in Moscow was one of the very big anonymous hotels, with a large and rather fierce lady guarding each floor, but we found it comfortable, and we had already welded into a closely-knit group. The nurses we were to accompany arrived over the next two or three days, while we became acquainted with our Russian counterparts. It was strange for us to be working directly with doctors rather than nurses. The programme was intense and well-organised, and in Moscow we saw hospitals, educational facilities, community care and the excellent ambulance service, which was an outstanding facility. At the end of each day, we met with our nursing colleagues who were participants in the seminar, and who included many of my friends, such as Rola Pratt of Nigeria and Docia Kissieh of Ghana. We discussed the events of each day and the programme for the next. Many of the events were very formal and Helen and I took turns to lead the delegation, and make the required speeches and courtesies. We were also shown all the famous sights of

Introducing members of the Nursing Committee of the EEC to HRH Princess Margaret at RCN Headquarters in London, 1977.

Moscow. After two weeks we travelled by plane to other cities, and the crowded planes did not fill one with confidence. The two places I remember most are Kiev and Tbilisi, the former having a strong feeling of greater freedom than we had felt elsewhere. We were also introduced to the holiday resorts on the Black Sea, where recreation was very organised. Outside Moscow the most fascinating part of our journey was the visit to a country village, where poverty was marked. Our travelling allowance was paid in roubles, which were pretty useless outside the country, so we joined the queues outside the famous store, Gum, and used our money on amber and records for presents to take home. We were accompanied almost everywhere, so it was a pleasure to do some shopping alone, and to stop for a hot drink in a local café. We had all enjoyed the experience, but it was with delight that we assembled at the airport for our flight home. It was the 22 November and we were told that the winter snows start on that day. They did, falling from the sky in a seemingly endless greyish white cloud. Flights were immediately cancelled, though we could hear planes flying overhead. We had all the nurses with us, going home via various routes, and the Russians who were in charge of us had said their goodbyes and gone home. Helen and the WHO staff had decided to take a short holiday in Leningrad, as St Petersburg was called at that time, and had headed off in a different direction, so everyone was looking to me for advice. I felt completely helpless and inadequate. Eventually, after some hours in which various nurses had been able to start their journey home, the rest of us had the offer of a flight to Berlin. It seemed best to take it, and with a group of nurses who were travelling through or staying over in London, we boarded the plane. Stupidly, I hadn't checked which part of Berlin, and we landed in East Berlin, without visas and needing to get through to West Berlin. Officials were helpful and we were escorted through 'Checkpoint Charlie' and to the right airport for London. By this time the remaining nurses were somewhat tearful, and on arrival we found there were no vacancies on flights to London but, after some waiting and juggling with numbers, everyone left and I was free to take the next flight to Geneva, where I received a great welcome from Mary.

After debriefing at WHO, I returned to the office to pick up the threads of ICN work. Frances Beck, the senior nurse advisor, had left on fieldwork, and we were still struggling with the minutiae of establishing ourselves in Switzerland. Christmas was almost upon us, and we had decided to remain in Switzerland for the holiday. We had established contact with the English-speaking Catholic community, mainly American, and became friendly with Joyce Duly, an English woman working in a senior position at WHO, who had been established in Geneva for a number of years. She became a close friend and was a great help and companion to Mary during my absences. She retired to the south coast of England and we visited often until her death in the first year of the new millennium. An English family whom we met at church had a father who was working at the British Embassy, in the same office building as ICN, and again the friendship continued after retirement to London until the death of the parents. The American Library was a real haven, being full of new English language books and journals, as television was confined to Swiss and French channels, and of limited interest. It is delightful in today's travel to be able to switch on to CNN, BBC World and Euro News, and keep in touch with what is happening in the world. We were both usually free at the weekend and decided to take advantage of being in the middle of Europe. We visited many of the Swiss mountain resorts, both near and far, and also went through the tunnels into France and Italy. We thoroughly enjoyed the beauty of Switzerland in all its seasons, and did a lot of walking in the mountains. Sometimes we were fortunate enough to spend a weekend with one of the WHO nurses in their chalet in Champery. When we did return to England, we continued to spend many short holidays in our favourite Swiss resorts. We both learnt to ski, but neither of us was brilliant and we tended to resort to cross-country skiing. All our friends from England decided to take advantage of our invitations to visit, and it did seem as if we were running a guest house-cum-tourist agency for the whole of the first year, but it kept us from feeling homesick.

The following year, 1967, we had the interim meeting of the Council of National Representatives, which fortunately was being hosted by the French Nurses' Association in Evian, just across the lake, but in France. We had two temporary English-speaking secretaries by this time, so life at the office was more organised, but even then we were struggling to get everything ready for the meeting, which was in June. Fortunately, it was easy to go over to Evian to arrange the hotel and conference rooms and to transfer documents, but we were still having many problems in Geneva with major matters such as the transfer of money from England. We had acquired a superb Swiss fiduciaire, or accountant, and he dealt patiently with the many problems relating to money, location and regulations, but it all took time. It also took its toll on Helen Nussbaum, in spite of the fact that she was in her own country. The new president, Alice Girard, came over two or three times and was a great support, but Helen went off sick and the officers, who were meeting formally as the Finance Committee, persuaded her to take three months' leave in order to rest and recuperate. When she returned it was obvious that she was pushing herself to the limit, and, with the extra work of the forthcoming meeting, her health broke down completely. She went into a clinic in Berne and was not able to return to the work she loved, but lived quietly near her friends and relatives until her death in 1985. I last saw her at my leaving party when I left ICN for a post in the United Kingdom.

Work went on for the meeting in Evian. The hotel was magnificent, in a perfect position, with all the facilities of a spa. The president and I had adjoining suites and I could not help thinking, as we sat on the balcony with the vista of Lake Geneva laid out before us, that it would be a wonderful holiday spot. The meeting was not one which solved major international issues, and the president's report was mainly on the joys and

A typical view of a packed hall at an ICN Congress in the 1970s.

trials of the move from the UK. It was obviously important to appoint a stable executive staff, but salaries and conditions had not been adequately adjusted for the considerable difference in the cost of living. The Finance Committee addressed this, but the pension scheme was more difficult. There was also great concern about Helen Nussbaum's illness, and eventually, with her agreement, she was given a long period with pay and then her resignation took place. The board appointed me as Executive Director designate, and then confirmed the full appointment when Helen's sick leave ran out. That year Mary and I rented a small chalet for a month high above the beautiful mountain village of Champery, and I took my holiday there, working on policies and procedures, and on articles for the *ICN Journal* as we were between editors. Mary was working, and drove up from Geneva on Friday afternoons, going back at dawn on Monday. The countryside really refreshed me and I returned to the office ready to pick up the work again.

Marjorie Duvillard, former head of the Bon Secours Nursing School in Geneva, had joined us as deputy director; she spoke fluent English and Spanish and, as a Swiss citizen, her local knowledge was invaluable. She left quite soon for professional visits to Latin America, which were long overdue, and on her return I left for another visit to the Caribbean. The main focus of my journey was Haiti, as contact had been established with two religious nursing sisters who came to the ICN meeting in Evian, the first contact with Haiti for many years. Guyana had also asked for a visit, as had Trinidad, and it was quite a relief to get away from the concerns and problems of Geneva for a while. My first stop was Jamaica, to see how their problems had settled down. The Custos of Kingston and his wife, a charming and delightful couple, had invited me to stay with them in their lovely villa above Kingston. The whole family was very hospitable and it was an enjoyable visit, especially as the earlier antagonism between various groups of nurses had settled down and a number of changes for the better had taken place in the nursing service. It was in Kingston that I had to ask the British Consul to arrange my visa for Haiti. This was done with a smile enquiring 'was my journey really necessary?', which did nothing to calm my apprehension. However, I boarded the Pan Am plane to Port au Prince wondering about my reception. I need not have been concerned because, as we touched down, an official came on board looking for 'the British Nurse' and escorted me off and through customs to the warm welcome of the two religious nursing sisters, together with a small group of nurses. They accompanied me to the hotel and told me that Madame Duvalier had lent me her car and chauffeur, and we were to have an audience of Dr Duvalier himself the next morning. Had I been acquainted with Graham Greene's book, I would have been more apprehensive than I already was, but the formal visit to the Palace the next day was very courteous and Madame Duvalier went out of her way to put me at ease. While we were in the waiting room, a tall American with his charming wife asked if I was the nurse that everyone had been held up for in immigration. He was apparently an oil magnate on important business and I felt more like Alice in Wonderland than ever. I was somewhat wary of my chauffeur with his very dark glasses, but he was extremely courteous and very patient, waiting for me at all times of the day. I spent the week seeing all aspects of the health service, and the poverty of the country and its hospitals was very marked. The sisters escorted me everywhere, and when our journey to Cap d'Haiti had to be cancelled because of weather, we visited a hospital in the centre of the country run on the same lines as the Schweitzer Hospital in Africa. The senior staff were American Baptists giving a year or more of voluntary work. It was interesting and refreshing to visit and to be able to speak

English, as the French used in Haiti was a patois which was often difficult to understand. Back in Port au Prince and at a cocktail party, I had obviously attracted the attention of both British and American Ambassadors, and it was with difficulty that I managed to persuade them that I was simply a nurse carrying out a professional visit. Nurses just did not get that kind of attention and an audience with 'Papa Doc'. After a farewell banquet attended by his aide de camp and the British Ambassador, I was seen off by the aide de camp and a posse of nurses, to say nothing of my chauffeur with the dark glasses. Obviously I found and read the Graham Greene book on my return, and have followed the unhappy history of Haiti with a great deal of interest and concern. I left a bit of my heart there with the delightful people who gave me so much in spite of their own poor and troubled lives, and I will always look back on my visit with affection. We kept in touch with the nurses who were able to come to ICN meetings for a few years, but there was little contact during the turbulent years after Dr Duvalier's reign.

While in the Caribbean I took the opportunity to make brief visits to the small islands, such as Granada, St Kitts and Nevis and Montserrat, where the nurses greeted me with delight and warm hospitality. Then it was on to Barbados and Trinidad for meetings with the associations there. In Trinidad I renewed acquaintance with a WHO nurse I had met in Japan, and had dinner with her and her husband at their lovely villa. It was a particularly hectic programme and I was relieved to move out of the capital city into the country. Unfortunately the weekend was interrupted as I had to return to the capital for a radio interview which had been forgotten. One unforgettable sight was of the scarlet ibis coming in to roost for the night on a lake in the country. At the weekend we went to Tobago, where I had my first experience of snorkelling in the Bucca Reef with one of their famous guides and swimming in the silk pool on the way back.

Guyana was to be my last stop before returning to Geneva, and as I had had no contact with the association or individuals, I was not quite sure what to expect. One of the officers of the association met me and took me to her lovely home where I met her husband, who was a doctor, and I enjoyed their hospitality throughout my visit. The association had very few members and had little activity, which was not surprising when I saw the impoverished state of their hospitals and of the nurses themselves. In spite of that, the nurses did their utmost to show me their health service and spoke freely of their problems. There had also been a lot of damage from a recent hurricane. My hosts were very friendly with the Chief Minister, the Hon. Forbes Burnham, and also with the head of a large British industrial firm in Georgetown, which opened many doors. First of all I was taken for a visit to the Chief Minister, who received me with great courtesy and offered me tea – I couldn't help noticing that the tray was rapidly removed from a secretary taking it in another direction! It was obvious that he was on very friendly terms with my host, and made suggestions for my visit. One of these was to go up country to the Rupununi and cattle country to have an idea of the kind of terrain outside the main towns, and he offered to make it possible for me to travel on one of the planes which shuttled back and forth daily.

Two days later, heeding a warning to dress casually, I was escorted to the airfield and climbed aboard an old Dakota. There were no seats as it was a cargo plane, and the pilot settled me on a chair lashed to the side of the plane. The noise of the engine made conversation impossible, so I watched the scenery during the two-hour flight. It was mainly jungle, but at one point it cleared to give an incredible view of a massive waterfall immediately below us. Otherwise the flight was uneventful, if rather bumpy. We landed on arid, almost desert-like, country and, on disembarking I was met by a wiry, middle-aged man, who was the local doctor, and he took me to his home for lunch. After that he showed me the small village and introduced me to the local priest. Both priest and doctor were responsible for a large tract of country, and they were interesting companions. We covered quite a bit of it by jeep, ending by a river which divided Guyana from Brazil, and where good coffee was bought. When I asked about my return, I was told it depended on the plane journeys with the meat. The large racks of meat hanging at the airstrip had not escaped my notice, and I gathered that a message would be sent to the homestead when the last load was secured and another to Georgetown with my arrival time. So we settled down to tea and discussion about life in that far-flung part of Guyana until the signal came to return to the airstrip. Sure enough the last of the meat was loaded and then my chair was secured; I said my goodbyes and thanks and picked my way over the carefully stacked piles of meat to my seat, which was more or less in the middle of it. The flight back was really bumpy and the smell of the meat was potent, to say the least, as it had been hanging in the sun. The flight seemed endless, and it was with great relief that I took my leave of the pilot and touched terra firma at Georgetown, to find my hosts waiting at the airport. They felt it would be nice to go out to a restaurant for dinner and asked what kind would I like; without any finesse I replied, 'Anything but beef.'

After one or two days of meetings with the nurses in Georgetown and visiting the hospital and school of nursing, it was time to see something of the nurses who worked out in the rural areas. The head of the industrial firm very kindly said that a flight could be organised to take me to another remote part of the country, but it was the small plane used by the factory and I was to be sure that I was on time. Early next morning my hosts drove me to another airstrip, where I boarded a little two-seater – for the pilot and me! It was with some trepidation that I climbed in and hung on while we lurched into the air and bounced in the warm currents. It was soon obvious that the pilot had only the odd word of English, and no one had thought to tell me where we were going or how long the journey would be. After a while I became quite fascinated with the country below us, especially when we came in sight of the huge Esequebo river, and nothing else but jungle in view. My nervousness returned when we were obviously descending without any possible strip for landing in sight. Suddenly we swooped down and hit the water. I was convinced this was the end, said a frantic prayer and was wondering how we could possibly escape, when I realised the spray was settling, the plane stopping and the pilot seemed completely unperturbed. I had not realised that it was an amphibian plane! But there was still no indication of what was to happen next. The wide estuary was empty apart from a small canoe in the distance, and then it gradually came near. The pilot opened the window on my side, signalled for me to get out and into the canoe – quite a feat with the plane tossing on the water – and said, 'Have a good day, man', his only words throughout the flight. Somehow I made the canoe right way up, and watched the plane vanish in a cloud of spray.

Communication was limited to smiles as the canoe was rowed back towards the edge of the jungle bordering the river. And there on the bank was a nurse, in spotless white uniform (including white shoes), who greeted me as if it were an everyday occurrence to meet strangers more or less tumbling out of the sky. Maybe it was! I returned her greeting and welcome with all the sangfroid I could muster, as if it were a daily routine to which I was completely accustomed. As we set off on the path through the jungle, she told me we were visiting a village with its tiny 'hospital' of six beds, and the attached clinic, where the nurse was holding a mother and baby class. The village was certainly remote and the facilities spartan but sparklingly clean. My powers of invention were put to the test when the nurse asked me to talk to the mothers about baby care and the health of the mother, but we ended up with smiles all round. Next there was a meeting with a group of nurses who spoke about their daily routine and their own training, and then we left to catch up with a member of the association who had come down to escort me back. I wasn't too enthusiastic about returning by the same means of transport and was relieved to hear it was to be a mixture of road and river. The four-wheel drive was the only means of negotiating the tracks down to a landing stage. There we took a small boat to the other side of the river, another four-wheel drive for a couple of hours, and then a crowded and rather ancient type of paddle steamer to the port of Georgetown. It was the last and certainly the most adventurous day of my visit to Guyana, and the following morning I left by plane with many thanks to my delightful hosts, and returned, with real regret, to Geneva with my memories.

Mary met me at the airport and home looked very good. We were getting quite near to the date of the ICN Congress in Montreal and there was a lot of preparation to be done. Most of the executive staff were at the office, but Biddy Shout was in Africa and not returning for a few weeks. Frances Beck had been working on the outline of a congress programme and, after discussing it the next day, she told me she had accepted another overseas post and would be leaving in a few weeks. She was the only long-serving member of staff with experience of a number of congresses, so it was quite a loss, but it was a post she obviously wanted and we could only wish her success. We were joined by a very able Jamaican nurse, Mary Jane Sievwright, and, though we were conscious of our lack of experience, we were all determined to make the congress outstanding. Secretarial staff had increased in numbers, but in those early years they all seemed very temporary and we had many changes. Gradually, however, we were able to build up a permanent staff. It was a joy to be working with Helen Mussallem as my counterpart in the Canadian Nurses' Association and, as our president was based in Montreal, help and advice were at hand. I made a number of short trips to the congress venue and a month before the event moved into a furnished flat to be on site for final preparations. It was hard work and major things went wrong, notably with the new Convention Hall, which would not be ready in time. We had to move the venue to an Exhibition Site, which had a monster of a main hall but was lacking in all the side rooms and offices needed for such an event. We were constantly changing plans and we had the largest number of bookings ever – 12,000 nurses had registered. Somehow, with superhuman efforts from the Canadian nurses, we were ready.

All the ICN staff had arrived and the president had made a formal entry to Montreal by visiting the Mayor to sign the Golden Book of the City. The preliminary meetings of the Council of National Representatives went well and, on the day it finished, Helen and I went to Place Bonaventure to make a final check. There we met a large group of well-known American nurses, who, in answer to our cheerful greeting, gave us the unwelcome news that something had gone wrong with the reservations and they had no hotels. Helen went off to sort it out and I returned to the Centre to meet lots of other problems. It was all resolved in the end and somehow we were ready for the opening on the Sunday. There was a church service at the great and beautiful Cathedral of Notre Dame, which was absolutely packed. It was multidenominational, but it also broke new ground in that the ministers were multifaith, headed by the Cardinal whose church it was. The two hundred or so members of the Council of National Representatives wound their way in colourful national costumes down the central aisle, but my main recollection of the opening ceremony was the blending of the saffron robes of the Buddhist minister with the scarlet of the Cardinal as they greeted each other in the equally colourful procession of the clergy. It was a beautiful and very emotive service, which ended after the president, followed by her vice-presidents and board members, moved in procession to a side chapel to lay a posy at the statue of Jean Mance, a famous Canadian nurse in the early days of the colonising of Canada. Helen and I were at either side of the president and it was vital that we got back to the congress hall in time to check that all was well for the main opening ceremony with the Governor-General. There was a small side door near the statue where we were to slip out and race ahead to the hall, but unfortunately it was closed. We struggled along with the crowds to the main entrance to find that we had lost our car and our expectation of arriving in time to greet everyone properly had gone sadly wrong, but eventually we arrived and changed into evening dress to be in our places.

The huge square auditorium had presented us with many problems but most of all for the plenary sessions, which could have as many as

With a group of Japanese nurses and RCN officials at the ICN Congress in Tokyo, 1977.

12,000 as an audience. We had settled for a square central podium, which, to ensure that all spectators could see what was happening, was a revolving platform with the control on stage. Everyone on stage had to be warned what was happening. For similar reasons the four major processions were to enter from different corners and, as Executive Director, I had the job of announcing and giving a commentary on the processions. It was a daunting task and acoustics were very bad, although participants were equipped with earphones and four-language translation. With my microphone on the platform, I had the best view of all, but twelve thousand looked an awful lot of people, although the colourful processions were dwarfed by the size of the arena. When all the main participants with the country flags had been seated, I slipped away to join the procession of the Governor-General, who was opening the congress, and took my place with Helen. On arrival on the podium it was then my task to manipulate the machinery to start rotation of the stage at given points, making sure it was facing the right way at the end of the procedures. It was effective, but a very odd sensation, especially for speakers who were alone on the platform during the week. At the end of the ceremony, the platform party retired to the Green Room but, to avoid getting lost in the crowd, the national presidents were to join on behind us, and continue to another hall while the Governor-General's party went into the Green Room. Helen and I were at the back of the Governor's procession but, as we turned to go into the room, we realised that the whole of the CNR were right behind us and had lost their way. The audience was breaking up and there was obviously going to be more than a little confusion. We looked at each other, Helen gave me a push, firmly closed the door behind us and we left the chaos outside to sort itself out.

It was a very spectacular but very wearing evening, and unfortunately the problems caused by the one huge hall continued through the week. It was quite a relief when it ended. Alice Girard had been a magnificent president throughout the proceedings and on the final day the elections were held for the new president. There were two candidates, Dame Muriel Powell of the UK and Margarethe Kruse of Denmark, both very well known and extremely popular. It was a close contest but Margarethe had become a household name. Her work with the International Labour Organisation, and the publication of the international report on Salaries and Conditions of Nurses, with the Copenhagen porcelain statue of the Danish Nurse pictured on the cover, was known in every country. Margarethe was elected and it was a very popular result, except for the badly disappointed British contingent. I had to break the news to Muriel Powell and, although she took it as the great lady she was, it was obviously a blow. We hoped there would be another chance but, as so often happens, the one precious opportunity did not return. Dame Muriel was appointed Chief Nursing Officer of Scotland and remained a greatly loved national and international figure, until her untimely death soon after her retirement.

We were soon packing up after the congress. So many months, and even years, to prepare and in a matter of days the event had moved into history and we were on our way back to Geneva with a new president for a new quadrennium. Only after my return to Geneva and a day or two away from ICN did I start to look at the future. Mary and I went to the mountains for the weekend to rest and collect our thoughts. The stress of the last few years had been enormous. The move to Geneva with all its ongoing problems, the illness and resignation of Helen Nussbaum, and the huge amount of work for the congress, together with the visits to member associations, had all taken their toll. It was also obvious that I had been coping as best I could with the demands of a huge job without any formal training, and I felt the need for a management course. There was no way I could cope with one in French, and America was far too costly, so I investigated what was available in the UK, with the help and advice of Harold Bridger of the Tavistock Institute, an adviser to the Royal College of Nursing, who was to become – and still is – a very special friend. As a result Henley Management College offered me an interview and then to my delight a place on their General Management Course – quite unusual in those days when only a few women had been accepted. Returning to Geneva I spoke with the new president who was very enthusiastic and supportive. The Leverhulme Foundation offered me a grant to cover what were considerable fees for the three-month residential course, and the ICN Finance Committee considered my request for leave. Sadly, they felt they could only offer me leave without pay, even though Marjorie Duvillard was willing to act as executive director during my absence. In a way it was understandable, because we had gone through so much staff change in Geneva, and the committee intimated that they would consider it later. It was a big decision to make and there was no guarantee that the College would give me a vacancy later. They had an upper age limit for the course and I was already a year older than the preferred age. The move to Geneva and difference in the cost of living had eaten into cash reserves, although the Finance Committee was trying to bring salaries up to similar posts in Geneva. After a lot of thought and discussion, especially with Mary, I worked out that two weeks' holiday was owing to me because of the congress, and by taking the whole of the current year's holiday for the course, it would reduce the time without salary to one third of the course. I made one more approach to the president, offering a guarantee to stay with ICN for at least a further three years if they would make up the deficit, but the committee felt it was not possible. With Mary's support I decided to take the plunge and booked in for the course starting at the beginning of October 1969. I made the proviso that, although I did not expect to move from ICN in the foreseeable future, there would not be any requirement for me to remain for any specific length of time.

The die was cast and I accepted the vacancy. It felt strange returning to college and to the UK as a sort of foreigner, especially where the job was concerned. I wasn't exactly in the general line of budding managers at a

Formal photograph on my election as RCN President, 1982.

business college, and I had real doubts as to whether I could hold my own. It was a pleasant surprise, therefore, to find myself different but equally capable of coping with the subjects and the course work. It was a most delightful twelve weeks. One other nurse in top management and another woman in general management were on the course, and we had our residence in the lodge at the gates to the college. Work was in syndicates, with projects and visits, and we had two long weekends when we were free to leave the college, and I went back to Geneva on both occasions. There was a delightful atmosphere and we lived well. The break from my usual hectic pattern of work showed up the extent of my fatigue, and I felt myself gradually returning to my usual energy. Mary's news was that her mother had deteriorated and she had been on leave to help her mother close up her home and move into a nursing home, in the same area and run by an order of religious nursing sisters, where she was very happy. Mary's cousins lived nearby and visited her often and Mary went over for weekends every few weeks.

A major reorganisation of the nursing structure in our NHS had just commenced. It was called the Salmon Structure, after Brian Salmon of the Lyons group, who had headed up the working party. He was also a great friend of the RCN and on the Finance Committee. Reading the Nursing and Health Service Journals and being in the country, I began to be aware of how the situation was changing and improving for senior nurses, both in career prospects and in salary. Catherine (Mary) Hall was an old friend from my student days at the RCN and was now established as the general secretary and a very influential figure in the UK. I visited her once or twice during my weeks at Henley, when she broached the idea of my returning to the NHS. She felt it was unlikely that I would want to stay in Geneva for the rest of my career, and there were some very large and interesting jobs coming up in the UK. It gave me food for thought but I intended to return to ICN, although I knew it was unlikely that I would remain there for the rest of my working life. Much as I enjoyed international work and was committed to the nurses, it was obvious to me I would always wish to return to my own country.

Decision time came very unexpectedly when Catherine Hall alerted me to an advertisement for the post of Chief Nursing Officer to the Southampton Hospital Group. The first new medical university and teaching hospital for two hundred years was to be set up in Southampton and, apart from the new medical school, a large new hospital was planned as its partner. A group of hospitals was to be formed, and the new post of CNO advertised. It was a big decision. I talked about it with Catherine Hall and with my colleague at Henley, both of whom encouraged me to apply. This I did, and went down to see the existing hospital and talk with the group secretary before interview. It was quite a daunting job. There were two older hospitals in the town and a number of smaller hospitals in the town and surrounding area to be served by the medical school. These had to be brought together to operate as a group, and one school of nursing and the new hospital had to be designed and built. However, the interview went ahead and I then returned to Henley to await a phone call. I felt myself out of the running but when the phone call came, to my surprise, the job was offered to me. I asked for time to consider, phoned Geneva to consult with Mary, discussed with Catherine Hall and returned to Geneva for the weekend, still undecided. It would be an enormous wrench to leave the international field and return, not just to a national situation, but a very local one. I had never held a management post in my own country and the NHS had changed considerably in nine years. It was doubtful whether I had the capacity and experience to take on such a large commitment. Southampton was a completely different part of the country and neither Mary nor I had any links there. Mary herself was quite sure it was time for her to return home, but we both felt that should not colour my decision. We had some sleepless nights and a lot of prayers were said for guidance. Finally, I came to the conclusion that, if the opportunity was turned down, it would always be a source of regret. The next day I telephoned the hospital administrator, agreed to accept the post and suggested a start date two months ahead. We exchanged letters of agreement and contract and the die was cast. Back in Geneva there was consternation at the news, but a very unexpected turn of events produced an excellent candidate for my post and she was able to start almost immediately. Adele Herwitz, a senior member of the American Nurses' Association, was leaving due to a reorganisation. She had been a member of the ICN Professional Service Committee for some years and was well acquainted with our work. We invited her to come over for talks and she agreed to take the post, at first on a six-month basis, and stayed for a number of years. It was a very happy appointment.

Then the process of winding up our apartment and going through all the formalities of relinquishing our right of sojourn in Geneva began, and was almost as lengthy and complicated as the formalities of arriving. But at last all was complete and ICN gave me a wonderful party at headquarters and gifts which are very precious to me and which include the Danish Nurse figurine. Biddy Shout saw us to the train next morning and we watched Mont Blanc disappear from view with many regrets, but we also looked forward to coming home to stay.

CHAPTER 7

Home and the National Health Service

FRIENDS HAD OFFERED US the use of their holiday apartment in Bournemouth until we found permanent accommodation. We started our journey from Geneva by train in the early morning, but it was not the easiest journey. We had a lot of luggage because furniture and other belongings were going into store until we had a permanent home, and our first problem was crossing Paris from one station to another. It was a holiday weekend and porters were non-existent, but we eventually found two willing students. After the train to the Channel ferry, we met the same problem, but eventually arrived in Southampton early in the morning and took a taxi to the garage from which we had hired a car for two weeks. As it was closed, we had to wait for the owner to arrive but, finally, with everything on board, we set off for Bournemouth where the apartment was easy to find near the sea front. After some essential shopping and the minimum of unpacking, we went thankfully to bed. I was beginning to wonder which was the more traumatic experience, to establish oneself in Geneva, or to return home.

Things looked much better in the morning, and Mary went to organise a temporary post at the Bournemouth Hospital while I drove into Southampton to meet the group secretary and matron of the general hospital. There was a warm welcome from all, and a pleasant office prepared next to the group secretary, but these brought me up sharply. In all my previous Health Service posts I had been in the centre of the hospital, very much part of the nursing staff, in uniform, well-acquainted with the life of a nurse, and it dawned on me that things were going to be very different. I wasn't at all sure it was going to work, but as my boats were well and truly burnt, I started with all the enthusiasm I could muster. The new team of which I was to be an integral part was already established in the group offices on the site of the general hospital. My colleagues were the secretary or administrator, treasurer, chair of the medical committee and the dean of the newly established medical school, all of whom made me very welcome. My induction period was short and intensive. The timetable for the opening of the medical school was moving very quickly, and the most important part of my role was to establish the Salmon Structure across the group. Once established, it soon gave way to what was to become a series of reorganisations for the NHS, but the Salmon Structure was not too popular with nurses and distinctly disliked by our medical and administrative colleagues. It was, however, invaluable in that it helped able nurses to move into management, and prepared them for the new role by a series of countrywide courses. Not all experienced nurses were adaptable to a new managerial role, and sometimes those who were preferred their former 'hands on' role. Until this point senior nurses could take one of the nursing management courses, but these were too few in number so senior nurses often moved into managerial posts in nursing without any real training for a new role. Many of them did not really want to leave the bedside, but had to do so in order to earn a reasonable salary and were quite unhappy away from direct patient care.

We had clear guidance as to how to go about moving nurses into the Salmon Structure. Eligibility to be interviewed depended on the grade the nurse already held and the numbers of beds or size of department, so my first move was to visit all the hospitals to talk to the senior staff in each. Everyone was extremely polite and helpful, but also very wary, and it was obvious that there would be no quick and easy acceptance. One or two senior staff, while friendly, were critical of the changes to come, and most of the senior medical staff were openly critical of the changes. One shortcoming of the Salmon Report was that it had not the remit or authority to include nurses working in the community. This was to come later, but at the time it did not make for a seamless service. The only way to handle the situation was to make friends with the community nursing and midwifery staff and agree informal rules of our own for cooperation and understanding of each other's role. This was achieved and made life much easier when the next reorganisation included the community medical and nursing staff. One very strong leader stood out and that was Betty Knox, the head of the community midwifery service. She was committed to cooperation and at that point had been a community midwife in Southampton for twenty-four years. She knew everyone and alerted me to all the pitfalls and personalities. She became a close colleague and a lifelong friend, head of the midwifery service, and succeeded me as Chief Nursing Officer.

Another important group of nurses were those employed at the region. They were very small in number, never more than three or four. I had a line relationship to the Chief Regional Nurse, Freda Gundry, a tall, striking woman with a very friendly, outgoing personality and a great style in hats! She had been on my interviewing panel, was a force in the region, and was well-liked and respected by medical, administrative and nursing colleagues; Wessex was a small but very happy region. My counterparts in the other districts of the Wessex Region, such as Portsmouth and Bournemouth, were also a closely-knit group. We had regional nursing meetings between the RNO and her nursing staff and the district chief nurses such as myself. I learnt an enormous amount from those colleagues, and am sure that the close working relationship we had was the reason that Wessex made the transformation to the Salmon Structure with the least upheaval and with very few disgruntled nurses. We all did our utmost to make sure that everyone was treated fairly and, if someone was unsuccessful in one post, he or she was able to transfer to another suitable vacancy. It was not without trauma – no such radical re-organisation could be – but it was reduced to the very minimum. Len Whitney, the group secretary, was always ready to give advice and help, and his wisdom and experience helped me to avoid more than a few pitfalls. Interviewing all eligible nurses throughout the country was a massive task. As a district nursing officer, I was automatically on the list of national interviewers, but for the actual reorganisation we were paired with a neighbouring region. It was a very hectic few weeks, moving from one district to another, and I got to know my fellow assessor, Rachael Worsley, very well and really enjoyed travelling around the region and recommending placements. There were very few nurses who could not be placed, and they were mostly able to find a position on a later round or to take early retirement, for which a few opted. One of the regional nurses, Angela Gould, was the nursing personnel and training officer, and did a great deal to keep up the morale of the nurses affected by the change, and her management courses were much sought after. Like so many nurses with whom I worked, she became a close friend.

At that time, the nurses employed at the Ministry of Health were quite a large group with considerable influence, both with the nurses throughout the country and, more importantly, with the ministers and civil servants with whom they worked. One nurse was appointed to one or more regions to act on behalf of the Chief Nursing Officer, and to work with the chief nurses of the regions and districts. The UK has always been fortunate in the calibre of its leaders, and the chief nurses at the Department of Health, from the first, Dame Elizabeth Cockayne, through to the present day, have all been giants in their field. I was particularly fortunate to know and work with Dame Kathleen Raven, who exerted an influence on nursing and nursing matters long after her retirement. She was passionate about the role and importance of the clinical nurse, and I was able to assist her with the setting up of a Chair in Clinical Nursing Studies, at her own alma mater, the General Infirmary at Leeds. She died soon after this appointment, and the UK lost a wise and determined leader of nursing.

In the district, with the assistance of the group administrator, we had organised a programme of interviews for eligible nurses, working down from the most senior group. Of the two major hospitals in the group, the old voluntary hospital, the Royal South Hants, with fewer than 300 beds, was in the heart of the town and had very little room for expansion. Its wards were old and not designed for todays' needs, and the school of nursing had already been absorbed into the group. It had a great history; most of the ward sisters had been in post for some years, as had the matron, and there was an obvious sense of pride in the hospital and its level of care, in spite of difficult conditions. The general hospital on the other hand was bigger, built more recently, had ample ground for expansion and more beds. The matron was London-trained, very able and up-to-date in her ideas and practice. The district was to be divided into two main areas under a Salmon Structure and indeed for total administrative services. The central sector – the acute area – consisted largely of the two main hospitals. The other area took in all the other hospitals, both in the centre and around the city, some of them quite large, others long stay, and also a number of small delightful hospitals of the cottage hospital type. The third area was midwifery, both hospital and community, including the small hospitals which had a midwifery section or a maternity home. One feature of the changes which did not seem logical was that the psychiatric and mental handicap hospitals and services were a separate structure from the rest of the district, with their own chief officers and hospital boards. It was felt that the standards of these often very large hospitals needed upgrading, and that this would best be done with their own management committees, but this decision was reversed in a later reorganisation.

It was obvious that one difficult problem was the appointment of the two nurses, directly accountable to me, who were to be responsible for the main city hospitals and the smaller but more numerous and widespread hospitals. Only three nurses were actually eligible for interview, but all wanted the post passionately and it was a difficult decision. The one person who was not fortunate stayed for a couple of years as my special assistant, before retirement. Unfortunately, the introduction of the Salmon Structure created a lot of these situations, however hard one tried. The smaller hospitals had their own problems, as each had its own matron and a small but very loyal community. They were to be grouped for closer working and a senior nurse was to be appointed in charge of each group. We asked the former matrons to keep their title in their own hospital, whatever the management structure called them on paper, and the senior nurse of each cluster was appointed from within their ranks. The trauma was minimised and the nurses ran their hospitals and departments extremely well under the circumstances, but there were one or two casualties of very unhappy professionals.

By this time we had moved into Southampton and Mary had become a clinical teacher at the group school of nursing. The first medical students had arrived at the university, the wards were becoming used to the students, and a culture of learning was established. At the same time the new hospital was being planned in three phases on the site of the general hospital. The Department of Health had been conducting research into a 'race track' pattern for the new building, and it was concentrated on the first phase of the Southampton project. The floors were of 120 beds around a central area, and planned to carry out a system of 'progressive patient care', with low, medium and high dependency areas, around which the patient progressed. We tried to imitate the idea in part of the old hospital, while we were planning the new wing together with a multi-disciplinary team of regional officers and department representatives. But patients are people and people don't always behave, nor their illness move, in a predictable manner, and when the wing opened we were only able to carry out a modified system. It was one theory which did not work out in practice and where the demands of patient care created the environment which best suited the time and place. By the time I left, the first block and the new nursing school were functioning. Now it is a huge university hospital and it is difficult to remember the early days. I was able to be present at the graduation of the first of the Southampton medical students. It was a great day. Soon after, Professor (now Sir) Donald Acheson left to become the Chief Medical Officer of the Department of Health and we missed the presence of a great man who had contributed so much to the infant medical school. We had many other founding professors who were equally committed and were the foundation of the famous medical school it is today. The Royal South Hants Hospital has undergone more than one transformation in spite of the problems of extending the site, and is now the centre of the Southampton Primary Care Trust. Management structures have come and gone, both in operational management and on the management board. Two important changes have done a great deal to integrate the service. One is the integration of the community medical and nursing staff, and the other is the inclusion of the psychiatric and mentally handicapped services into the overall health care system. Obviously there have been many changes in education, management and methods of working of nurses and we have been proud to see nursing education brought into the mainstream of university education in Southampton. My own links with the university and medical school came just after my retirement from the National Health Service, when Southampton University conferred an honorary degree upon me. It was a day to remember and a special link which I will always cherish.

We found Southampton a pleasant city, and spent a number of weekends exploring the South Coast and the country around. Then we were offered a prime site in the grounds of Wickham Lodge, half a mile from the lovely village of Wickham. It was next door to the lovely small church and pastoral centre of Park Place, which we already frequented each Sunday and where we occasionally stayed over for one of the excellent residential courses; we had made a number of friends. A house next door sounded a perfect idea. We knew nothing about house building, but with the help of one of our surveyors, we found a plan, modified it, engaged a builder and set off. It didn't go smoothly, of course. Roots of trees required much deeper foundations than expected, with the relevant increase in cost and time. Having sold our flat, we had two months' delay, so furniture went into store and we remained at Park Place over Christmas. But at last it was ready – a truly beautiful bungalow in ideal surroundings. Now we were only a few minutes' drive from the sea and, from another aspect, the Hamble River. We both loved the sea and it wasn't long before we found the river on our walks and cast envious eyes on the small boats. We were introduced to one of the boatyards, ventured into the purchase of a small fourteen-foot boat with cabin and outboard motor and were very lucky to find a berth upstream. We made lasting friends with a family building their own boat and obtained a lot of instruction and advice. Most of our weekends were spent on the boat during the summer months. In the beginning we just went up and down the river and enjoyed the sun and fresh air. As we became more confident, we would go over to Yarmouth on the Isle of Wight for the weekend and use it as a floating hotel. We then upgraded to a larger boat and engine for more comfort and safety in inclement weather, but had the misfortune of having the boat vandalised one weekend and the engine stolen. We kept the boat for quite a few years and had enormous pleasure from it, but there was a point where Mary's health began to fail, and it was obviously not safe to be single-handed, so we reluctantly sold it. We maintained close friendship with one family, sometimes going out with them for the day and, when they sold their boat for the same sort of reason, we continued our friendship on dry land.

My post was both absorbing and time-consuming, but I missed the added interest of being involved with the profession, its advancements, politics and problems. I was asked to stand for nomination to the Council of the Royal College of Nursing, our professional body, which is also the UK member of the International Council of Nurses. I accepted willingly, and was elected. It brought me into the national arena, which I thoroughly enjoyed, but there were many times when it seemed that nurses did not look beyond the confines of their national identity. It was certainly an interesting period to be involved in nursing and Health Service politics. The Salmon Structure had hardly been implemented when one of the many NHS reorganisations reared its head. This time it was bringing the various professions in the service into a system of 'consensus management'. At the same time the committee or board structure was changed. Instead of individual hospital boards or committees, the service was divided into regional, area and district levels, each with its own management board. Again there was a lot of disappointment for small hospitals which had their own committees, the members of which took a great interest in the hospital, its patients and staff, and had close working relationships, especially on fund-raising. It was obviously an effort to improve efficiency, but there were differing opinions as to whether that was achieved. One long-standing institution did survive, however, and that was the Leagues of Friends of the various hospitals, without whom all our hospitals would miss the extras and luxuries raised by their efforts, though sometimes it was a question of also providing the necessities. They carried on the long tradition of voluntary work which we have in this country. This reorganisation was the point where the medical and nursing services of local government became merged with the NHS. It was badly needed, but understandably many of the local employees disliked being moved into such a large organisation, and it took some time to settle down.

The creation of an area tier caused more movement within the staff and often more insecurity. Generally speaking, the districts tended to follow the town or city boundaries, except where the towns were very large and were divided into more than one district. It was also at this point that the hospitals for psychiatric patients and for people with learning disabilities came into the overall structure. By this time the movement for breaking these often large hospitals into more homely and domestic units was gathering pace. The service has quite a different face today, and very many of those large hospitals have disappeared. All four chief officers in Southampton – doctor, administrator, treasurer and nurse – were appointed to the area authority which covered the County of Hampshire and monitored the district performance of Southampton, Portsmouth, Basingstoke and Winchester. New chief officers were appointed to Southampton, including Betty Knox, who succeeded me as chief nurse. The area officers moved into offices in Winchester, and we were a small team, not having direct managerial control of the services in the districts. It felt a strange situation, and it was not long before this feeling spread across the country, for it seemed as if at least one level was too many for the smooth running of the NHS. It took quite a while for this to translate into action, but eventually it led to another reorganisation. Before this happened, however, Freda Gundry retired from her post at the region, and persuaded me to apply for the vacancy. I hesitated, feeling a younger person was needed, but Freda was great at getting her own way, and although we had a number of applicants, I was appointed. It was not easy to integrate into a well-established regional team, especially to replace a person as popular and outgoing as Freda Gundry, but I thoroughly enjoyed my tenure. There was a first-class team of nurses at the region, and my fellow chief officers were both able and very easy to relate to. The post brought me into the national arena in another way, with meetings with the government nurses, working on various national committees and as a national assessor for senior posts. Apart from that aspect, I had a wide remit in the Wessex Region, and plenty of contact with my former colleagues. In addition to regular business meetings, we were able to have two special meetings once or twice a year with special speakers, and all the senior nurses of the region joined for a residential weekend. It was stimulating and it also enhanced the professional and friendly links within Wessex.

By this time I had been on the RCN Council for some time, and had been elected vice-chairman, bringing me much more into nursing politics and having my colleagues on council look to me for international information and comment. I fear the latter wasn't always appreciated! Then matters took another turn in that the RCN International Officer, who was particularly involved with the growing interest of the European Community – as it then was – in the training of nurses, fell suddenly and seriously ill and could not return to work. Catherine Hall, the very able general secretary, asked me if I would take over the representation for the UK and go to the next meeting in Bled, Yugoslavia. It was assumed that because I had been with the ICN for so long I must be well versed in EC matters. The ICN had been involved for a few years when it appeared that Brussels had an interest in the harmonisation of nurse training, and Nellie Goffard of Belgium, a former ICN Board member, alerted the ICN to the need for professionals to keep abreast of what was going on. New Zealander Margaret Pickard of the ICN staff held the watching brief on the subject and I did not have too much knowledge of it. There was also another very important complication.

Since I had left ICN, it was having problems with collecting dues from members. This was not a new problem, but having ICN headquarters in Geneva was expensive, and the organisation needed the money. Some organisations gave large numbers of members, which those of us doing fieldwork were aware were far more than the actual numbers of the association. When it came to paying dues on a per capita basis, the numbers often suddenly shrank. So ICN sent out one of its reminders about paying full dues for members, including students. The RCN took this to mean that all members of our very large student association should be included in payment, and wrote to ICN to say they would have to withdraw as they could not meet this financially. Because of my position with ICN I kept out of the discussion, though with hindsight it might have been wiser to suggest mediation, and to my dismay the rumour spread that I was orchestrating the RCN's withdrawal from ICN. There was nothing further from my mind, but feelings were running high among the membership both for and against the proposed withdrawal. ICN then suggested that officers should come over to meet the RCN officers. The meeting took place at the RCN, to the great interest of the Nursing Press, who were invited to meet both sets of officers for a press conference. Adele Herwitz, then ICN Executive Director, was unable to come to London due to illness, but the President, Dorothy Cornelius, an American nurse, came with her vice-presidents to meet with the RCN officers. Winifred Prentice, the RCN President, was our spokesman, and I could see the misunderstandings arising, but I felt, as merely the vice-chair of Council, that I could not intervene. The Nursing Press were present, and the RCN was looking very inept in what was obviously a real misunderstanding of the content of the ICN letter, which was perfectly clear in American English, but not so obvious to us. However, the misunderstandings were cleared up and the RCN officers agreed to take it back to council with a recommendation to withdraw the resolution passed at the last council meeting. We all went to dinner and parted amicably, but I was relieved not to be representing RCN at the next ICN meeting. The incident had caused more than a few ripples round the nursing world, and we had letters from a number of nursing organisations begging us not to leave ICN. The next council meeting unanimously voted to withdraw the resolution, to the great relief of council, as the news had caused a great furore in the UK. I was mildly amused at that, because ICN was usually placed at the bottom of the council agenda, and nobody seemed very interested in it until our membership was threatened. I remember Dame Muriel Powell, then Chief Nursing Officer of Scotland, being especially distressed by it. The quite newly formed Standing Committee of Nurses of the EC was also very concerned and wished to talk about it at their next meeting in Bled, at which Adele Herwitz would be present. So it was not surprising that I had absolutely no wish to attend.

However, it was obvious that no other council member knew any more about the subject than I did, so the journey was planned. The International Department had a new assistant, Sue Russell, a young graduate who had fluent command of the French language and who had already been to one or two of the meetings, so it was agreed that she would accompany me and act as translator. We both set off with very mixed feelings, mine because it was going to be a diplomatic minefield and Sue because she was new to the College, was used to accompanying the president and I was an unknown quantity. However, the day dawned and we set off with Sue on her best behaviour. The flight was by British Airways but we had to change at Frankfurt to a Yugoslavian airline which took us to Lubliana. For some reason we had a security problem at Frankfurt, and the luggage for those continuing by air was left on the tarmac. We had to recognise our cases and take them to the handlers to place in the hold. Once on board we were settling down when someone realised that Adele had not taken her luggage. We were about to depart, but she felt sure it would be all right. Unfortunately, when we reached Lubliana, only one piece of luggage arrived for Adele and the smaller of the two which were missing contained both her papers and her cosmetics. It was quite a catastrophe as luxuries were impossible to obtain in that part of Europe at that time. We then discovered that Bled was some distance away. Usually the host country gives careful instructions or will meet the plane but, on this occasion, one nurse appeared and collected Adele and they departed to try to rescue her luggage. Not a very good start for the meeting. Next, there did not seem to be any transport to Bled and the group looked to me to sort it out, thinking me still ICN! One of the porters showed our little procession the way to the market square for a bus. When one came it was very full, and the lack of space was not helped by our luggage, large bags of market produce and a good few squawking hens. At each stop more piled on until the bus came to a complete stop with no sign of our destination. More broken English and sign language and we needed yet another bus, even more packed than the first. Finally, we reached Bled and piled out; we sorted our luggage from humans and hens, only to discover that we were at the wrong end of Bled and we had to get back into the bus again. The long-suffering passengers were giving helpful advice in loud Yugoslavian but, as we didn't understand, it didn't help much. Finally we arrived at the terminus, discovered we were at different hotels and eventually arrived at the correct ones looking a trifle dishevelled. Yugoslavia was still under Communist rule and life was obviously quite difficult at times.

The next problem we met when checking in. All rooms at the hotel were allocated centrally from the capital, and Sue Russell and I had been allocated a shared room. Neither of us was very happy about this, and we spent ages trying to explain, but to no avail. This was the way the rooms were to be allocated and there was no flexibility. Sue probably felt much worse than I did. As a new member of the RCN staff, the vice-chair of the governing body could not possibly share a room with her. But when one recognises a no-win situation, the only thing to do is to make the best of it. My main concern was that the RCN president was changing over with me at the end of the meeting, as she was the representative for the following meeting, and I was returning home. They might think it obvious that she could take my place in the room, but fortunately they did not make the connection. Winifred had a single room and Sue could relax in sole occupancy in hers. All the concern was probably unimportant, but things can look very different in an unknown situation. As the meeting progressed, we ran into more than a few other problems, but we somehow got round them and turned to the business of the meetings.

The most difficult part was yet to come. On the first morning, the chair, Mlle Florin of France, asked Adele and me if we could explain the unhappy situation which had arisen with the UK following the letter from ICN regarding dues. I was asked to explain the British position first, and while this in itself was very difficult, Sue was in an even worse position because she had to do the translations both into French and English. It was quite a problem for me to put the RCN position, because I was aware that it was an incorrect reading of the ICN letter. I could hardly explain that it had also happened because of the way it was expressed in American phraseology, but that really was ninety per cent of the problem. I was conscious that Adele's reaction to the correspondence sounded much more logical that the line we had taken, but felt there was no point in making the situation worse. Marie-Paul Florin was obviously anxious to smooth things over, the situation had been reversed anyway and there was little more to say.

Adele and I had been friends since the time I called in to the American Nurses' Association in New York on my return from that memorable first visit to Jamaica, but relationships were never quite the same again, although we both tried to pick up the pieces. However, we all tried to get on with the meeting. The atmosphere was much better by the time Winifred Prentice arrived for the following meeting and I was quite glad to have it behind me and to be heading for home. I certainly hadn't been at my best but at least I was forming an impression and getting information about the impact the EC was going to have on nursing. It was strange but I doubt if many nurses within the Common Market countries, as they were then called, had any idea of the problems ahead of us in the 'harmonisation' of the education of the general nurse. Specialist nurses, such as psychiatric nurses, were not affected at this point, and neither were midwives, although the latter soon were involved. It was thanks to Nellie Goffard of Belgium, who had the foresight to see what was coming, that the profession was alerted and began to understand that wide-sweeping changes could have been made without representation from the profession. We had started out on a long journey which was to involve us for over a decade and ended favourably with a harmonisation of nursing education in the EC countries. But it was a long road, with many anxious meetings and discussions, and I became closely involved in the work in a way I had never expected.

I pondered all these points on the long journey back to Southampton, but at least the first part to the airport was easier, as I travelled with one of the Danish representatives who had also to return early, and we shared the fare. Back at home, I sent my report to the RCN and settled down into sorting out some of the work waiting in Winchester. It was quite an uneasy period for work as we were sandwiched between the district and the regional tiers, without a clear line structure. In addition to myself as a nurse at the area headquarters, there were also two nurses working to me, one a general nurse and the other responsible for child health. If it had not been for very good relationships throughout the area, it could have been quite unpleasant. My transition to the region made life and work much more interesting and with more job satisfaction. The RCN council occupied two to three days a month, and I usually took part of my annual leave for the congress. Winifred Prentice had combined the roles of president and chair of council for two years, and the time had come for re-election to those roles. In her report the president commented on the growing workload and felt the two roles had to be split. She was re-elected as president and another member became chair of council. The council then elected me as the second vice-president. The senior vice-president was Sheila Collins, the Director of Nurse Education at the London Hospital and a former chair of council. She was an eminent nurse and had been involved in RCN affairs for many years, and I learnt a great deal from her. My new role was very light, mainly supporting and standing in for senior officers when required, but it gave me a closer insight into the multi-functions and work of the college, and I was still a member of council. I gave my report on the Bled meeting to Catherine Hall and she then asked me formally to take over the RCN representation on the Standing Committee of Nurses of the EEC, with the assistance of Sue Russell. I agreed, and it was the beginning of a very close working relationship with Sue, who soon acquired an astounding knowledge of nursing and the EC, and we happily worked together for something like the next twenty years. Our friendship still continues. Another international secretary was appointed but she had no experience in international work, and I kept the EC brief. After a few years she left to become Chief Nursing Officer of Moorfields Eye Hospital in London, and we had to make another appointment to the RCN. This time it was Shelagh Murphy, a nurse with a vast history of working in other countries, latterly holding a senior position in Saudi Arabia. She also had an infectious personality and a great gift of making friends quickly with nurses of any nationality. The three of us soon became used to working and travelling together and our journeys were long hours and hard work, but full of laughter. We still lunch together frequently and reminisce about our travel years.

I had envisaged working in a senior capacity in the Health Service, being able to participate in professional forums and play a part in nursing politics. I did not expect to be involved in international work except at ICN congresses, but I was now committed to a long period of government negotiations and meetings in Brussels. It was important work, the outcome of which would affect the profession for many years. At the same time, knowing that I am not good at legislative work and tiresome detail, I was very ambivalent at the decision made. Having spent a number of years at ICN working for the improvement of salaries and conditions of work of nurses, I thought I was probably much more in tune with the non-stop battle we had to improve the situation in my own country. However, there were very able people already doing extremely good work in that area and hardly anyone else with international experience, so, in spite of many trepidations, I moved into the work.

CHAPTER 8

The Rich Professional Years

THE PROPOSED Nursing Directives of the European Community were not the first attempt to agree a common curriculum for the basic education of nurses. During the 1950s and 1960s a working party of the Council of Europe discussed the possibility for nurses in its member states. My colleague, Ingrid Hamelin, of the ICN Education Division, represented ICN, and the chairman of the committee was another international colleague, Yvonne Hentsch, of the League of Red Cross Societies, who also presented the report. 'The European Agreement on the Instruction and Education of Nurses' was signed in 1967 and during the course of the next few years was ratified by some of the member states. It was a valuable baseline when the EC discussion started on 'Training of the Nurse responsible for General Care'. At the time there were only six member states (later extended to nine) and in each of these there was a nursing organisation which was a member of the International Council of Nurses. Within ICN, some of the associations had formed into regional groups. The oldest and most closely knit group was the Northern Nurses' Federation, comprising the associations of Denmark, Finland, Iceland, Norway and Sweden, but the European Nursing Group (ENG) was formed in 1953 and, by the time the directives were being discussed, had a membership of twelve national nurses' associations. Initially, the main work of the ENG centred on the Council of Europe and its 'European Agreement on the Education of Nurses', but it widened its contacts and membership later.

At the ICN Congress in Melbourne, Australia, the council asked Alice Clamergeran of France, the newly elected ICN president, and Nellie Goffard of Belgium, an ICN board member, to make contact with the officials of the Commission. This was the beginning of a dialogue which lasted for a number of years. The individual nurses' associations had meetings to agree on the main points concerning training to be put to the Commission. Draft texts were drawn up in the 1960s and submitted to the European Parliament and to the Social and Economic Committee.

Only those six countries which were members of the EC (and later the nine which included the UK) were able to make formal representation. In 1973 there was a public 'hearing' and for the first time there was a move away from a quantitative to a qualitative approach. Then we launched into a long but important argument about the total length of training before reaching full agreement. Another important step was the setting up of a committee, known as the Standing Committee of Nurses of the EC, with a representative of each of the nine member states. Through this, an approach was made to the Commission for recognition in the same way that the doctors had recognition as a formal advisory group. This was finally achieved and the first formal meeting was held in Brussels in 1971. One of the privileges is the right to make formal representation to the Commission and that right has been well used.

It was a very wary group at its first meetings. The two languages used were French and English, and the ability of members to express themselves in one or other language varied considerably. Sue Russell acted as our interpreter, and was brilliant in getting across to the meeting the real meaning behind some very fractured language. She became the confidante of those who were struggling, and was often to be found in corners comforting someone who simply could not make us understand. It was a situation which required enormous patience from the members, and it was quite some time before there was confidence in the group and with each other. After all, this was not a formal committee of the Commission, but one of nurses themselves from some twelve different countries, not used to international collaboration. Somehow, through incredible patience on everyone's part, members opened up and ceased to be afraid of admitting the problems of their own health and nursing service. It also required a lot of patience from the chair, and there were times when I retired late at night almost in despair about our lack of progress; however, with relaxed social occasions and talks in the corridor, a frankness and openness developed. The group really was anxious to work together, and our discussions did give individual nurses' associations the information and arguments they needed to work with their own governments. When Bob Tiffany joined the group to lead the EC cancer nursing developments, he was brilliant in identifying and understanding points made in very fractured French or English.

Some associations had very little money to spare, and generally we had to work on a shoestring. Many members had to travel the cheapest way possible and we knew that some paid their own expenses. This produced some amusing situations. Even the RCN was short of finance at the time. Sue and I travelled together and the travels were often a story in themelves. On my first journey to a meeting with Sue, the cheapest way was from Lympe airport in what were transport planes which also carried passengers. On this occasion we were the only passengers on the return journey, we could see the sea through gaps, and were more than thankful when the plane lumbered in to a safe landing. On hearing of our adventures, Catherine Hall said firmly that she wasn't having her council members travelling like that. So travel changed for the better, but Sue and I vied with each other in finding cheap packages to wherever the meeting was to be held. The general secretary didn't see the various hotels we used to stay in on cheap packages that we had discovered. We had meetings in the member countries, but not every association had the facilities, so we also had some interesting venues from time to time. Residents of one Elderly People's Home were very interested in this nice group who had invaded their sitting room, and started to sit and listen, until they got tired of the peculiar language. We met in hospitals, schools of nursing and education centres, which required a long coach journey to places we couldn't find on the map – rooms in tiny hotels of dubious vintage where the only typewriter had so many spikes and missing keys that it made the draft report very interesting reading.

On one famous occasion we met in Spain. It was winter and as usual my flight was very early and it was dark when I went down to the garage to get my car. In haste, and not putting on the light, I tripped and fell down a short flight of stairs, wrenching my ankle badly. Time was short and I thought it was probably all right but by the time my flight was boarding at Heathrow there was considerable swelling and a lot of pain. The flight was uneventful but on disembarking I found it agony to put my foot on the ground and the stewardess found me a chair. The Spanish nurses who met me were concerned but we made it to the hotel, where the British contingent was waiting. After a lot of fuss from both my colleagues and our hosts, they moved me to the hotel where the conference was to be held. Bob Tiffany was also at the conference and he came to my room with Sue, both with armfuls of gifts from the Spanish nurses, a huge bouquet of flowers and a large Lladro figure of a nurse. Bob was his usual bright self, full of fun and wild suggestions, and the Spanish president produced a crutch and a wheelchair! After a somewhat sleepless night, they helped me to the conference room to chair the day's events, of which I remember little. Then I was whisked to a hospital to deal with what fortunately turned out to be only a bad sprain. However, we had a formal dinner that night with the health minister. Mindful of the importance to the Spanish nurses of this first occasion for a meeting with EC representatives, I dressed with difficulty and set out for the restaurant, again with willing helpers. When I discovered that the dinner was in a private room up a narrow, winding staircase, I was about to admit defeat, but my escorts hoisted me up the stairs and carried me up in triumph. The minister did not arrive until later, so he knew nothing of the drama. As is customary in Spain, the dinner went on very late and our main dish was the delicacy sucking pig. Somehow I survived, but I've never eaten that dish since. The next day Sue and Bob helped me through the air journey to Heathrow where Angela Gould, my regional nurse, somehow got me home. Mary's reaction was unprintable, but it was just another incident for Sue and me to add to our diary of EC nursing folklore.

The first time we met in the UK we made it a big occasion, mainly because we wished to bring the importance of the Nursing Directives to the notice of the profession. Former members of the committee will remember with laughter and affection our early beginnings, but we shared a comradeship which helped us to build up our experience. What a relief it was to have a permanent office in Brussels in the 1980s and now a permanent nurse staff member. All the current committee has grown with European membership, and it is a very well-organised and effective operation.

All this sounds both dull and complicated and it is not surprising that very few nurses knew much about it, much less appreciated its importance. I was actually at ICN when the debates started in the early Sixties, and had rather brushed it aside as being 'Education' and of little importance to me as it was not in my Economic Welfare brief. The RCN representative on the Standing Committee had a considerable influence on the committee, and it was soon after the initial formal meeting of the committee that she became ill and had to leave the RCN. It was at this point that they turned to me to replace her, and understandably assumed that, with my ICN background, I would know all about it. It was with some reluctance that I took over the role, as detail on training and legislation was never my strong point, but once having accepted the role I did my utmost to safeguard the interests of the profession. One positive feature was that all the representatives were well known to me through ICN. However, my main job at the time was the National Health Service, and the time I had to give to EC affairs was limited. At this point Sue Russell was appointed and became our expert on the subject, so much so that everyone forgot she was not a nurse and expected her to know everything about nursing – and she more or less did! We travelled together, and the travels were often a story in themselves. Sue was the real expert on the subject and I often felt I was unfairly 'fronting' the discussions on Sue's knowledge. I remained on the Standing Committee until 1991, and from 1983 was its president, eventually handing over to Kirsten Stallknecht of Denmark, another nurse who was one of the giants of the profession and a very close friend. So I was launched into Europe and was closely involved with the EC and the wider European profession until my retirement in the late 1980s.

Two persons concerned with negotiation for nurses had a considerable influence on the meetings. One was Kirsten Stallknecht, the new president of the Danish Nurses' Association, who had a formidable ability for negotiation, and became an international figure and later a president of ICN. We did not always agree, but were firm friends and enjoyed each other's company and professional expertise. The other was Sydney Allman, a former British diplomat seconded to the Commission and secretary to the professional advisory committees, including nursing, who made his home with his family in Brussels. He continued to live in Brussels after he retired from the Diplomatic Service and carried out many commissions for the professions. I often stayed at their home when in Brussels and we still keep in touch.

My work at the region and at the RCN council continued, interspersed with meetings in Brussels. It was time for the election of the RCN president, and we said goodbye to Winifred Prentice, who had completed her second term of office. She was a well-known figure and a very well-loved president. We missed her greatly on council. Her successor was a long-standing member of council, Eirlys Rees, a Welshwoman, who was a small, neat figure with a mercurial temperament. She was very able, but was a completely different personality from her calm predecessor. At the same meeting, the current chairman had resigned from council because of home commitments, and I was elected in her place. Council, its work and protocols were still new to me and I felt nervous at accepting the leadership. When Eirlys got to her feet and raised a point of order, which she did from time to time, I always went into complete panic, as she was invariably right. Committee procedure was not my strong point. However, the general secretary was more than helpful and would always come to my rescue. We tended to think the same way, so we enjoyed a happy relationship until her retirement.

The interim ICN meeting had taken place, but only the general secretary and president attended the meeting. I wanted to distance myself from ICN for a while so as not to confuse roles. The next ICN congress was to be held in Tokyo, when it was time to nominate a British nurse to stand for election to the board of directors, and council was asked to consider the name of a well-known British nurse. They unexpectedly turned it down and nominated me. I pointed out that many nurses still felt me responsible for the threat of the RCN to resign from ICN, and we risked losing the seat on the board and an important voice in international affairs. When it was obvious that they were determined to nominate me, I gave in gracefully, but not without some concern.

A small contingent of RCN members went to the Tokyo Congress and, apart from myself, no one else in the delegation had visited the city. The president and general secretary went on ahead for the closed meetings of the Council of National Representatives and I took the rest of the party for a three-day stopover in Seoul, Korea, with the RCN director of education to support me. On arrival we were met with the news that bookings had gone awry in Tokyo, a perennial problem for ICN congresses. There were hardly any single rooms available, and our members would have to share twin-bedded rooms. Having passed the bad news on to the delegates, there was almost a revolt, and I left the tour representative to sort it out. We invariably had this problem, mainly because our members are fairly senior nurses and not used to sharing rooms. The congress organisers, on the other hand, could not see what the fuss was about. I remember little of Seoul itself on that first visit, except that I stopped in a small hairdresser's near the hotel and my sign language was good enough to have a girl come to wash my hair. It was a little disconcerting to be led out the back and have ministrations carried out in the street. It is much easier to go to the hairdresser in the hotel, but not half as much fun, and it is a habit I have always maintained, sometimes to the astonishment of any companion who asks to accompany me. I was to visit Seoul again many years later, and the hotels had become beautiful and luxurious, but something always seems lost of the feel of the country. It is easy to be cocooned in one of the luxurious international hotels in familiar surroundings and experience very little of the real life of the country. When I travel nowadays, it seems that the large hotels really do try to mirror the culture and traditions of the country, which makes them so much more interesting.

We carried on to Tokyo, which was again much changed. The hotel was beautiful but very European, and I missed the tranquillity of the Japanese-style decoration and the bath. One very helpful change was that English characters and names were being used, and I could find my way round the underground network. Although rooms had finally been sorted out, Margaret Green, our director of education, and I still had problems, this time with half the luggage missing. All we knew was that it was somewhere in Tokyo and we eventually located it in two different hotels at opposite ends of the city, but we sorted it all out and left cases at various hotels for their distracted owners. Then we had to register for the congress. I was sure we could find our way across the city to the venue, and we did, but got lost coming back and ended up with a long walk through the park. The congress proceeded. It felt good to have no responsibility for the organisation and I sat back and enjoyed it. ICN had its own problems, as Adele Herwitz had resigned as Executive Director six months before the congress, and one of the board members had taken over but, to their credit, all ran smoothly although there must have been some panic behind the scenes. Fortunately there was little or no reference to the differences between ICN and the RCN. When it came to the elections, to my relief I was elected to the board and remained for the post-board meeting while the president and general secretary had a day out. I was very wary about that first meeting as a board member, making sure I did not appear to take advantage of my previous role with ICN. After the meeting, as I waited in my room on the twenty-sixth floor to join the others for dinner, I had my first experience of a Japanese earthquake. It was mild, apparently, but didn't appear so to me with the room creaking around me.

Back home there was a busy two years ahead. Politics were already playing their part in the EC committee on nursing, although one might have expected nursing matters not to be involved in politics. The arguments centred on the length of nurse training, the acts which nurses were allowed to perform and the nurse in each country recognised under the EC agreement as 'the nurse responsible for general care'. The latter was a very sensitive issue because of the different ways in which countries had educated their nurses. Understandably, each country wished to safeguard the position of its own nurses, and there were times when debate became quite heated. The governments in each country were involved, but not all had a chief nurse at government level, so civil servants and doctors were closely involved in decisions. We were very fortunate in the UK to have a strong nursing department at the Ministry of Health, led by Dame Phyllis Friend, and the General Nursing Council which was responsible for the education and registration of the British nurse. As chair of the RCN Council and also president of the EC Advisory Committee at the time, I was able to help maintain close relationships as far as British nurses were concerned, and to take quite a lead in the delicate negotiations taking place with some of the countries. As always in such formal committees, much of the negotiation was done outside sessions over a cup of coffee or between meetings. The fact that most of the nurses leading their delegations were well-known to each other through ICN, PCN and other professional committees certainly helped things along. There was a widespread sigh of relief when the news came through that the European Parliament had agreed to the nursing directives and they were formally signed in 1977. Such was the relief of the RCN International Department, that it bought out HMSO's entire stock of the Official Journal of the EC in which the directives were published – and complained that HMSO could not provide the French version. I guess they were not used to having such a run on EC documents.

After the signing, the RCN held a conference – 'The Directives are signed – what now?' It was extremely well attended and all the European members of the committee participated. At the RCN we were very fortunate to have three royal patrons at the time – the Queen, the Queen Mother and Princess Margaret. The Princess was extremely interested in the college and its work and was always ready to grace special occasions. She came to the evening reception for the European nurses, and I had the pleasure of introducing the nurses to her. I remember how beautiful she looked that night in a fragile daffodil-yellow dress which was a myriad of tiny pleats. She spoke effortlessly in fluent French to each of the European nurses, and left them spellbound. It was my privilege to host Princess Margaret on quite a few occasions, both in my role as the

European member of the committee and later as RCN president. My memories of her are of a charming lady, always interested in the people she was meeting and what they were doing, especially if they were from the Commonwealth or Northern Ireland.

As I write these chapters just over a quarter of a century later, I can't help reflecting on the enormous amount of time spent on the directives by many nurses and officials. The provisions of the directives and the detail were hotly debated, but they have slipped into the background now. While still operative, more emphasis is being placed on the free movement of all professional personnel throughout the Community. It was noticeable that there had not been much movement of nurses. The largest number was between the UK and Ireland, a situation which had existed long before the directives were thought of. Today's concerns centre on our own nursing shortage, but incoming nurses are largely from developing countries. This raises considerable ethical concern, because recruiters often target developing countries, such as Africa and India. Qualified nurses are only too scarce in these countries and they are badly needed in their own health services. Nursing salaries which do not equate to the education and work carried out by nurses affect both the recruitment and retention of nurses in the UK, but to the nurse in a developing country our salaries are very attractive. These nurses do not always get the best of treatment and professional recognition here. There is a great deal to be done, first in this country to make sure that we have an adequate professional nursing work force which is properly paid. At the same time there is a need to help the developing countries to develop their own nurses and equate their salaries to those of other professionals. I spent my years as the director of the ICN's Economic Welfare Division trying to influence the situation of nurses in those countries, and headway has been made, but not nearly enough. If we cannot solve our own problems at home without poaching professionals who are badly needed in their own country, our manpower planning is sadly lacking.

To be chair of the RCN council is a fascinating but arduous post because it is virtually the elected business head of the college. We had an able and committed council, which included, as Nurse Honorary Treasurer, Trevor Peel, a young man with an amazing capacity for organisation. He came from Hartlepool, and motivated a group of nurses in setting up an annual, national professional conference in Hartlepool. He asked me to give the keynote address. I accepted and was amazed at the professional attention to detail which the local nurses displayed. Nothing was left to chance and it was a brilliant success. I participated for five years, with the event getting larger and more sophisticated each year. Eminent nurses were invited as speakers and very rarely refused. Hartlepool became a well-known town to us. My attendance ended with my presidency, although the conference continued for a further year. Trevor, who had finished his term on council, was promoted and left the area. When we met recently at a London event, I learned that he had changed his work and was pursuing a successful career in the Prison Service. I was delighted for him, but sad that such an able nurse had been lost to the profession.

The role of Regional Nursing Officer in Wessex was very enjoyable, and I particularly liked my close contact with the district nursing officers, who made me very welcome when visiting their hospitals. We had monthly meetings at region which were professionally very productive, as we shared both problems and progress. On the whole recruitment was good, the new University Hospital in Southampton was taking shape and the first medical students had graduated. I was particularly fortunate in having Angela Gould as one of my regional nurses at headquarters, for she was responsible for personnel and training across the region and was very popular with the senior nursing staff. We had special residential weekends for the district nursing officers at least once a year and sometimes more often. We were able to invite first-class speakers, perhaps nurses who had pioneered something special, and we always had our liaison nurse from the Department of Health, who kept us up to date with national issues. This welded our senior staff into a close and relaxed team, where we were able to share our problems and successes. There were also regular meetings of regional nurses in London, sometimes with the Chief Nursing Officer, which also made for easy relationships and sharing of problems and successes. I cannot help but regret the demise of the Nursing Division at the Department of Health, while recognising the excellent work which has been done and is still carried out by succeeding Chief Nursing Officers. There is merit in seconding nurses for a particular period and for a specific piece of work, but there is also continuity and wisdom in having a core of nurses who have spent time working closely with politicians and top civil servants. I wonder if we would ever have had the Salmon Structure for nurses if it hadn't been for a determined Kathleen Raven bearding the then Minister of Health, and travelling along with him to his next appointment while persuading him of its merits. The system had many critics, of course, but I don't think I'm the only one who benefited, and grew up in terms of management because of it.

The RCN had been growing in membership at an increased rate, and was no longer seen as an elitist organisation, but one which was leading the way in professional matters. It had seats on the Whitley Council for Nurses and Midwives and was therefore a strong voice in salary negotiations. Relationships with the traditional unions were cordial and we cooperated on many matters. There were others, of course, in which we had opposing views and competition for membership. One of the most important moves of the RCN was when it balloted the members and on the result became an independent trade union. We had checked beforehand with the Privy Council to make sure that it was compatible with our Royal Charter. This was the most important feature in our upsurge in membership. When I first became a council member, the membership was in the region of 40,000, and today it stands at over 350,000 and includes students. That transformation was not achieved easily or quickly, and there were many members who did not believe that trade union membership was compatible with a professional organisation.

About the same time, council decided to establish an award for distinguished service to the RCN and nursing at large. This was the RCN Fellowship, and the first few fellows were elected and included some very distinguished names, with Catherine Hall heading the list. They were inaugurated at a special occasion in London, which was attended by many distinguished guests from government and medicine. This became an annual award, with nominations and citations accepted from any member. The fellows have grown in number, have their own convenor and meet at least once a year for conference. Council granted me the privilege in 1977 and, as the council was meeting in Edinburgh that year, my award was presented in the historic Signet Library. International nurses can be elected as Honorary Fellows, and we were all delighted to honour the famous American nurse, Virginia Henderson, who must be the most loved international nurse of our time.

1977 was a special year for me. Not only had I been created a Fellow of the RCN but, on the Queen's official birthday, I was gazetted a Commander of the Most Excellent Order of the British Empire (CBE). On that same day I had to leave home and drive to Harrogate for the annual RCN congress. Because of the calls from the press and friends, I set off late from home, leaving Mary to make my excuses to further callers, and arrived tired, and late, in Harrogate to find everyone waiting dinner for me, and a special celebration. That whole week of congress seemed to be a series of parties and it was a week to remember. The most exciting event was yet to come, when my turn came to visit the Palace to receive my award from the Queen, and the memories of that special morning are as clear now as at the time.

The driving force behind the changes to the RCN and the key to their success was Catherine Hall, my friend from the days when we were both students of the RCN. She not only had strong professional views but also the ability to see when the time was right for major moves and the strength of purpose to see them through. I was a member of council throughout these events and shared in the ups and downs of the membership reactions. She was in the last decade of her work as RCN general secretary and was determined to leave a strong and healthy organisation for her successor. The quite small annual congresses gave way to much larger and dynamic gatherings; the members became very vocal and lively debates ensued. Although we had become a trade union, we were not registered with the TUC, and we realised that was important if we wished to influence national negotiations in the best possible way. Again, we took advice from the Privy Council and duly registered. We did lose some long-standing members, but the membership increased considerably. This had another major result, and that was the demand for increasing democracy and a stronger say by members in the general work of the college and its decision-making. One result was the change of the annual congress to the representative body, or the RRB as it was termed. Delegates were elected from the branches, with the right to speak and vote, and from the major professional societies within the RCN, and expenses were paid. Attendance went up very rapidly, discussion was strong, animated and well-presented, lobbying went on between branches and the floor came to life. The RCN has not looked back. It has lost its reputation for elitism and the power is definitely in the hands of the membership.

Another feature was the changing character of council. The membership was astute about elections to council, asking prospective members for their policy and inviting them to branch meetings for questioning. I found myself in the middle of this at the end of my term as chair of council, as it coincided with the election of council. This had been a large body, but at this stage council decided to cut down its membership. In Wessex we were cut to one seat and I lost to a very able occupational health nurse from Bournemouth. In my own mind I had been quite realistic about my chances and was not surprised, but it did hit the headlines for a while. It certainly felt strange not to be involved, but in other respects it was quite a relief to be able to concentrate on my regional role and to spend more time at home. Mary had her own time-consuming job and had to go home frequently to visit her mother who was in a nursing home in Liverpool. She was longsuffering about my absences, but we did enjoy more time together for a while.

Another democratic change made at the same time as changes to the composition of council was to the mode of election of the president. Until these changes, both chair and vice-chair of council and the president and two deputy presidents had always been elected from among the council members only. The council was to continue to elect its own officers, but there was a demand for the right of the membership to elect their president and only one deputy. This was obviously democratically correct, and it certainly changed the character of the election. For this first event it became a real national lobby and election. I was nominated to stand, together with Sheila Collins, a long-standing council member and deputy president, Sam Richards, a most popular former council member and very vocal member from the North of England, and a completely new RCN member from Wales, Marion Morgan. Electioneering and politics are definitely not my style and I endured, rather than enjoyed, the requests to visit branches and defend my election manifesto. Nor had I any illusion about the outcome, accepting that I would be viewed as the establishment figure, and expecting Sam, who was a really popular figure at the representative body meeting and one of its former chairmen, to win convincingly. We were all surprised, except for the general secretary, who had read the feelings of the membership correctly. Marion Morgan was elected president with a large majority, and I came second and was therefore deputy president. I was aware that many people expected me to refuse, but it never entered my head to do so. The membership had stated their choice and it was up to me to support the new president, even if I was not too thrilled about it. I think Marion was as surprised as anyone, but she was obviously delighted. We exchanged telephone calls but did not meet until our first council meeting, which was in Northern Ireland, where the new president and deputy were inaugurated at a special event the same evening.

As the president and deputy are ex officio members of council with full voting rights, I was welcomed back to council very warmly. Marion and I had discussions with the general secretary as to how best to split the duties between us, and one thing I was asked to retain was the chair of the college refurbishment group. This was a huge and expensive project, including what had been the Cowdray residential club, which was linked with the RCN building. The extra space provided gave the RCN much needed room for expansion. There was also a great deal of work with modernising the RCN part of the building. At that time, the RCN also housed the RCN Institute which had grown considerably and occupied a good share of space. It took two or three years to complete the project which, although very costly, was funded by the RCN with the assistance of many influential and hard-working friends. Needless to say, in a few years we were again constrained by space, but the mode of working between the institute and the university had changed, and more space was released. Very early in the new millennium yet a further transformation of the college was unveiled, with imaginative use of the upper storeys and open-plan working. Hopefully, the increasing workload can be contained in our historic and well-loved headquarters in Cavendish Square.

Catherine Hall's retirement was drawing near, and council agreed to her suggestion to appoint a 'designate' to ensure a smooth turnover. Council and most of the membership had known only Catherine Hall as general secretary, and the thought of the future without her was daunting. After wide advertisement, we had a small short list for interview, and the interviewing committee was set up. It included the president and me, one of our external advisers, who was chair of our finance committee, and the new chair of council, Ian Hargreaves, a most able young man. After his term on council, he joined the college staff and became the staff member leading the north west of England. One candidate stood out and was appointed without hesitation. This was Trevor Clay, who had already won a name for himself as a strong and wise leader. He joined the college first as deputy general secretary, then became designate, and took over the reins in two years. These were very productive years, and when we said farewell to Dame Catherine with a huge party, we knew the college was in safe hands. Actually, Dame Catherine did not leave active nursing at that point, but changed to an honorary post with the UK Central Council for Nursing, Midwifery and Health Visiting. This was the body responsible for the education and registration of nurses, and was undergoing major change. Dame Catherine was offered the part-time post of president, in order to see through the changes of this very important statutory body, and it was another two years before she retired completely. The role of chief executive to the council had also changed, and Maude Storey moved from her post as regional nursing officer to become its registrar. Maude was another outstanding nursing leader who came into her own as a very wise leader of the council and was to succeed me as president.

The RCN council at that time was very strong and had some interesting figures serving on it who became leaders in their own posts within the health service. One of these was Robert (Bob) Tiffany, Chief Nursing Officer of the Royal Marsden Hospital, famed for its cancer care. The hospital was already famous, but Bob kept it so. He was always ready to catch the public eye and imagination and he made the hospital a household name for excellence in nursing. At that time I was one of the leaders of the EC Advisory Committee on Nursing and Bob made use of the fact that there was a European year against cancer to launch a nursing initiative, which the EC committee took up. We had at least three major European conferences on the topic, two in the UK, and as the UK lead for the practising profession in Europe, I was heavily involved. It was an era when nursing seemed to be very much to the fore with the emphasis on excellence in care. The meetings in Brussels were equally productive at that time. Kirsten Stallknecht was the leader of her country's delegation, and it was a delight to work with such able people who were committed to their profession and to excellence in care. Trevor Clay had moved easily into the role of general secretary and was very successful. Unfortunately, he had a long-standing and progressive lung disease, and the strain of work began to tell on him. He made light of it, but it was particularly noticeable on travel abroad and we were all concerned.

The demands on me as deputy president became unexpectedly heavy, as Marion was in a difficult position with a chair and management committee who were unhappy with her frequent absences to carry out the role of RCN president. It was made more difficult because travel from her home in Wales was quite lengthy and even a short commitment to the college or a branch meant at least overnight stays. Because of this, I had to stand in for her quite a lot, but I had easier travel. The biennial elections for president came round again, but the elections didn't seem to produce the same high profile as the last time. Marion and I both stood again, as we were allowed a second term of two years if successful. Surprisingly, our positions were reversed. The vote may have been affected because there were not so many candidates standing. At the next annual general meeting in Cardiff, I was inaugurated at a ceremony in the lovely town hall, with Marion as my deputy. She was as gracious to me in my success as I hope I was at hers two years before. It was without doubt the happiest point of my professional life to wear the beautiful and historic chain and to serve the membership for what was to become a four-year term, as I was returned unopposed for a second term of two years.

The college building had been open for business throughout the major changes, and at last it was finished and handed over to us. We were delighted with the outcome, especially the new dining-room with its domed glass ceiling. It was to be run cafeteria fashion for members and, as it adjoined the refurbished Cowdray Hall, it was ideal for functions. For a number of years we were able to restore our annual dinners and hold them in the hall. We had a number of eminent guests, including cabinet ministers, but during my second term of office, the Prime Minister, Margaret Thatcher, accepted our invitation to be guest of honour. Relations between her and the College were decidedly cool, as she had agreed yet another NHS reorganisation, which, on this occasion, was detrimental to nurses, removing them from the top tier of management.

For a time it looked as if the Prime Minister would have to cancel, as the event took place just after the Brighton bombing, but to our delight she agreed to come as she wished to carry on normally. The difference it did make was in security, and during the day we were besieged by officials going through the building. We had one great treasure in the college building, and that was what we always called 'the painted staircase' – a broad sweep of stone stairs running up from the hall to the first floor with an original seventeenth century mural with flamboyant colours covering the walls and ceiling. We always received guests at the top but, on this occasion, security decided it was too public and Trevor Clay and I were asked to receive guests as usual until the Prime Minister was within three minutes of the building. When alerted, Trevor and I were to move to the back door and wait inside until she had been safely ushered in. As we invited her to join the other guests to mingle as she had requested, Trevor mentioned our disappointment about her not seeing the staircase, whereupon she immediately turned round to see and admire it. She was a delightful dinner companion and we did not touch on controversial topics. Norman Fowler, then the Secretary of State for Health, warned me that they had a three-line whip and must leave at 9.55p.m. He promised that Mrs Thatcher would speak for ten minutes, which would give me six minutes to reply, and this seemed fine. The report on NHS re-structuring was by a gentleman named Griffiths, who was also a guest and sitting at the top of one of the side tables opposite to us. At 9.40p.m. we halted the courses and the Prime Minister rose to her feet. She began by extolling the virtues of the Griffiths Report and then continued for twenty minutes. I looked at Trevor in horror as she finally sat down, having thoroughly roused the nurses present. Norman Fowler leant across to me and whispered. 'You have only three minutes.' Trevor looked desperate as this was our only real chance of getting across how the profession felt. As I got to my feet I had a sudden burst of courage, thought to myself 'You weren't elected to be polite in these circumstances' and, without notes, set out the College case and said what we thought about the Griffiths Report. It took me ten minutes and, to her credit, Margaret Thatcher showed no irritation and the nurses felt they had had their say. I proposed her toast and she was given a great ovation before we hastened to the back door where we waited while her car was summoned. In the few minutes' pause I apologised for keeping her late for the division, and she smiled at me and said, 'Don't worry, the bell won't ring until I'm in the precinct.' Although the whole assembly seemed furious at her overlong and very political speech, I had only admiration for her courtesy to me in the circumstances. I have been a great fan of hers ever since, and do believe she was a very great lady and one of our finest ever prime ministers.

There was one other great occasion to come during the second term of my presidency, and that was the royal opening of the new building. To our delight, the Queen Mother accepted our invitation and was at her charming best when the great afternoon arrived. A small crowd, one or two of whom had already identified themselves as people who try to be at every occasion in London, gathered to greet her on arrival and it was noticeable that she gave each of them a special wave and smile, before coming in and greeting Trevor and me. We had agreed to do a short tour

Escorting HM Queen Elizabeth the Queen Mother around the refurbished RCN headquarters in 1984.

With the late Trevor Clay watching Prime Minister Margaret Thatcher sign the visitors book at RCN headquarters, 1985.

of the building and had small groups in some of the rooms to present to the Queen Mother. The students of the Institute had been warned to stay in the classrooms as they weren't on the tour but, understandably, they opened a door and peered round it. Noticing this, the Queen Mother instantly went in to talk to them and it was obvious why she was so well-loved. Moving on to a room where some of the friends of the college were gathered, Trevor, who was attempting the introductions, looked at me and said desperately, 'Who are they?' to which I replied, with equal stupidity, 'I haven't a clue.' Needless to say, they were people we knew extremely well, but all common sense seems to go on these occasions. Fortunately, my PA saved the day by prompting in a whisper. Passing through one of the historic rooms, I commented that it was a room where Queen Mary used to visit 'to take tea with council', and immediately the Queen Mother replied, 'I would like to do that. Please invite me.'

During my last year of office we remembered the Queen Mother's words and did invite her. It was deliberately a much less formal occasion and concentrated on council and the staff who served it. Tea was arranged in one of the elegant first-floor rooms, with a special round table for Her Majesty and the senior college officers. Other members of council and staff were brought up to the table to sit beside the Queen for a few minutes' conversation with her. She has a very happy knack of defusing the awe and stage fright of her guests, and there was a lot of laughter on what turned into a very special but quite informal afternoon. Her eagle eye spied the Adam fireplace and wanted to know if we ever lit a fire in it. I also remember her leaning across to one of our senior council members, Stan Holder and, addressing him by name, remarking that he wasn't eating, and urging him to have a good tea. It was these small touches which endeared her so much to people. We bade farewell to her at the door, a small figure in a deep-blue velvet coat and hat which were so much her own inimitable style.

Having been elected to the ICN board at the congress in Tokyo in 1977, we had two board meetings in the two years before the next meeting of the Council of National Representatives (CNR) which was to be held in Singapore. ICN had been through a difficult time in finding a replacement for Adele Herwitz. Barbara Fawkes had held the fort nobly at Tokyo, but wished to leave afterwards to return to her home, which at the time was in Australia. Winifred Logan, from the UK, was appointed and served until after the Singapore meeting, then Doris Krebs, the senior nurse adviser, stepped in for two short periods of time, but was near retirement and wished to return to her own country in Latin America. After a further advertisement, Connie Holleran from USA was interviewed and appointed at our board meeting. She took up her appointment very quickly, and was a very successful executive director until she retired, following the congress in Madrid in 1993, to be succeeded by Judith Oulton of Canada. Nurses often comment to me about what an exciting post it must be, and so it is, but it is also one that is consuming of one's normal way of life, and is very demanding. ICN is now a vast organisation, and very different indeed from the one I joined in Dean Trench Street in London. One very interesting board member was Eunice Kiereini, the Chief Nursing Officer of Kenya, with whom I was to work very closely. Muringo, as her friends knew her, was nominated for ICN President in 1981 when the RCN was nominating me as a vice-president. The elections took place at the ICN congress in

Los Angeles. Muringo was returned unopposed, with me as her first vice-president, Rebecca Bergman, of Israel, second and Eileen Jacobs, of USA, as third vice-president. We had held the interim meeting in Nairobi in 1979 where Muringo was host, and it was a delightful and very colourful occasion. Kirsten Stallknecht also became a board member, and the four years to come looked to be fruitful with a good experienced board and a well-established executive director in Connie Holleran. In fact, it turned out to be quite different.

Our first ICN board meeting went very well, and Muringo and I established a good rapport, but, soon after the board meetimg, she phoned to say that she had had telephone calls from Connie and there were problems within the staff. A meeting of the officers was coming up and we had long discussions. One executive member had been asked to leave because of concerns about her work, and two of the general staff were also leaving, all with very adequate notice. Connie was still quite new, and it is not easy to understand the industrial relations and employment law of another country, especially when they are very different from our own. Official grievances were laid down. Connie and I had difficult meetings with the union officials who took an aggressive stance and were effectively challenging the right of the executive director to hire and fire. There was an obvious language problem which didn't help, and we found ourselves facing a case in the 'Tribune des Proudhommes', which could be loosely described as similar to our Industrial Tribunal. Muringo had a very large job at home and could not always get over, so we asked another board member, Kirsten Stallknecht of Denmark, to help. Denmark is well known for its good employment practices and labour relations and Kirsten led the national negotiations for nurses and was a formidable negotiator. Our Swiss lawyer was a tower of strength and, with Kirsten's skill, we reached a good settlement. It was helped by the fact that we had already given generous leaving pay. All turned out well, but it took a very large slice of time out of the first two years of the quadrennium, and we had to catch up with work for the interim meeting in Singapore, and rebuild staff. It was a most unfortunate time for Connie at the beginning of her ICN work, but she soon picked up on the work and preparation for the Singapore meeting and all went well. A major event was the move from rented accommodation in Geneva, which we had occupied since moving there from London and had grown out of, to the purchase of our own headquarters in a newly-

Presiding at my last formal dinner as RCN president, with ICN president Muringo Kiereini as guest of honour, 1986.

built block closer to the lake. It was a wise move and is a delightful headquarters, but it took a large amount of time. Connie continued as a very fine leader, gave ICN stability which was badly needed with all the changes which had taken place, and, when she left after the Vancouver congress, she handed over to her Canadian successor, Judith Oulton, a well-run organisation with clear objectives and a happy and competent staff. My four-year term on the board ended with the congress in Tel Aviv, Israel.

During the four years of my RCN presidency, I participated in four annual congresses. These are always hard work for the chair of council in particular, but as president it was possible really to enjoy the occasions. After the presidential address at the start of the meeting, one largely assumed the role of host and attended all the social events being held every night, quite time-consuming in themselves as there were more than one on each evening. We still had formal congress dinners at that time. These were changed later to a huge congress party to which all members attending congress were invited, making it quite a night out. The congress dinners usually had a key guest speaker, often from the locality, and it was relaxed. Everyone enjoyed dressing up, but it was much better when we extended the party to all comers. This was started at my last congress as president and, as the numbers attending congress have grown considerably, so has the party.

We always had a political speaker on the opening day, usually from the government and often a Secretary of State for Health. RCN members had grown in their ability to ask questions of the various politicians and I saw more than one vanishing in relief from the spotlight, often, I fear, feeling aggrieved and badly done by. It was never a comfortable situation to be the Chief Nursing Officer accompanying the politicians. Their sympathies might well have been with the nurses as members of the RCN themselves, but it could not have been easy if there had been a somewhat rough reception. The nurses had learnt how to question relentlessly, and even the chair had difficulty in controlling the meeting at times. The session I remember most was when Neil Kinnock attended. As he could only come on the first day of the congress, he was to follow straight on after my main opening speech. He obviously expected it to be critical and, after greeting me, said he would remain in the Green Room until I had finished my address, as he did not want to interrupt my session. However, he asked if he could have a copy of my speech while he was waiting. I had a habit, which I knew irritated a lot of people, especially the press, of speaking without a script. My speech was always completely prepared and the press had a copy of all the parts in which they would be interested, but I have a photographic memory and feel more comfortable without a script because I can then make eye contact with the audience. Having explained this to a disbelieving minister, we continued the session and then welcomed him formally on to the stage. Instead of the usual polite greeting, Neil Kinnock said to me with a chuckle, 'So you really didn't have a copy. I was sure you were just keeping it away from me.' The congress warmed to him and gave him a standing ovation, and I personally found him a most interesting and likeable guest.

At home in the dying months of my RCN presidency, a most unexpected event took place. I was about to leave the office one morning when I turned back to take a phone call. With some disbelief (so much so that the voice enquired if I was still at the telephone) I heard the caller announce himself as the Master of the Household. He went on to say that the Queen wished to invite me to lunch and he was checking the date with me. Having seen names in the newspapers, I was aware that the Queen held small informal lunches, but one never expects in one's wildest dreams to be a guest. I did, of course, agree to the date and listened to some of the very helpful instructions as in a dream; only in the car on the way to work did I realise that I should be in Geneva on the appointed date. However, I informed the executive director that I would be a day late in joining the meeting and only Muringo knew of the reason. I was not a complete stranger to the Palace, having been to two investitures and garden parties, but this was very different and nerves were very much to the fore. I stayed overnight on London, not daring to risk British Rail's punctuality, and arrived in good time. The welcome and careful briefing of the courtiers did a lot to relieve my nervousness and along with five other guests I had a glass of sherry while waiting for the Queen and Prince Philip. It is just not possible to describe the incredible courtesy and friendliness of the occasion, but it passed all too swiftly and about 3p.m. we were seen off; as a last thoughtful gesture, we were given the menu and seating plan as mementos. It was a great highlight with which to remember four incredible years, when I handed over to Maude Storey, my successor, a few months later.

Time had passed very swiftly those last years, and it was also time to retire from my post at the region and have a quiet life. But before that happened I had a telephone call from the British Red Cross Headquarters to ask if I would like to go and meet the director general and one of the vice-presidents, as they would like to discuss my becoming the Chief Nursing Advisor to the organisation. I had been active with the Hampshire Red Cross, and for a time on the National Council, but this was quite a surprise. The current Nursing Advisor was Eirlys Rees, who was about to retire. I met Countess Mountbatten and Lady Victoria Palmer, both delightful people who made me feel that it was I who was doing them a favour by accepting the position. This was for two to three days a week, and didn't sound too onerous but, of course, it did mean travel to London on those days. I accepted, and returned to the region to give a definite date for my departure. I had started my working life in the hospital service, which soon became the NHS, and it felt strange to be leaving. However, it wasn't quite the end of my NHS service, as I found myself appointed first to the Dorset Family Practitioner Committee and then to the Dorset Health Authority as a member, after it had absorbed the former body in one of the reorganisations.

It was a busy last few weeks at the region, preparing for handover to the new regional nursing officer, Jacqueline Flindall, another well-known nurse leader. The signs of further changes, especially for nursing, were on the horizon, and while I was sad to have completed my work with the NHS, I was very pleased not to have to tackle another upheaval. The strong managerial role of nurses has been eroded considerably, and I cannot help feeling that it is one of the main reasons for the many complaints made about the deterioration in care. The new 'modern matrons' will do their best within a much smaller remit, but only time will assess their success. That very traditional British figure, the matron, has, I fear, gone forever, and if the ghost of Florence Nightingale haunts our wards today, she must see much to sadden her. There are other new initiatives, such as the nurse specialist and nurse practitioner, in which nurses are really beginning to use their education and skills to the full. We must turn our attention to growing these posts and encouraging nurses to use this opportunity to influence patient care radically.

Chapter 9

Retirement and After

It was a few days after my official departure from the region before my successor, Jacquie Flindall, could start, so I returned for a morning in order to hand over to her and we were chatting about events when the phone rang. Jacquie answered and handed it to me. It was the Chief Nursing Officer from the Department of Health, Dame Ann Poole, who asked me if I would be free to carry out an assignment in the Far East. Somewhat puzzled I agreed, and then she explained that the British Council had received a request from the Chinese Embassy for a small group of British nurses to carry out a few weeks' lecture tour of China. She wished me to lead the delegation, and suggested I might like to recommend some names and phone her back. I left my phone number with her and departed from the region thinking that it looked as if my travelling days were not over after all. I talked it over with Trevor Clay, discussed some names, and then went along to see the British Council to get a better idea of what was expected. There were meetings with Ann and her colleagues, because of the importance of the mission. It was the first time since the cultural revolution that an official group of nurses would be formally welcomed into China actually to teach and give a series of lectures. When the Red Cross became aware of my assignment, they asked me to call in Hong Kong to talk with the director of the Red Cross and visit the blood transfusion service there, as it was their most important project. At the same time, having had such close contact with the Hong Kong nurses, I notified them of my visit but stressed it was not in an official capacity. In preparing my itinerary, I allowed for a few days in Hong Kong, in order to see how the hospital and nursing service had developed in the twenty years since my visit to the nurses' association.

A lot of thought went into the choice of the four nurses to accompany me, as we had a very wide remit, which was to visit schools of nursing, and observe continuing nurse education, administration of nurses in hospitals, organisation of specialists units and intensive care, and community nursing. After a long session at the British Council, the group was finally composed of Peta Allen from the UK Central Council for Nursing, Midwifery and Health Visiting, Christine Hancock, Chief Nursing Officer of a London health authority, Thelma Holland, Director of Community Nursing in Nottingham and Joan Wheeler from the Nursing Division of the Department of Health. Between us we felt we could cover most aspects of nursing.

In Hong Kong messages were waiting for me at the hotel both from the Red Cross and the Nurses' Association. To my delight it was Paula Chow who greeted me the next morning. She had become the Director of Nursing of the large new Christian Mission Hospital in Kowloon. We had coffee together and discussed an itinerary for the three-day stopover on my way back from Beijing. She also gave me a lot of information and advice for my China visit and asked if I could collect some basic information for her. It was good to see her again and I looked forward to my return. Soon after Paula's departure, the Red Cross director arrived and we went off to visit their headquarters and hear about the services. We continued to one of the major hospitals where the Blood Transfusion Centre was situated. Then I said goodbye to the director and greeted my new host, who was the woman doctor in charge of the transfusion service. We formed an immediate rapport and spent an interesting morning visiting various clinics both in Kowloon and on Hong Kong Island, meeting nurses, volunteers and blood donors, a part of the health service I had not seen before.

All too soon it was time to return to the hotel, pick up my case and head for the airport. In the departure lounge, the other nurses were collecting and we all turned our attention to the task ahead, with anticipation and not a little apprehension, on my part at least. It was the first visit to China for all of us and we were strangely nervous as the plane circled the airport for landing. It looked a comparatively rural scene as we approached and then we were into a small and crowded airport, very different from today's gleaming and modern one. The senior British Council official met us and was responsible for our programme and overall care while we were in Beijing. He and his wife introduced us to the president and general secretary of the association, who had planned our programme, and to the interpreter for the duration of our visit. The senior nurses we met were quite fluent in English, having learned it many years back in nursing school from English and American teachers. The officials then left us with a promise to meet for dinner at the hotel

As Nursing Adviser to the British Red Cross at the London HQ, 1987.

and we were escorted to a minibus by our hosts. After some thirty minutes' drive, we arrived at the hotel at which we were booked. The interpreter went in and we waited in the bus, but when she eventually emerged it was to say that we were not staying there, but must wait to find out which hotel was expecting us. It was a distinctly low point, but at that moment there appeared a small cheerful Chinese, who introduced himself as the coordinator for the medical association. Full of good humour he announced, 'You ask what you want. I make you happy.' His laughter was so infectious that we continued to the next hotel hopefully, and sure enough they expected us. It was one of the huge anonymous buildings which abounded in Beijing at the time and rooms were small but quite adequate. Its restaurant also had a good reputation, so life looked brighter. Our British Council hosts appeared and we had dinner while collecting information about our programme and about various points of protocol. It soon appeared that, as leader, I had a precise role and was given instruction as to my behaviour, to the amusement and relief of the rest of the party. If things didn't go right, it would be my fault!

Next morning we arrived at the medical association, where the nurses' association shared accommodation, to discuss the programme. As planned, it was full of sightseeing and one or two basic visits to hospitals in a journey which included three more cities, but the carefully worked out lecture programme for the tour was conspicuous by its absence. It soon became clear that the nurses had not understood the reason for the visit and when we raised the question it was suggested that one lecture in each city would be fine. We retired for the night and next day came up with a scaled down version of each lecture, which could be put together in a shorter time. We adopted this method for audiences of around thirty senior nurses in each city. They were very keen to ask questions and enter into discussion, so the programme was changed again, reducing the time for sightseeing. We felt more comfortable with this.

In the course of the tour we visited several hospitals, including a large one for traditional Chinese medicine. Here we observed a number of treatments, often given by nurses. Many overseas doctors, including British, were taking courses in traditional medicine, especially in acupuncture. We visited home care and small clinics, but rarely saw nurses carrying out care. This seemed to be the role of the doctor, but more because of a shortage of nurses than any other factor. The situation is very different today, with large schools and colleges of nursing, including university programmes, and nurses carry out treatment as they would in any other country. Outside the cities we visited a commune and medical station, and a home for elderly people run by the commune. An elderly gentleman suffering from advanced cancer of the lung gave us a demonstration of exercise and relaxation response. He explained how he could relieve the pain with it and improve his quality of life. He was a charming character and had a good command of delightfully stilted English. We were always accompanied by our young interpreter, who was amazingly good at translating our concepts, and also by one of the senior nurses from the association. The president, Madam Lin, spoke perfect English and was a very well-qualified nurse. When I returned to China some twenty years later, I saw her name and picture in the main Medical University of Beijing, where she had been the nursing director at one time. She had also studied and obtained her degrees in the USA and had been retired from active nursing for some years. The vice-president, Madam Wang, was also a qualified nurse, and had been trained in a missionary school. She told us that there were very few nurses who had had this early training, and it was her mission to help nurses understand

With interpreter and delegation of senior British nurses to China, 1987.

their profession and to be proud of it. At that time she was just under eighty years old, but she was a very vigorous woman. A few months later she came to the UK at the invitation of the RCN, both to see something of our nursing service and to attend the annual congress in Harrogate, where she was elected an Honorary Fellow of the College and received a standing ovation.

All the time we were in China we heard about the English language programme which everyone, from student nurse to elderly citizen, was following on the radio. The person giving the course was called Cathie Flower and, everywhere we went, we were asked if we knew Cathie Flower. Some weeks after my return home, the phone rang. I picked it up to hear a female voice at the other end saying, 'You won't know me, but my name is Cathie Flower.' I dissolved into laughter, explaining that I seemed to have followed her across China. With a similar reaction, she told me that when she was in China everyone asked her if she knew me! She was to make a programme in English with Madam Wang to be sent back to China and, although I was given a copy of the video which included the Fellowship ceremony, I still haven't actually met Cathie Flower! The third official who looked after us was the secretary of the association, also a very experienced nurse. She was a very efficient and practical person, who accompanied us throughout our journey, making sure we knew what we were eating and where it came from, though often we would rather not know. After the first ten days or so, we could no longer cope with huge lunchtime meals, and said firmly 'No lunch', which she very reluctantly accepted. Halfway through our journey, I had a very bad cold and sore throat, common to most travellers in China at that time. I really did feel awful and, at one stage, was offered Chinese Medicine and insufflation. Having seen the instrument in use, I declined hastily and, as we had quite a formidable collection of medicaments between us, I survived with familiar medicines. We were always in good hotels and if they were not the luxury hotels one finds in China today, they were comfortable. Breakfasts were the one meal where we just couldn't cope with the Chinese version and opted for orange juice. We had a particularly fierce waitress in one hotel who glared at us and announced firmly, 'You pay,' and we agreed meekly, 'Yes, we pay.'

There was still plenty of time for sightseeing and each town we visited had its special features. In Beijing the Forbidden City completely lived up to our imagination, but we fell in love with the gracious Summer Palace, with evocative names such as 'the hall of wind through pines'. We walked down the great route to the ancient Ming tombs and gazed at the huge stone figures lining the way. We also walked along the Great Wall, crowded with tourists, and later looked down on it from the air as we left China. After Beijing we continued to Nanjing, although we were to return to discuss our experiences and reactions with Madam Lin and her colleagues. We were pleased that our travel was by overnight train so that we could see something of the countryside, and it was certainly an experience. Facilities for washing were sparse and we all decided to arrive dirty and have a shower at the hotel. We hadn't allowed for the enthusiasm of our hosts, and left luggage in the bus for some essential sightseeing. By the time we reached the scene of the Mausoleum of Dr Sun Yat Sen, it was midday and the sun was very hot. The beautiful edifice in white marble was before us, with over 400 steps leading up to the actual tomb, and we regarded it with awe and a little misgiving. One of the party verbalised what we all felt. 'Do we really have to climb to the top?' she asked hopefully, but our looks were adequate reply and we commenced the ascent, which got slower and slower. One by one we reached the top and leant thankfully on the marble balustrade looking down on the tomb, which was very similar to Napoleon's tomb in Paris. We stayed quite a while in contemplation of the simple doctor who had done so much to start China on the road to modernity. I was particularly moved, as I had visited Macau while in Hong Kong and seen the hospital where he had first practised medicine. Eventually we had gathered enough breath to start the downward journey. It was almost as difficult as the way up, because the steps positively danced in the sun and made it quite hard to maintain balance.

We were very grateful to go to the hotel and have half an hour to shower and change and to feel human again. Later we went to the school of nursing and carried out the lecture programme for an audience which was intensely interested and asked very many questions about the British nursing service. This programme was repeated once or twice in each of the cities we visited. We always had a delightful audience and lots of questions, which at times we found strange and difficult to answer. One afternoon we were driven to the top of a mountain, where we had a refreshing tea in a beautiful house which we were told had belonged to the sister of Madame Chiang Kai-shek, then living in America. It was a lovely afternoon; time seemed to stand still while we sipped green tea and looked down on the wooded hillside, with the city far below. Our young interpreter was adept at creating an atmosphere, no matter what situation, professional or otherwise, she was describing. Before we left Nanjing we had a visit from the smiling and energetic provincial president of the association, who had looked after us in the city. She was very enthusiastic about Shi-gong and the relaxation response and had us all practising in the beautiful lobby of our very elegant hotel. We must have looked very odd, and certainly clumsy, foreigners, but no one seemed in anyway surprised.

We continued by bus to Suzhou, famed for its many and beautiful walled gardens, each with a name describing its history, contents and architecture. We were fortunate to have a doctor from the Medical Association for a guide, as he made the gardens live. One really intrigued us, as it was called the 'Garden of the Humble Administrator'. Health service administrators are not always universally popular and would be unlikely to be described as 'humble', so we were amused, although our hosts could not understand our laughter. It was at this point that I developed a cold and throat infection and was glad that the pace was much slower and that there was some time for rest.

The new Honorary Doctor of Southampton University after the ceremony, with friends Bega Hood (left) and Mary Niven (right), 1987.

Our next visit was to Shanghai which lived up to all our expectations. We walked along the Bund and gazed with awe on the mighty Yangtze River on a very tranquil evening. Our hotel was nearby, close to the English and French quarters. The next morning we visited both a school of nursing and a hospital called 'Number 5', in line with the older method of naming them. We were intrigued by the tiny and neat student nurses and the information about their training, which included a very good introduction to English. Recruitment and training of nurses has changed considerably these days, as I discovered on my visits some years later. I was carefully instructed in protocol towards our hosts at each place, especially on what was expected of me as leader. The group used to tease me on my ultra-polite introductions and discussions, but there were some advantages, such as driving with our host in the official car, while the rest followed in our rather battered minibus. Our host at the Shanghai hospital was the medical superintendent, a very courteous elderly gentleman who told us something of his background during the cultural revolution. Most professionals spoke very simply about their life during that period, without rancour, simply saying how much there was to catch up with, both for doctors and nurses, and they saw this as a real mission. All the professionals we met throughout our tour were very fine people, and we warmed to them and remember them well to this day.

It was time to return to Beijing and we left late at night in a very old plane which was certainly packed to capacity. I was told that most of the airline pilots had received their training in the armed forces. It made us feel safe, but the heavily laden plane was manoeuvred as if it were a fighter plane. We were pleased to see the same hotel we had stayed in before, and we had a two-day lecture programme before we left Beijing. We reported our impressions to the council of the association, and had dinner with the British Council officials to report to them and say thank you for all the arrangements. All too soon it was time to leave for the airport, where we said our farewells with genuine regret and boarded the plane for home. I left the others at Hong Kong to spend three days with the Hong Kong nurses. They were equally curious to have my impressions of nursing in China because, as they pointed out, most of their contacts till then had been with South China, particularly with Canton. That changed very quickly, of course, as the pace of integration with China speeded up and, as I visited quite frequently over the next few years, I was able to observe and follow the major changes.

Once home I settled down to two to three days a week at the British Red Cross headquarters in London. It was a much slower pace of work than the National Health Service, but I enjoyed the staff and the volunteers with whom I worked. There was at least one senior nurse at each branch headquarters responsible for the programme and training of volunteers. We had an annual conference at Barnet Hill, the delightful old house which was the Red Cross training centre in the Surrey countryside, and various lectures were also organised for the nurses in London. As I had been on the branch council while working in Southampton, I knew many of them. I was also involved with the selection and employment of those nurses who were assisting the work of the Red Cross in emergency situations across the world. These were mainly young nurses who volunteered from time to time when disasters such as earthquakes or the Ethiopian famine produced a need for medical teams. They were enthusiastic people, ready at short notice to fly to any part of the world, and I came to know many of them. Understandably, it affected their own work at home. Health authorities were willing to second nurses for one or even two disasters, but once having worked in the emergency field, some went out again and again, and worked on a temporary basis at home. I used to suggest to some of them that the time had come to consolidate their own career, but they rarely took the advice and I could well understand them.

We had some very eminent persons on the national committee, and two were particularly notable. One was Lady Victoria Palmer, who was the vice-chair of council, and a charming gentle person with a great interest in nursing. We became friends and continued contact after she had completed her term of office, until her death a few years ago. Another was Countess Mountbatten, the chair of the Joint Committee of the Red Cross and St John. This was not an easy committee with two similar yet very different organisations, and she was a delightful chairman. She had a relaxed, friendly approach to people and was extremely kind to me. As patron of many organisations, she was in great demand and tried to visit each of them every year or two. She was one of the vice-presidents of the Royal College of Nursing. I met her again a year or two ago at a major College function where she had registered, and was walking into the auditorium, by herself and without any fuss, when I saw her and went to meet her. 'How very nice to see a friend' was her greeting and she was perfectly at home talking to the nurses. She is a very great lady in more ways than one. During my time with the Red Cross, a young Princess Diana came to visit headquarters, as she had just become the Red Cross Patron of Youth. She spent some time talking to each of us about our work, and came across as a charming young woman, anxious to please, but a bit ill at ease among rather an elderly group of officials and staff.

While at the Red Cross, I received a letter which was quite overwhelming. It was from Southampton University, asking if I would accept an honorary doctorate. It was an amazing experience and utterly unexpected. Usually with something like this, there is a feeling in the air which makes one suspicious, such as pertinent questions being asked from unusual sources, but on this occasion I had no hint and the letter came out of the blue. There was a meeting at the college later on that morning and, when I mentioned the letter to Trevor Clay, he chuckled knowingly and said they had all been quite sure I would find out. It was a very well-kept secret. At the ceremony in September, Mary and Bega were my two guests, but the university had thoughtfully invited many of my colleagues from the NHS and the RCN, and I was surprised to see so many in the audience. The day coincided with the graduation of the first

Outside the House of Lords with Lord and Lady Westbury, my hosts to a celebration lunch, following my investiture as a Dame of the British Empire by Her Majesty the Queen at Buckingham Palace.

B.Sc. nursing graduates, an event which I had worked towards throughout my tenure in Southampton, so it was a doubly happy event and an honour in which I take great pride.

The Red Cross headquarters was in Grosvenor Place, and those of St John further down at the corner. Apart from meeting at the Joint Committee of the Red Cross and St John, I had little contact with St John until a new senior officer, Lady Westbury, was appointed. One of the first things she did was to invite one or two of us to lunch to get to know each other. That was the beginning of a close friendship which continues today. Ursula Westbury is a tall, elegant woman with an easy charm, and her husband, David, was a very senior official of St John and a great fundraiser. Lord Westbury was everyone's idea of a British peer, as my American friend remarked. He was tall and handsome and a real charmer. I enjoyed a lot of their company when in London and spent a delightful weekend at their Yorkshire home.

Two days a week at the Red Cross left me plenty of free time, but not for long, for there were a number of interesting requests for help. One was to become a founding member of a new organisation, the Continence Foundation and, although my days of practical nursing were well behind me, and I knew little about the subject, I agreed. The chair was a very well-known consultant, most of my fellow members were knowledgeable professionals and the foundation rapidly took shape and carved a niche for itself. I personally learnt a great deal and when I resigned from the board some five years later, it was with real regret. I left a thriving organisation fulfilling a vital role, and I still follow its progress with interest.

Another organisation which invited me to join was the Edith Cavell and Nations Fund for Nurses, the link being Dame Ann Bryan, who was closely connected with the Red Cross and the chair of the grants committee of the fund. As the name suggests, it was an endowment set up to assist nurses in difficult circumstances and it included a few smaller funds and the various grants. Dame Ann was a splendid and distinguished lady who was a great friend to nurses. When she retired she asked me to take over the office, and the main committee agreed. She always teased me by referring to me as 'the young Dame', which I suppose I was in her view, even though I was well past retirement age. The work was useful, practical and very interesting, but we were a bit hampered by a number of small funds with their special conditions, and changing times had brought different needs and problems. I remained as chair for a number of years, but since my departure the various funds have been brought together under the title of 'Nurse Aid', thanks to the efforts of the chairman, and its able administrator, Ann Rich. A year or two after my retirement from the fund, I had an interesting invitation to a ceremony at the National War Museum, when a recently discovered letter from Edith Cavell, written the night before her execution, was donated to the Museum, to be kept along with other mementos of her life. I found it strangely moving to read her words written almost ninety years ago – 'standing as I do on the brink of eternity…' and, returning home, my thoughts kept coming back to them and the quiet faith and courage which inspired them.

It was during my appointment with the Red Cross that I was promoted to the Order of Dame of the British Empire, although it was for my services to the RCN and the Health Service. My friend Joel Bishop from New Orleans came over for the ceremony, together with Mary, Bega Hood, my long standing-friend from Blackpool, and my cousin Joyce, also from Blackpool. Only two guests were allowed into the ceremony and so, as Mary and Bega had come with me for my CBE some ten years earlier, it was the turn of Joyce and Joel this time. For an American it was clearly the occasion of a lifetime and, when I met Joel at the airport, she was laden with luggage. On arrival home she revealed three hats and even more outfits to see which we thought was most suitable for the palace. The Red Cross provided a limousine to take us. Bega and Mary left the hotel later and joined the crowd outside the palace.

Although I had been to a previous investiture for my CBE, it was still a daunting occasion as I climbed the steps and was directed into a small room where three gentlemen receiving high awards were already waiting. An official kept polite conversation going and introduced us to each other, and then the Lord Chamberlain arrived to brief us and to allow the gentlemen who were to be knighted to practise with the faldstool. I was very thankful it was not required for a Dame!

The Lord Chamberlain went on to tell me that my guests were in the front row. He had been making conversation with the guests generally and, when he asked one lady from where she came, her answer was from a town in the north of England. He remarked that it was quite a long journey and then spoke to the next person and asked the same question. It happened to be Joel and he admitted to being quite taken aback when she replied, in a strong Southern States of USA accent, 'New Orleans.' Then it was time to be escorted to the ballroom, past a large number of other recipients awaiting their turn, and catching the sound of the music of the band before waiting at the side entrance for the Queen to arrive. She was wearing a very simple yellow dress, and looked as serene as her photos. Only one of the knights was before me and I had no time to be nervous before I was standing in front of the Queen and answering her gentle remarks. I remember my fear that I might catch my heel in my dress as I moved backwards and curtsied, but to my relief no such disaster occurred. The rest of the investiture passed in a dream; there were photographs in the quadrangle and then we were off into the limousine, picked up the other two as we left and headed for the House of Lords for lunch as the guests of David and Ursula Westbury. David was a delightful host and, for the sake of my American friend, showed us round the House. I remember very clearly that he paused before one painting and said simply, 'That is my ancestor, the first Lord Westbury, and Lord Chancellor of England.' Joel obviously was absolutely fascinated but for

With the late Trevor Clay waiting for the moment of presentation of the Christiane Reimann Award at the ICN Congress in Madrid, 1993.

me it was a moment to pause and wonder at our great history, and to feel that I was a small cog in that great procession of our tradition through the ages. It was a wonderful day, not least for Joel, and I think she dined out on the story for many a year back at home. We ended with a dinner given at her home by the Countess of Limerick, who was chair of the Red Cross Council at the time. The other guests were senior Red Cross officials. It was another generous and delightful occasion, and we returned to the St John's House Club, where we were all staying, before we went our separate ways in the morning. Mary and I felt quite exhausted by it all and were glad to have a rest from the excitement. We saw Joel off at Heathrow, but we were both to see her again quite soon, as we visited her for a couple of weeks later in the year.

One of my frequent visits to New Orleans was quite special, as the biennial convention of the American Nurses' Association was to be held there. I had been invited and Trevor Clay was also going and participating in one of the panel discussions. Although Trevor was staying in one of the main congress hotels, I stayed with Joel and joined him for the congress events. It was a busy but enjoyable time, and I had been to New Orleans so often that the city was familiar and I even dared to drive round it. The busy motorways are quite daunting and I spent a lot of time getting lost. It was not very long after our return to the UK that Trevor informed me that he was retiring from the RCN due to ill health. It was devastating news. He was only in his mid-fifties and had at least another ten years of productive work in one of the most important nursing posts in the country. He had really made his mark as the RCN general secretary, and was extremely popular with the membership as well as being very successful in his role. He went on to tell me that he was having to think very seriously about a heart transplant, and I had noticed for some time that the least exertion was causing him difficulty. We gave him a great send off with many mixed emotions, as those of us who knew the true situation were very concerned about his future. He had followed me at ICN in the role of vice-president, but I gathered that the work and travel were beginning to take a great deal out of him, although everyone tried hard to make his stay in Geneva as easy as possible. He had to enlist the help of a wheelchair but understandably wished to finish his second term on the ICN board.

The college then had to make plans for recruiting his successor. It always surprises me that there are never many applicants for this type of post, probably because of its size and the commitment needed. There were two sets of interviews before an appointment was made. The successful candidate was Christine Hancock, quite a young nurse who had already made her mark in a very senior position in the NHS, and the same Christine who was a member of the group which went to China. She was a completely different personality to Trevor, but quickly made her mark, steered the college skilfully through many difficult periods, and oversaw the second, and even more complete, rebuilding of the RCN headquarters. This required the building to be completely empty for over a year, and the organisation had to operate in rather difficult temporary accommodation near Euston station. The fact that this was achieved with a minimum of disruption to work was a great credit to Christine's leadership and vision, and she oversaw the move back to a very new headquarters in Cavendish Square. Soon after the return, she retired, as she had always intended to do so before the official age. She was elected ICN president at the Copenhagen Congress in 2001, the first British president for over sixty years, and is showing the same leadership and vision in this post as she has done throughout her career.

After the Madrid presentation surrounded by the flags of participating countries.

It was good to get home to Mary, for I was conscious that her health was deteriorating and she looked very fragile. For this reason we decided to move into Southampton from our lovely bungalow in the village of Wickham. We had designed it ourselves and watched it built brick by brick, so it was quite a decision to make, but Mary felt it was time to give up her car and Southampton would be near facilities. In Wickham we were in the next property to a new pastoral and conference centre, run by a French order of nuns. We had entered into the life of the centre with its many activities and had made many friends, and the decision to move wasn't easy. We had watched an old hotel pulled down at the corner of the main avenue in Southampton and opposite the large common which has ancient common land rights. A complex of rather special apartments was being built on the site and, after visiting in its various building stages and wondering if we could afford one, we eventually took the plunge and bought an apartment. It was a happy choice. Mary was near transport and all the other facilities she required and, to our good fortune, Mary and Tommy Thomas, a married couple who were very old friends, moved into a flat further down the road. Mary had a passion for cats and we were adopted by a stray tabby in Wickham whom we christened 'Fred.' Needless to say Fred moved with us, adapted very well to town life and lived to the ripe old age of twenty years. We were fortunate to have a flat with lovely views over the common and could watch magnificent sunsets. From my own bedroom at the other side, there was a wonderful view over the rooftops and down to Southampton Water. As an early riser, I also enjoyed the sunrise. As Mary became frailer, Mary and Tommy were great companions and gave a lot of practical help. In addition, we had a very beautiful and active church just a few minutes away, where we both became absorbed in the life of the parish and the outgoing and friendly people who made it. After a few months I decided to indulge my love of singing by joining the choir, and I have never regretted it. They patiently put up with my fairly frequent absences, and gave me stability while satisfying my love of music and liturgy.

Chapter 10

New Horizons

RETIRED COLLEAGUES were always telling me how busy they were and that they did not know how they had ever found time for work. I never believed them, but soon changed my views. The visit to China came hard on the heels of my retirement from the Wessex Regional Health Authority, the post with the Red Cross followed, and although my RCN presidency was coming to an end, work with the European Nursing Directives continued and was very time-consuming. I had edited a book on the directives as soon as they were signed, with a nurse from each of the nine EC countries writing a chapter on the situation in their own country and how it affected nurses. This was an attempt to spread knowledge among the profession. More countries became members of the European Union and, with the basic curriculum agreed, the Committee on Nursing considered additional matters, such as the work on cancer nursing. and care of older people Our professional nursing committee (PCN) debated how we could keep nurses in the various countries informed, and decided that another book was needed. The whole subject had wide implications for the profession and the first book was out of date. I agreed to do it, but this time in partnership with Sue Russell. The result was a book of greater depth and with chapters from each country showing the degree of change. It seems curious that I had spent so many years both working on the directives and writing about them. Legislation and the minutiae of the directives had never been my favourite topics, and the meetings in Brussels seemed very tedious. They were important for the profession and we all did our utmost to get the best results possible, but it was the fellowship and cooperation with my nursing colleagues on the committees that really motivated me. We had interesting journeys in and out of countries and, while it was time-consuming work, we had a lot of fun and various adventures. Most of my travel was with Sue Russell and on some occasions we were joined by Shelagh Murphy, the new head of the RCN international department.

A number of my roles were coming to an end within two years. My period of time on the ICN board and as first vice-president would finish at the forthcoming congress in Israel; the presidency of the Royal College of Nursing would end in November 1986 and my work with the Red Cross would soon follow suit. I was beginning to wonder what it would feel like to retire from a busy life but there was not much time for reflection as we were in the midst of preparations for the congress in Tel Aviv. We all had mixed feelings because of the unstable situation, and it was not the happiest of congresses, but it was very well attended, in spite of the fact that some countries declined to send a delegation. Because I was involved in the programme and general arrangements, I arrived early, travelling by El Al airline. I was exposed to the intense security measures before boarding for the first time and, like most people, found the in-depth questioning quite intimidating, but the flight was uneventful and we arrived at the hotel very early in the morning. Somehow I had managed to lose the key for my hand luggage, which held all the working papers needed, and it took two or three hours to get it opened.

The planning for the congress was superb and nothing was left to chance. When we had finished preliminary meetings, we had a free day and, as a friend had arrived early and had a hire car, we spent some time visiting one or two of the holy places. My main recollection was of taking a trip across the Sea of Galilee, sitting on the side of the boat watching the movement of the waters and pondering on those events of two thousand years ago. When we arrived at Capernaum, there were very few people around, and it was another quiet experience to sit by the ruins of the synagogue where Christ had so often spoken to the people. I was very glad to have experienced Galilee for the first time without being surrounded by people. In spite of the usual busy pace of the congress, we did have time for quiet exploration of Israel. We all had a free half-day, and, with Trevor Clay and another friend, we took a trip by car into the desert, which conjured up the biblical scenes of the wilderness.

The congress itself was perfectly organised, and we were made very welcome by the Israeli nurses. Muringo Kiereini of Kenya and I had both served on the ICN board for eight years and, in the last four, Muringo was president and I was first vice-president and we enjoyed working together. She was an striking figure in her national costume, and presided over the congress with calm and dignity, but there was a certain tension throughout and we were both quite relieved when it was over and we stepped down from office on the final night. For myself there was a curious feeling of loss. ICN had played a large part in my life for almost twenty years and it was difficult to imagine the gap it would leave. Most participants went home after the end of the congress, but the Israeli nurses had arranged a sightseeing tour for all of the Council of National Representatives on the day following the closing ceremony. First we went to Bethlehem and, although there were no tanks in Manger Square, parts of it were barricaded and armed military were in evidence, but we had free access to the Basilica where all was calm. We were indeed fortunate to see it before the square and Basilica were under fire and the Basilica out of bounds. Then we went on to Jerusalem, but it was a rushed tour through the main holy places, and left one feeling frustrated. It was by no means the fault of our guides but resulted from the general oppressive situation. I suspect that my feelings were shared by very many of the congress participants. It was memorable to visit the Holy Land and we appreciated the efforts of our Israeli colleagues to show us as much as possible, but we could not help feeling saddened by the general atmosphere and were quite relieved when it was time to board the plane home.

It was probably the rather unsatisfactory nature of my visits to the holy places in Israel that prompted me to join a small group organised and led by a young priest from our church on a pilgrimage to the Holy Land. It lasted for ten days, which gave us time to see all the main sites. For the first half of the journey we stayed by one of the main gates into the old city of Jerusalem, and the second part was spent on the shores of Galilee near to Capernaum. Father Ray Lyons had a unique ability to make the sites come to life, and it was an amazing spiritual experience. Each of us had our different special places. For me this was the small and ancient church in a very beautiful and quiet garden, and is thought to be the point on the way to Emmaus where Jesus met and walked with two of his disciples and 'they recognised him in the breaking of bread'.

My eight years on the ICN board came to an end with the closing ceremony of the ICN congress. It had been a fascinating period, and I was glad to see the organisation from the point of view of a board member, as well as from my former role of executive director. Muringo and I had worked together closely and became firm friends, weathering the various crises that most major organisations have to cope with from time to time. During the final year, the then executive director, Connie Holleran of the USA, had discussed the possibility of following up the history of ICN published in 1965 and written by Daisy Bridges, who interviewed me for my first post with ICN in London. ICN had expanded rapidly, membership of national nurses' associations had almost doubled, ICN's place in Geneva was assured and activities had greatly increased. After a lot of thought I felt it would be possible for me to write the book. I was neither qualified nor willing to undertake the writing of a fully annotated reference book but there seemed to me to be a need for a readable, accurate history which nurses could enjoy. Connie agreed and *ICN Past and Present* was published in time for the next quadrennial congress in 1989. This was held in Seoul, South Korea and, as I had not attended the interim congress, it was the first for many years in which I did not have a specific role and which I could enjoy as a participant. The Korean Nurses' Association had matured very rapidly, led by their president Mo Im Kim, who at the time was the very influential Minister of Health.

I had spent a few days in Seoul on my way to the congress in Japan a decade earlier, and the city and the country had made considerable progress since then but retained its special character. My journey was not without its adventures. A large contingent of British nurses were on the plane, and were following me through immigration. The usual problems of translating passport details into a language for the Korean computers slowed the queue. There was a longer pause than usual with my passport, then the young official looked at me and a rather fractured conversation ensued.

'What is this "Dame?"' he asked.

I replied, 'Is title.'

Pause. 'Ah, title like mother, father?'

'No. Title given by Queen.'

Longer pause. 'Ah so,' (brilliant smile) 'Meesis Thatcher!'

The waiting British all collapsed with hilarity, and I grabbed my passport and fled in the interests of international relations, before I too gave way to mirth.

A car was waiting for me, and I checked into the hotel, to a most delightful room with welcoming flowers, before going to the front hall to see if there was anything I needed to do. One of my former regional colleagues was travelling with me and we were quickly hailed by Shelagh Murphy, who was in charge of the newly-arrived British contingent. She was quite frantic because of a muddle with room reservations. They had been given in error to another party and none were available. With everyone very tired after the long plane journey, feelings were running high. Eventually rooms were found, but in one of the hotels they were Korean style and that caused further chaos. The evening had practically gone before Shelagh returned to us for a restoring drink to calm her nerves.

There were still a few unexpected episodes, but that was part of the charm of a country with many customs and practices dear to its own culture and at the same time moving fast into industrialisation. Most people have very happy memories of the congress. It was very efficiently run, with a lot of concern for individual welfare. I presented my book to the ICN president at one of the sessions, and spent a lot of time on the stall in the exhibition, signing copies. The Korean nurses were wonderful hosts. We had a number of special banquets, one hosted by the Prime Minister in the beautiful State House. Naturally, participants were very anxious to take advantage of the wide variety of shopping at attractive prices in the special shopping streets. Most of them returned home with examples of lovely Korean handicraft, but also with a suspiciously large selection of famous name watches, silks and leather goods. As Angela and I were moving on to circle the world for two weeks' holiday, there was no place for such souvenirs in our luggage.

One adventure which turned out well was when we decided to go into central Seoul for mass at the cathedral, only to find ourselves turned out of the taxi because of a large student demonstration. It was quite a daunting sight. We were near the Cathedral Square, which was packed by students on a 'sit-in'. Police were very much in evidence and the atmosphere was volatile but, as we did not know our surroundings, the sensible action seemed to be to get into the cathedral and hope that things would be quieter when we returned. As we picked our way over lines of bodies, no one stopped us. Unfortunately, the situation was just the same when we came out and there was obviously no hope of a taxi. Just then, a courtly gentleman came to our assistance and offered to escort us to the nearest underground station, where we thankfully boarded a train and returned to the hotel safely. Only minutes later Mo Im was on the phone to me expressing concern, and I couldn't help responding that, had we known of the problems, we would not have been in the area. There was such a sense of pride in their country and concern that their guests should see the very best, that we had not been warned of the demonstrations. But my lasting impression of South Korea was of a very beautiful country, rich in tradition and anxious for the comfort of their guests. It is still on my agenda for a promised return. Angela and I continued round the world on our holiday journey, with an all too brief stop in Hawaii, and some lovely days among the Rockies in Banff before returning home.

While I was still in a senior position in the National Health Service, I was approached by one of our nearby health authorities. A nurse was required on each authority, but it had to be one who was not actually employed by that authority. I was appointed to the Dorset Health Authority, our neighbouring county, whose meetings were usually held at the headquarters in Bournemouth, an easy twenty-five mile drive away. It was work that I knew and enjoyed but, after two or three years, the policy changed and members had to come from the area. Then, just after my retirement, an unexpected phone call asked me to be the nurse member of the Dorset Family Practitioner Committee. This brought me into a new area of health care concerned with medical, dental and pharmaceutical services in the community, which again was quite a learning experience. For the first time I met a very able lady, Wilma Mulliner, wife of a well-known anaesthetist, who was designated chair of the Dorset FPC, as it was known. The committee was a mixture of health professionals and able business and professional men and women and it worked extremely well. Alas, after another two years it was 'all change' again, and the FPC was merged with the Dorset Health Authority, with Wilma Mulliner as chair. I began to feel part of Dorset and its health service, and the work was both interesting and time-consuming, with a very hard-working and brilliant chief executive of the authority, Ian Carruthers. He was, without doubt, the finest executive I have worked with and richly deserved his knighthood in a recent Honours List. But it was too good to last, and yet another reorganisation slimmed down the authority and required members to live in the area. So that was the end of my experience on a health authority. It was hard work and enjoyable, and my fellow members were dedicated and very able. I've lost count of how many reorganisations I experienced since the days of Hospital Committees and Regional Health Authorities, but it does seem a lot more complicated and the personal approach somewhat lost. That is probably old age speaking but I watch, with interest and some amazement, the continuing saga of reorganisation. There has been a great multiplication of work throughout the NHS, but from observation and the comments of those who have experienced the service, it does not appear to have improved.

Then an intriguing offer came my way. It was from an organisation called the International Hospital Group, which as its name suggests was concerned with management of hospitals in other countries. I took up the invitation to meet them in their gracious headquarters at Stoke Park, now an extremely expensive and gracious hotel. The organisation had a medical committee, composed of very well-known consultants, to help with recruitment of personnel and make visits to the hospitals to assess progress and quality of service. It was felt that a nurse should be added to the advisory committee and I was asked to join to assist with senior nurse recruitment and carry out occasional visits to two or three major hospitals in Saudi Arabia. It was not too onerous and the Middle East was a new area for me and promised to be interesting and good professional experience. Dame Kathleen Raven, a well-known former Chief Nursing Officer of the Department of Health, was consultant to the organisation, and a delight to work with. Some of my trips to Saudi Arabia were with Dame Kathleen, who was obviously revered by the senior officials in the country, and doors opened very quickly. It was a strange experience to visit Saudi Arabia, having to conform to its special customs in dress and behaviour, and I had great admiration for the nurses who took contracts there. Some had been out for a number of years and had adapted well to the country. The hospitals were very modern and well-equipped, but the language barrier was a problem, and I admired the way that nurses had adapted to the use of interpreters; most had obtained at least a basic knowledge of the language. My own visits were rarely for more than two weeks, and I made sure that my mode of dress was acceptable. A driver was responsible for my travel in the city and IHG staff looked after me in the evenings. It was a bit frustrating never to be out alone, but one adapted and I was never exposed to any difficulty while in the country. It was very obvious that I was treated as an honoured guest and it is not possible to compare my short experiences with those of nurses who had accepted contracts of three or more years. I doubt that I could ever have worked there, even for a short contract of two or three years. The five years spent with IHG passed very quickly; when the hospital contracts changed companies, my work with IHG came to an end, but it was an enjoyable experience.

Nursing has been high on the agenda of the World Health Organisation over the last decades of the twentieth century, mainly as a result of the vigorous lobbying of the international and national nursing organisations. In the early years of the 1980s, my work with the WHO came to the fore again. Emphasis throughout most of the decade was on standards of care. I was drawn into this quite early with the WHO European Region, based in Copenhagen, as one of a small working party of nurses from other European countries. Marie Farrell, Chief Nurse to WHO Europe at the time, was the driving force behind the programme. A newcomer to the WHO working party was Alison Kitson, then recently appointed to the RCN as a nurse adviser with a particular interest in the Standards of Care programme. She was to become a key player and consultant to WHO and largely led the programme during the years it operated. Alison is now the Director of Nursing and Policy at the RCN, working very closely with its general secretary, Beverley Malone, and has carved a unique place for herself in the nursing life of the UK. She is well known and highly respected internationally for her work on standards of care.

WHO then called the first European Conference on Nursing in Vienna in 1988 to publicise the key role of nursing as a major force for change in health care and stressing the role it can play in the WHO strategy of Health For All. It was not an easy meeting. There were wide variations in the education and role of a nurse in the various countries and we had some heated debate both within groups and at plenary sessions. My Danish colleague, Kirsten Stallknecht, was the president and I the chief rapporteur and we both had difficult roles but, in spite of many conflicting opinions, a consensus statement eventually emerged. On the last evening Kirsten and I were responsible for producing the draft report and we were nowhere near its completion. The only space available for work in the hotel was outside the lift shaft on the top floor, where we set up tables. A constant procession of nurses en route to bed passed us with puzzled looks, and some thoughtfully offered the contents of their mini bars to keep us going. I can still see the amazed gaze of the president of the Norwegian Nurses' Association as she emerged from the lift. We still meet at international meetings and Marthe invariably recounts the story to current friends, who may be under the impression that international work is glamorous. We settled for black coffee at intervals and handed the finished document to our long-suffering secretary at 6a.m. and the report was available for distribution at the morning session. It was finally agreed, but the work was not finished and the pressure had to be kept up.

At the 42nd World Assembly in 1989, a debate took place on the need to strengthen the role of nursing and midwifery personnel. A second Ministerial Conference on Nursing and Midwifery in Europe was held in Munich in 2000, considerably strengthened by the participation of Ministers of Health of member states. For all its powerful membership and strong language, the situation of nursing and midwifery across the world does not seem to have changed a great deal. Individual countries have made great progress, but so much more is needed in the poorer countries and the developing world. I cannot help reflecting that it is nearly half a century since I joined ICN with great resolve to improve nursing worldwide but, looking at the global scene, improvements appear to be small and slow to take effect.

One very interesting event took place at the end of the Vienna conference, when we realised that a papal visit to Austria had just commenced. There was an invitation for two nurses to be present when the Pope visited a concentration camp some 100 miles outside Vienna. As members were all dispersing that morning, Amelia Maglacas of WHO and I were asked to go. We were accompanied by an official who was carrying a large bouquet of flowers and was also the driver, and he informed us that we were to travel quickly because we were late. And quickly we went, in a rather ancient four-wheel drive, with a rooftop flashing light and siren, which our driver used most of the way. We expected to be stopped by police at any moment but arrived without incident, except the effect on our nervous systems. Once there, we were ushered into a small section of the grounds, and we realised that our guide was a Jew and it was a very emotional visit for him. He took the flowers down to lay at a small monument and was obviously distressed. The helicopter bearing the Pope touched down inside the main courtyard and he stopped to pray for a while in one of the cells. Then he walked past us through the main grounds, accompanied by some members of families of those who had been imprisoned and died there. It was a very moving occasion and we didn't speak much on the way back, which was taken at a much slower pace. The next morning we left Vienna. After the Vienna conference I moved out of the working party on standards and Alison continued to make an important contribution, not just to the WHO programme, but to Europe in general.

Work with the World Health Organisation and the European Community has occupied a large part of my working career, and sometimes one looks back and wonders what positive effect it had. We still seem to struggle with the same problems, and the shortage of nurses in my own country appears to get worse rather than better. We are bringing in considerable numbers of nurses to help us to continue day-by-day care in our hospitals and community services. We would certainly be in dire straits without our overseas nursing colleagues, but what does it do to the services of the country they have left?

My role at the Red Cross was taken over by Stanley Holder, a colleague of many years' standing, especially with his roles with the Royal College of Nursing. He had been in post about eighteen months when he telephoned me one day to say that the president of the Hong Kong Nurses' Association was trying to get in touch with me and he had given her my address. It was Paula Chow, whom I remembered from my early visit to Hong Kong, now the president of the association and also chief nurse of the United Christian Hospitals. On getting in touch with Paula, she explained that the association wanted to review its work and activities, and asked if I was able to help and come over for a few weeks. As my work was fairly quiet at the time, I offered to go over for two weeks in the first instance to assess the situation and see how much help I could give. I stayed in a central hotel and had two or three meetings with the committee and then with key people. The professional associations in small or developing countries do seem to have problems of membership and interest after the first few years of enthusiasm. The impetus to start comes either from a senior nurse or from someone who has spent time in the UK and has seen the growth of the RCN or who has been to an ICN congress. While there is a strong and influential president, the association grows but, without a full or part-time person to keep things going, enthusiasm dwindles, membership drops and money becomes tight. It becomes a vicious circle.

We spent a lot of time discussing strategy. The association had a very adequate centre in Hong Kong Island, but it took money to maintain and it was being rented out on occasions to help with finance. We visited hospitals, talked with groups and eventually decided on a part-time organising secretary. A nurse from the UK applied and remained for a year, but then took a post at one of the universities, and a local nurse who followed was not very successful and was not replaced. I did not feel I had been very much help, except to participate in study days and the national conference. At the same time Paula spoke to me about the major changes taking place in the organisation of health care. A new body, the Hospital Authority, had been set up and she was the nurse member. The authority was to appoint a panel of experts, and the chairman asked to have lunch with me to discuss nurse membership. I was very conscious of the sensitivities of the government nurses, and relationships with the 'subvented' hospitals and private hospitals, all of whom were now to come under one roof. The forthcoming problems were only too evident and I didn't fancy getting involved with local politics, but the restructure was badly needed and very worthwhile.

At the end of lunch, the chairman asked if I was prepared to join the group of experts, which was to be multi-disciplinary and expected to meet twice a year for a week each time. I agreed to this and, as Paula Chow was a member of the authority, I felt she would fill in any gaps in my knowledge. We had time for further discussion about the work of the authority and, though I still felt there were nurses more knowledgeable for such an important task, I saw the advantage of having someone who was close to the development of the profession in Hong Kong and quite well-known.

I left with a small pile of documents to study, and looking forward to what was a new and bold approach to re-structuring the health service in Hong Kong It was a few months before a formal invitation came for the first meeting of the group, which was both multi-disciplinary and made up of different nationalities – Cyril Chantler from the UK, a well-known medical consultant, now Sir Cyril, a professor from a College of Health Studies in Australia, finance and governance experts from the USA and a medical consultant from Singapore. We also had help from counterparts in Hong Kong.

I was extremely apprehensive about the first meeting, as the aims seemed very high-powered and I certainly felt inadequate compared with the other members. Cyril Chantler reassured me and we enjoyed working together. We had many colleagues in common and, more important, our doctor/nurse relationship helped us to view the service in a similar way, and we tended to have the same approach. Doctor/nurse relations in Hong Kong were much more hierarchical than our collegial approach, and we made a point of joint discussions on structure and patient care. On one occasion we took a seminar of top professionals together. I like to think we helped to break down some of the barriers between the professions. There were other sensitivities. As in many former colonies, the health service was centralised, usually with expatriates in the senior posts. This changed in time to local officers, but the service stayed centralised for many years. This was the situation in Hong Kong, and the reason for setting up the hospital authority with a new approach. It brought together the very large government and university hospitals, and the sub-vented hospitals such as the United Christian Hospitals, which had a percentage of government funding but were independent as regards management. There were also a number of private hospitals and clinics, often owned by a religious organisation or a local doctor and usually small. These were to remain outside the remit of the authority, as well as the community care side of the government health service. The latter seemed an unfortunate decision, as hospital and community health services need to be integrated if they are to give seamless care. But at the time it was felt that the reorganisation of the hospital service was more than enough to cope with.

The nursing staff of government hospitals were obviously part of the government service, with a chief nursing officer and her staff. The hospital schools of nursing were also under government management, with the exception of the universities, sub-vented hospital schools and those of independent organisations, all, however, having to follow the syllabus of the Nursing Council. There had never been a strong relationship between government nurses and the association, and I felt I was viewed with some suspicion and would not have been their choice for the group. If this was the case, it was well concealed and we worked together very well. The senior government nurses were very close to retirement, but in the meantime they were extremely helpful. We had one joint meeting of the Expert Group a year, and then one with our own disciplines, which we arranged in advance and set out our own programme. The entire exercise was helpful for the nurses' association, broadening its view and also bringing it into close contact with the nurses' union. The president of the union was an extremely able male nurse with a high standing in the profession, and later became a member of the interim legislative council before Hong Kong returned to China.

The part I played was small compared with the changes taking place, and the chief officers of the authority were outstanding, especially the chief executive, who was a medical consultant and, at the time of writing, had become the Secretary for Health. All senior posts were available for competition according to grade, and multidisciplinary management was set up. It was hard for many of the nurses to adapt, but the authority set up short but intensive training courses, and I have felt very proud of the role the nurses have played in what is now a huge and very sophisticated effective health service. I have had opportunity to observe the change on a number of occasions when I have been in the country for other programmes. On my last visit, Hong Kong was recovering from the major problems brought about by the sars virus. It was an occasion when I was also visiting Macau and China. We seemed to have a mass of health forms to complete at each airport and the health checks and system of checking temperatures were very highly organised. It was a relief when Hong Kong was declared free of the virus and the health service could return to normal working.

By this time I was involved in many more church activities and had quite a wide circle of friends with similar outlook and involvement. One of the groups which is still especially important to me is the Parish Liturgy Group. It has widened my love of singing and choir, opened my eyes to the development of the liturgy and deepened my faith, as well as giving me the stimulation of working with involved, like-minded people. My faith has always been a key part of my life, but I was now finding new depths in it.

As a church community we had been active in assisting with aid for Bosnia during that fierce nationalistic war which caused so much damage and ethnic violence on a horrific scale. The initiative arose from the concern of a young parish worker. Francis Davis was a young man with a great concern for social justice, and he was responsible for motivating the parish to give generously We raised money for lorry loads of food and other needed requirements, and Francis led the transport by road to its destination in Croatia, from where it was distributed as needed. He was supported by the parish priest and the catholic bishop of Portsmouth. After a few distributions of aid, it was decided that a small group should go over to observe the situation and see what more the parish could do to help. The group was led by Bishop Crispian Hollis, with the parish priest, Canon Nicholas France, Francis Davis and myself. Mary was desperately worried. We tried to reassure her that we were staying outside the conflict zone in Zagreb, capital of Croatia, but she was quite convinced we would all be shot. I have to admit that I had some trepidations myself, but we need not have worried; we were well looked after.

We were there for a few days and the bishop was the guest of the Bishop of Croatia in his palace, while the rest of us stayed in a very pleasant hotel nearby. We were all invited to supper with the Bishop of Zagreb, and were fascinated by the historic, round, fortress-type building dating back to the twelfth century. During the day we were looked after, and accompanied on our fact-finding travels, by a sister from the nearby convent, who was closely involved with organising and distributing relief and who had been our contact. She briefed us on the situation and organised and accompanied us on our journeys by minibus through parts of Bosnia. In those few days we saw sights which shocked us deeply and heard first-hand accounts from victims who had horrific stories to tell.

Each day began with mass celebrated by the Bishop, before we set off on our programme. On one morning the Bishop decided to delay the celebration of mass until our first stop, which was a badly wrecked hospital, which had been plundered but was providing a refuge where a lot of very old women, whose homes had been destroyed, were sheltering. They had lost everything. Mass was to be celebrated in a nearby hall, mainly used for the service of meals to the refugees and, when it started, first one or two, and then a large number of women crept in quietly and fearfully. It was one of the most moving episodes of the tour. After mass we visited the wrecked hospital and were surrounded by refugees telling us their stories. One of the features which shocked us was their description of their neighbours and friends turning on them, killing the men and destroying their homes. While in Bosnia we also visited temporary camps and new housing being erected. We saw one large hospital and were shocked by the number of children there without one or more limbs, mainly due to mines having been laid indiscriminately. Near the frontier there was a large psychiatric hospital full of war victims in serious states of psychiatric illness, and we stood at one frontier crossing point and spoke to the sentries on duty, who warned us to move back because of the activity by weekend snipers. We were also privileged to have an interview with the vice-president of Croatia, who gave us a chilling account of the damage done to Bosnia and the size of the reconstruction required.

We returned to the UK feeling almost ashamed of the peace and comparatively luxurious life we lead at home. We redoubled our efforts to send the aid required and the materials to help with reconstruction. Over the years and in the midst of the conflict and terrorism around us, the memories of the bitter fighting and the other atrocities have receded, small in the context of the major conflicts of today. It was very bitter and, as we were told so often, atrocities broke out in peaceful villages, neighbour turned on neighbour and families on their own kith and kin. It was an unforgettable experience which remains with me. Last year, on a very short visit to Dubrovnic, while exploring the town I came across an exhibition which brought it all back. It is good to know that peace has overcome the conflict, injuries and poverty, but the scars will remain in the hearts of those who suffered for a very long time.

Soon after my return, Dame Kathleen Raven contacted me to ask for my assistance in her dream of setting up a chair in clinical nursing at her own alma mater, the General Infirmary at Leeds. Dame Kathleen was quite a legendary figure to me, as I had known her from afar in my days as a ward sister, when she was the Chief Nursing Officer of the Department of Health. After she retired to her beautiful home near Wing, she continued to take a great interest in nursing affairs. She set up an Annual Lecture at the Royal College of Nursing, and I was privileged to present one of the early lectures. She was passionate about the art of nursing and the importance of good practical care, and it followed naturally that she should want to set up a chair to recognise the value of nursing and its good practitioners. She had been twice to Leeds for talks with the vice-chancellor and all was set in place to recruit the right nurse. Unfortunately, she was no longer able to travel to Leeds for the appointment and asked me to go in her stead. I had to make more than one journey but eventually we made an appointment of Professor Claire Hale, and we were able to meet Dame Kathleen, who was delighted that the chair had been established. Sadly, Dame Kathleen died very soon after the meeting. It was a great loss to nursing and to those of us who knew and loved her well.

While I was Executive Director of the International Council of Nurses and just before a board meeting, we had a strange letter from Christiane Reimann, who could be said to be the very first general secretary of ICN. She was a Danish nurse who owned an estate in Sicily, to which she had retired to live, and she was a very old lady. The letter invited the president, then Alice Girard, and me to visit her and to discuss her offer to leave her estate and fortune to ICN for a special award. We duly set off after the board meeting and were met at the airport by Christiane Reimann herself, very old but absolutely clear about what she wanted to do. We stayed as her guests in her large and historic villa in the midst of an extensive orange grove, which she owned together with other orange and lemon groves. The house itself was very old and somewhat eerie, not too surprising when we realised that the remains of an ancient cemetery were in the garden. We talked about Miss Reimann's wishes for the gift, and she told us that she wanted to set up a 'Nobel prize for nursing', as she described it. We discussed it as far as possible and returned to Geneva to report to the board. Negotiations continued for some years, and agreement was finally reached a number of years before Miss Reimann died. By that time I was a member of the ICN board, and a small committee of three eminent nurses was set up to make the choice of the first recipient of the award. To our delight it was Virginia Henderson, then well into her eighties, known and beloved throughout the world. It was a tremendously popular choice, and a cause of great celebration at the presentation ceremony at the congress in Seoul in 1985. The second recipient was another well-known and popular international nurse, Nita Barrow of Barbados, who had the distinction of becoming the Governor General of her country.

After leaving the ICN board in 1985, I had no further formal connection, but obviously remained a very interested spectator of ICN's progress, and participated in the international meetings. One day in early summer, I had just returned home from a weekend speaking engagement in Scotland when the phone rang. It was Connie Holleran, who gave me the astounding news that the ICN board had just approved the recommendation of the Reimann committee that I be the recipient of the award for 1993 and it would be presented to me at the forthcoming congress in Madrid. Mary came in a few minutes later to find me in a state of mild shock, and then the phone calls began, led by Trevor Clay and Bob Tiffany, who were on the ICN board at the time. We decided to have a small party of close friends to celebrate, and it was a delightful occasion.

The prize was a considerable amount of money and it seemed logical to donate a large part of it to ICN and also to the RCN to help visiting nurses from less wealthy countries. Then I persuaded both Mary and Bega to come with me to the congress in Madrid. It was a wonderful week, with ICN having a banquet in my honour and the RCN holding an evening party for all the large number of British participants and friends from other countries, when the RCN Fellows presented me with a most beautiful framed address. The presentation itself occurred at the final spectacular closing ceremony. Apart from the beautiful brooch to be worn on special nursing occasions, a figurine of a Danish nurse in Copenhagen porcelain is presented with the award, to remind recipients of its Danish origin. It is a treasured possession, which I can see from my desk while working.

Madrid was one of the high points of my life, but was to be followed by many months of great sadness with the loss of my closest friends. Robert Tiffany, or Bob as he was known to his friends, was very much in the forefront in European and international work, and the chief nurse of the Marsden Hospital, world renowned for its role in the treatment of cancer. Bob was very much a leader in the overall work going on in nursing, but he was passionate about his own speciality, cancer care. He was a great ambassador and a faithful friend. We had worked together for many years, and it was with surprise that we heard of his early retirement. At the time he was on the ICN board, and the last conversation I had with him was when he phoned to congratulate me on the Reimann award. Only weeks later I heard he was seriously ill in hospital, followed very soon by the devastating news of his death. It was a shattering blow to the profession, both as an outstanding leader and a very dear friend. We still miss him, his humour and no longer hearing him say 'I think you're wonderful' or 'Quite right, love.' He touched more lives in a positive way than anyone else I know. The church was packed for his funeral, with Marsden staff from near and far. There was hardly a dry eye in the congregation and, as I stood on the steps of the church waiting for the hearse to depart, I was aware of the great grief-stricken atmosphere. I doubt we shall see his like again. A few months later there was a memorial service, again with a packed church, crowded with friends, especially his international colleagues, who could not be at the funeral. The very moving address was given by his personal and professional friend, Trevor Clay, the general secretary of the Royal College of Nursing. I was devastated at being unable to attend, as I was on one of the multi-disciplinary visits to Hong Kong.

New Orleans had become my second home, with visits every year over a long period of time, sometimes accompanied by Mary when she was well enough. Joel's friends, as typical Americans, were among the most friendly and hospitable people it has been my pleasure to meet. Southern hospitality is quite famous, and rightly so. Joel had spent so many years in India working on the US AID programme that her heart was there. It was also the place where I first met her at the Nursing Congress in Delhi. She had told me that she was returning to India to stay with the friends she had made there and whom she regarded as her second family. I was not too worried at first when there was no answer to her home telephone, but after a few days I phoned again and a strange voice answered. It was one of her close friends, who told me that Joel had returned from India gravely ill and was in hospital. I followed this up with one of her friends and discovered that she had an inoperable malignancy, but was returning home with a live-in carer.

After discussion with her friends, and at Joel's request, I went over to visit her and was very upset at the situation. The carer was excellent; Joel also had support from a visiting specialist nurse and her friends rallied round her, but Joel herself could not come to terms with the situation and was intensely angry. She had a superb young doctor, who visited frequently and was a great help and friend to her. She had a relapse while I was there and my flight home had to be postponed for a few days until the situation was clearer. On phoning Mary with the news, she told me that Trevor Clay had just died, two weeks after a heart transplant. She had been holding the news until my return but, with the delay, she felt she had to tell me. Joel rallied and I returned after another few days, as Mary's state of health was such that I did not like to leave her alone for too long. It was not an easy homecoming. Mary was distressed and shocked at Trevor's death. Like so many nurses, she saw him as a superb leader and a very fine person, with the best of his career ahead of him. There was not too much time to talk, because the RCN congress was in progress at Bournemouth and, as I knew there would be much shock and grief at the news about Trevor, I just went down for the day. The atmosphere was as if the whole of congress was in a state of shock. Christine and the president, Maude Storey, were trying to carry on with the week's events, but no one's heart was in it. The actual funeral was only attended by the family and a few very close friends. I left as soon as possible and went home. Mary admitted she didn't feel very well, and didn't look it, so the doctor was called. He put her on antibiotics and she retired to bed. I was pretty tired myself by this time, so thankfully also retired to bed but woke in the middle of the night. Going in to check on Mary, I found her very restless and in some discomfort. Early in the morning I called the doctor again and he came straight out, diagnosed pneumonia and admitted her to hospital as an emergency. After that the events of the next few weeks were of nightmare quality.

Mary went downhill rapidly and descended into a restless and agitated semi-coma, and in spite of all possible care went into kidney failure. She was in the Royal South Hants Hospital, the smaller of the two general hospitals in Southampton, which of course I knew well. The nurses were superb, and I remained with Mary throughout ten days and nights, as she gradually drifted from life. My close friends and the local priest were an enormous support, relieving me from time to time, and I was able to stay with Mary throughout. However, because she was in coma, there was no opportunity really to say goodbye. Dialysis was suggested, but Mary had always felt strongly about treatments of last resort and had left a note in her papers to that effect. I went along with her wishes but it was an extremely testing time. Eventually, Mary just slipped quietly away and I returned home to cope with the aftermath and try to return to normality. Bega Hood had already come down from Cumbria to assist me, and I notified Mary's friends and relatives, talked to our local priest and prepared for Mary's funeral. I went to see her one last time. We then brought her into church on the evening before her funeral. It was the feast of Pentecost, Whit Sunday, and we waited with the hearse for the church to empty following the evening mass. The children had gifts and balloons and it seemed quite wrong to be grieving. Then we took Mary into church and, after a very short informal ceremony of reception and a few prayers, I was able to stay with her for some time, before leaving her in front of the altar in the quiet and darkened church.

Mary's cousins and friends arrived for the service next day, and we followed her wishes with her favourite hymns, continued to the crematorium, and then said goodbye to the friends and relatives at home. Bega remained until the next day and was a great support, but, as we were preparing to go to the station, the phone rang. It was Joel's doctor from New Orleans to tell me that the end was very near. A neighbour offered to see Bega off and I booked the next flight. Although I left within hours, I wasn't in time to say goodbye to her and remained for the funeral next day, staying with a friend of Joel's who was extremely kind. I experienced the American way of death and, although it seemed strange to me, it was exactly as Joel herself had requested and all was beautifully done. I was very touched when we arrived at the Funeral Home for the service to find Joel's doctor waiting to talk to me. I was unable to change my flight home, so spent two days with one of Joel's closest friends and helped to clear the house I had come to know so well. Apart from my family and Mary, Joel had been the person closest to me, and we also shared much professionally. Her death left a large gap, and though I had many invitations from her friends to visit and be their house guest, I have not been able to bring myself to visit New Orleans again. It held too many precious memories.

I travelled home to a flat which seemed strangely quiet and lonely, as I began to come to terms with Mary's death. Our cat, Fred, had been very much Mary's cat, and I was afraid he would be distressed at her absence, but he adopted me, slept at the foot of my bed and appeared quite settled. It was not easy to cope with him, being out during the day, and often away for two or three weeks at a time. He was used to a cat door and, with the help of friends who looked after him while I was away, and others who came to stay with him from time to time, I managed to keep him. It was a real blow when he died about three years later, of old age and kidney failure at the age of twenty years. It seemed the last link with Mary and the flat was very empty. We had chosen a ground floor flat, as it was easier for Mary but, because of my frequent absences, I now looked for one higher up and was fortunate to be able to buy one on the top floor of the next block. It was a wise move, but it did finish any question of having another cat.

Chapter 11

Charities, Home and Abroad

LIFE SEEMED as full as ever but, as the Hong Kong programme ended after a busy five years, my international work also seemed to be drawing to a close. It had not been easy to adapt to living alone and, after Fred's death, I would have loved to have another animal. However, it wasn't practical, especially when I moved to the top floor. My new apartment was much more spacious, which was quite important, as being completely free lance as regarded work, I had to create a home office.

Just after my retirement from the Health Service, Sir Ronald Gibson of Winchester wrote to invite me to join the board of a newly-established charity for older people called Brendoncare. I knew Sir Ronald only by reputation as a former president of the General Medical Council and of the Society of General Practitioners, and had never met him. Brendoncare was an organisation he had founded in 1984. He felt very strongly about the care of older people, and was convinced that they were often let down by the institutions which looked after them. His vision of a home was one which would accept people at the point of need, whether physical or social, and would be a home for life, whatever happened to the individual's circumstances. It sounded intriguing, but I had only just retired, needed time to adjust, and was still heavily committed with the Royal College of Nursing and ICN. However, I was drawn to the idea which was so different to various care homes I had seen, and we arranged to meet at Brendon, a home in Winchester from where Sir Ronald had developed his philosophy. Unfortunately, he was unwell, but the development officer met me, answered all my questions, showed me the home and spoke of its philosophy. I had seen too much of care which fell short of the individual's need, but this was different and I decided to accept Sir Ronald's offer.

In those early days board meetings were usually held in London at the Royal Society of Medicine or other suitable location. I felt decidedly a 'fish out of water', as the board seemed to be composed entirely of eminent doctors. One rather strange custom was to start the meeting with a glass of sherry and drink the health of the Queen Mother, who had graciously accepted to become our Patron; and then one full glass was left in the middle of the table. At the end of the meeting it was to be drunk by any member who had not spoken during the discussions. I made sure to make some comment, however slight, to escape that embarrassment. Sir Ronald was extremely persuasive, or I would have backed out there and then, but the doctors eventually dropped out one by one, and a multidisciplinary group began to emerge, one of whom was Professor Michael Hall, whom I knew well as the first consultant for elderly care at Southampton. The small staff were also very friendly and informative. So my connection with Brendoncare began. It has survived more than twelve years and and I am now vice-chair of the board and chair the care committee. A well-known surgeon, Harvey White, succeeded Sir Ronald as chair and has carried the organisation through various crises to become the successful and forward-looking organisation it is today. Sir Ronald kept in close contact after he resigned as chair, would attend my nursing meetings when he could, and was quite sure that any Brendoncare Home should be managed and run by the head nurse, with doctors, administrators and other key personnel in support. This is the situation we have today and it is a principle we hold very dear as one of the keystones of our philosophy.

To be a member of the board in the early days was quite a rollercoaster experience, as we had very little money, and were trying to put the bricks and mortar of a home into place with little more than enthusiasm and a driving desire to test our philosophy. We did have a model in the home in Winchester set up by the Brendon Nursing Trust, which had followed Sir Ronald's philosophy of care, while remaining a separate trust. It was quite a pilgrimage in those days, following up leads which didn't quite come off, or seeing opportunities which never fulfilled their early promise. But eventually things began to happen. A small residential home in Exeter run by the Soroptimist organisation was proving too much for them and it was offered to Brendoncare. It is a small home without a lot of ground, but it has had a lot of improvement, a superb Head of Home (or matron), a staff second to none, and has gained a high reputation for care. The Duchess of Somerset Hospital Charity in Froxfield near Hungerford, Wiltshire, in conjunction with Sir Seaton Wills, offered us land and, with grants and a frightening loan, our first 'new build' appeared. Next came The Old Parsonage at Otterbourne near Winchester, at first an elevenbed residential home to which a twenty-four bed nursing wing was added. The paddock next door was acquired for twenty-two 'close care' dwellings. There is a lot of sharing and communication between the two communities and, with the gardens around the total complex, it is a delightful home.

Then in South London a small hospital for elderly chronically sick patients was closed and we were offered a site in the grounds of a psychiatric hospital nearby with a contract to care for these patients. So Ronald Gibson House brought us into the London area. Next, there was a similar opportunity in Stone, near Aylesbury, where a large mental hospital was closing. We named this home Chiltern View because of its lovely views. We also took on the staff as well as the patients and soon found out who was the most institutionalised.

With five homes and very tight finances, the trustees took stock of the situation. We had in our new Chief Executive, Ron Staker, an able and professional entrepreneur, and together we had seen a home with a complex of close care housing, were intrigued with the concept and saw it as a possible way forward. When the building of another new home came up, we put our views forward. This time the possibility of the new building came about through a local initiative in Alton, Hampshire called the Mary Rose Trust. It was too large a project for the local group; they turned to us, and we were offered a piece of land, due to the closure of the small local hospital.

This seemed ideal for our concept of a central home with a curtilage of attractive flats, but a number of board members, especially the financial experts, thought this was a 'bridge too far'. Not to be discouraged, Ron and I went into battle for our ideal and, in all fairness to the board, they finally agreed on the concept, notwithstanding a great deal of concern. In fact, as the scheme progressed, with all its setbacks, the successful sale of those apartments went a long way to help with paying for the building. It was just as well, because we did have a lot of problems in the early stages. Finances were so tight that we had reluctantly to shrink the size of the building to fit the budget and we were able to open only two of the three wings. They were still well-designed and furnished and allowed us to develop the Brendoncare philosophy from the start. Then, with the help of a large legacy, the third wing for psychiatric patients was opened. We had also allowed for a large day care provision, but this was never used to the full, and it was a mistake we would not repeat. Serious financial problems were made worse by the acute nursing shortage of recent years. At last, however, we seem to have turned the corner, and we have taken a few groups of Filipino nurses, giving them the adaptation programme to enable them to be placed on the UK Register. Alton is now becoming the leading nursing home we had envisaged it should be.

About the same time we were discussing Alton, another small charity, with a beautiful old house in East Grinstead used for elderly people, approached us with a view to our taking over the home. It was set in lovely grounds, but the house was difficult for its residents, and it was becoming more costly to maintain than the trustees could afford. Our budget was very much under strain with the building of Alton, and we could not afford to spend a lot of money on conversions. It was eventually agreed to accept the gift but we knew we would have to wait some years before we could contemplate a new building. The residents were quite happy with that decision. They were very fond of their lovely, inconvenient home and had no wish to move to a modern building. Eventually, in 2003, a large grant was given to us by another charity and we managed to find the rest. The new build started alongside the old in the extensive grounds, and the day eventually arrived for the old house to come down and the residents to move into the one wing of the new home. They were sad to see their old home with its happy memories go, but all of them now tell us that the new home is even better. Along with the continued building of the second wing, some close care apartments have been built, and although they have only just come on the market, they show every sign of being as successful as the Alton apartments.

Care in the community is also changing rapidly; the growth of housing associations has provided very many older people with the pleasure of their own secure apartment. Over the years managers have realised that more care is needed for people living in this type of apartment. This would release space in what used to be large homes for elderly care, and at the same time provide older people with new accommodation to allow them to live independent lives. Sir Ronald would certainly agree with us. As with most active organisations, once we have a home established we tend to take stock and think in terms of the future tense. Life does not go on for ever, but our philosophy is to maintain independence and active living for as long as possible. We have begun to think about smaller central homes with more apartments suitable for close care. We believe it is not just a matter of treating illness and infirmity, but of trying to prolong activity and wellness for as long as possible. I might even see the next phase. I do hope so.

Our Heads of Home, all registered nurses with a high degree of organisational ability, are the key to the success of Brendoncare. They need highly skilled support from administrators, planners, finance officers, caterers and many other people to help them run happy and successful homes. Like all buildings, the homes need extensions, repair and innovations, and money is always a worry. Brendoncare was fortunate to attract a brilliant small group to steer a fundraising programme over a few years and they were able to raise considerable monies to allow each home to have badly needed developments and extensions. We are just at the end of this programme, and it has given all the homes the opportunity to take more residents and to offer even better facilities.

Brendoncare has taken a lot of my time and interest over a decade and it is good to see so much work and hope of a large number of people come to fruition. Sir Ronald always said there should be a Brendoncare Home in every town, and while we can't achieve that goal, we like to believe that we have changed the lives of many for the better when they needed our help.

Running almost alongside my work with Brendoncare but starting a few years later was my work with the Southampton Care Association, now known as SCA. It started with our young parish social worker, Francis Davis, who organised the parish contribution to Bosnia and our fact-finding visit there during the conflict. He had involved the parish in a number of community projects, and we had a small group to coordinate them, which I was asked to chair. Francis and I became very involved with some of the projects, and one day he asked if he could introduce me to someone who was starting an organisation in Southampton. I agreed and was introduced to an Anglican clergyman working in the field of social care. He was not like any other clergyman I have met. Reverend Brian Strevens was a real entrepreneur who, like Francis, had a great sense of social justice. His dream was to set up a local organisation which could give good care in the community in and around Southampton with the help of contracts from Social Services. He was working out of a small office lent by Social Services, had one contract with social services, some day care centres, an assistant and two or three like-minded people, such as Francis and myself, and Jonathan Farrow, who was involved in residential care for young people. That was in 1991. Today, not much more than twelve years later, SCA stretches its services the length of the M27, between Portsmouth and Bournemouth, but is centred on Southampton. It occupies space in three different offices and is leasing a new build to house the staff in one place. A glance at its index of services includes day care, community transport, domiciliary care, mental health support and 'welcome home from hospital', to name but a few. A small central staff and a few hundred care staff are employed, and both the work and staff are growing steadily.

When we met in Southampton those few years ago none of us, except perhaps Brian, could have foreseen the growth. We set up a not-for-profit, businesslike organisation with charitable status, to deliver community care. We started a venture to meet a need, and we are still stretching ourselves to meet that need, which is growing faster than we can keep up with it. We were not even sure how the organisation would develop, and although we have had some disappointments and made some mistakes, the growth and achievements of SCA have gone way beyond our expectations. I chaired the organisation for the first five years of its life, was then followed by Jonathan Farrow for the next three, and Francis Davis, now a family man with four children, has taken over as chairman.

Brian Strevens had always kept SCA involved in training, and a large proportion of our care work force is training for National Vocational Qualifications (NVQs). Training Centres are scattered and no one organisation is specifically devoted to the caring service. Brian's idea was to set up a partner organisation devoted to NVQ training for the care sector, and also to have the facility for research and consultancy services. It was to be independent of SCA, although much of the membership was common to both organisations.

At the time I had had a particularly heavy year with overseas work and had missed one or two meetings. It was with disbelief, therefore, that I opened mail one morning halfway through 2002 to read a letter formally announcing the setting up of the centre, and informing me of a unanimous decision of the board to name it 'The Quinn Centre', and asking for my formal permission. I seem to remember picking up the phone to Brian and saying bluntly, 'You're crazy!' which simply brought a chuckle at the other end. After the first shock, and realising that the board really wanted it that way, I agreed, and became even more embarrassed when I saw the formal announcements going out with introductory leaflets and a résumé of my career. I did ask wherever they had found all the detail, to which the amused reply was 'the internet'. We had two launches, one at the House of Commons new complex of meeting rooms, hosted by MP Alan Whitehead, where the gathering included some of my Brendoncare friends. The other was in Southampton, where the centre is currently based in the new Third Age Centre, and the reception was graced by the Lord Lieutenant of Hampshire, Mrs Mary Fagan. Only a few weeks ago we had the pleasure of a reception to present certificates to the first carers to achieve NVQ level two at the Centre. I am still on the SCA board and delight in the expanding community care. It is so badly needed and we could do with many more SCAs around the country, but that would need more Brian Strevens, and he is unique!

It was during this period that another close friend and colleague died. Catherine Hall, or Mary as she was known to her friends, was the person that I met when I commenced the Sister Tutor course at the Royal College of Nursing, and we used to walk through Hyde Park to the college together each day. We came together again when Mary became general secretary of the College, and I was with the International Council of Nurses. During the ten years before her retirement, I was on council, then office holder and finally president. We worked together very closely and knew each other well. After retirement Mary lived in Buckfastleigh, so we did not see each other very often. The news of her serious illness came as a great shock. Although she was seeing few visitors, she said she would like to see me, and I went to visit her in the local hospice. She was obviously very near death, but was as lucid as ever. We both knew the situation and didn't waste time with social talk. We talked of her faith, which was very great, and her attitude to death. I remember her saying she knew she was dying and, if one believed in eternal life, there was no point in trying to delay it a matter of a few days or even weeks. When it was time to leave, I got up to say goodbye, hardly knowing how to speak, but she looked up at me, smiled and quoted Thomas More – 'till we meet merrily in heaven'. I couldn't do more than bend to kiss her and say 'Goodbye', and somehow I got out of the room with a smile for her.

Some months later the college had a memorial service for Mary in the Chapel of the British Empire in the crypt of St Paul's Cathedral, as she was a Dame of the Order. It was packed with her friends and colleagues and many senior officials with whom she had worked in her long career. I had been asked to give an address about Mary's life and I spent a long time in preparation. It was extremely hard to speak when the time came, but I finished with the words of Mary's farewell to me. Her grave is in the peaceful cemetery of Buckfast Abbey, in a plot which looks directly on to the Abbey Church. I would like to think I had the same strength of faith that enabled Mary to face death with such serenity and certitude of eternal life.

The new millennium coincided with my eightieth birthday in September. I had intended to let it pass quietly but, the year before, the choir startled me by presenting me with a large bouquet and wishing me a happy eightieth birthday. It threw me completely and, without thinking, I said, 'But it isn't until next year' and caused so much embarrassment that the only thing to do was to say that I would have a big party the following year on the correct date. To keep my promise I booked the church hall for a lunch after the 11a.m. mass on the Saturday, and the choir promised a sung mass with my choice of music. I was then abroad for a short holiday and came back to find a letter from the parish priest to say that he had invited the bishop to celebrate the mass, and the bishop intended to present me with a diocesan medal. My original hopes of keeping it quiet had gone out of the window, and it was just a question of being gracious about it. So I invited my cousins and close friends and decided we might as well make an occasion of it and enjoy the celebrations. In fact, it turned out to be one of the happiest and most moving occasions of my life. With having special friends over, we also had two extra dinner parties to accommodate everyone, and the house overflowed with flowers for a week.

I thought I had left work with the Red Cross behind me, although I accepted an invitation to become a trustee member of the Hampshire branch. It was not a very demanding assignment, but during my period of office, the very long-serving and greatly loved Betty (Elizabeth) Balfour retired. She had served as director for a very long time, and change was inevitable. One applicant for the post stood out from the rest – John Derben, who had a history of long involvement with the Scout organisation, and he was appointed. I resigned as trustee some few years after his appointment, and was surprised one morning to have him on the telephone. 'Sheila,' he said, 'I want your help.'

'What for?' I countered warily, and he went on to tell me that, with a recent reorganisation, the Red Cross were divesting themselves of their clubs for the elderly, as not being a core activity. John pointed out that many of these clubs were in Hampshire, and he would like to try to keep them operating under new management, as it were, but he needed help. I really had as much as I could cope with, but it is difficult to refuse such a request, and I agreed to act as chair for two years, if he could bring together a group of trustees. John was near retirement, and he collected a keen group of people, interested and ready to make the venture work. It was some months before all the formalities were completed; John retired and became our director and was joined by another former Red Cross officer, Edwin Ingleton. Small offices were found on the outskirts of Winchester, and Club Hampshire came into being. Our main asset was a grant from the Hampshire Social Services, and we had a very small subscription from each club member, but that still left an income gap which we endeavour to fill with fundraising. We have managed to take on four new clubs as well as almost doubling the membership of the existing clubs, and are now into our second year. The organisation is not yet on a firm enough footing, but it is moving in the right direction and we have faith that this will continue.

However, not all ventures are successful, and one that turned out to be very disappointing was the attempt to start an international organisation called Action in International Medicine, the brainchild of a well-known doctor, Sir Gordon Wolstenholme. He had worked for one of the major international companies in health care in a number of the poorer developing countries, and in his retirement wished to set up an organisation of doctors and other health personnel to help. I was one of the nurses he asked to join. It survived for a few years supported by Sir Gordon's friends and colleagues, and originally there was some modest funding. A part-time director was recruited, and work was carried out from a small office in London, but support and finance dwindled.

On one of Sir Gordon's visits to New York, he passed an address which seemed familiar, and he remembered it was the office of an American colleague, who was the director of a charity called the Dreyfus Health Foundation (DHF). They had a long conversation and felt that the two organisations could cooperate. The director, Dr Barry Smith, came over to London on a number of occasions, and we cooperated in an international workshop in Cape Coast, Ghana. I was one of the last to arrive, travelled alone and arrived early in the morning in Accra to be greeted by a young doctor as we had to stay overnight in Accra before continuing to Cape Coast the next morning. Also waiting, and just off the plane, was the director of finance for DHF, Lenin Gross. Our cases were eventually cleared, and we were escorted to a nearby hotel. It looked delightful even in the small hours of the morning, but we had little time to assess it as we were to set off by car to Cape Coast at 5a.m., less than four hours away. My case arrived but, as the locks were broken and toiletries missing and scattered, sleep eluded me and I was ready and waiting long before departure time. My companion, the finance director, was a large man with strong spectacles, and appeared to be a man of few words. The four-hour drive looked as if it was going to be fairly uncomfortable and rather dreary. The car was not exactly new and the driver monosyllabic. He turned to my companion and announced, 'We need petrol. You pay.' That had the effect of sending both of us into fits of laughter, which broke the ice. Once Lenin had sorted out the petrol situation, we had a most entertaining journey. For the next few years, Lenin was the leader of most of the workshops in which I participated; he had a great sense of humour and was a very congenial person to work with. The director of AIM and I participated in the Cape Coast workshop, but once back home we could not escape the fact that finance was the major problem of AIM and was not adequate to maintain the office, staff and a programme.

The small executive committee met and reluctantly decided that the only way forward was to wind up the charity. It was not an easy decision to take and quite unpleasant to carry through, with all the legalities of winding up a charity, closing the office and sorting out the finances. Dr Smith and the Dreyfus Foundation gave a lot of support and understanding and asked me to continue to assist them with their workshops, which were held in a number of countries throughout the world. I was only too glad to accept the offer and have continued to be involved since 1997.

In some ways the Cape Coast workshop was different from the other workshops in which I began to participate. The latter were mainly for doctors and medical students in the early days of my work with DHF, but became multi-disciplinary. Dr Smith expressed his wish to help the nurses, many of whom had not had a very wide professional education, and whose function and status needed a great deal of improvement. He felt that some workshops could be restricted to nurses and that they should be encouraged to carry out projects relevant to their work. Otherwise, the numbers of nurses compared with doctors and other health personnel meant that if they did not have their own workshops, only one or two at a time would ever be able to attend one.

Following Ghana and the demise of AIM, my first experience of working with the DHF team was in Bulgaria. It was rather an unknown country to those of us on the other side of Europe, and I did not know what to expect. I was met by the country coordinator, a university lecturer by the name of Yanka, whom I have come to know well over the years as a most able and enthusiastic leader. She spoke perfect English and was a prodigious worker. She also had the knack of squeezing the most out of every workshop and the limited time available. Now I look upon Bulgaria as a well-loved country to visit and have had one or two workshops there every year.

Poland and Romania followed, first with multidisciplinary health personnel, and later we again organised some workshops solely for nurses. Jan Sobotka, of the Polish Society of Hygiene, was the Polish organiser, and is now the coordinator for Europe, and was a most able and likeable person to work with. Nurse education in the various countries of Eastern Europe was very different to our own in the UK, but more importantly it differed from the rest of Europe. This was important, because most of the countries were working towards EU membership, and some have just been accepted. A lot of effort is required to bring the nurse education in those countries up to the level agreed in the EU. The position of the nurse and her professional status and work differ greatly among the various countries. Lithuania came along somewhat later than the other countries mentioned, and I have been involved once a year in multidisciplinary workshops in the lovely city of Vilnius. Mid-December seems to be the time we arrive there, usually with snow, biting cold and early darkness. We are all enchanted with the old town and its beautiful buildings and churches, and experience temperatures as low as minus eighteen degrees. We particularly enjoy their 'hot wine' in those circumstances, and our hosts offer great companionship and delight in introducing us to their culture.

The only Indian workshop I attended was in Trivandrum, and it was strange to return some thirty years after the visit made for the ICN. The nurses' home where I had stayed looked much the same from the outside, and the hospital did not appear to have altered very much; the work going through it looked just as hectic. We were working in the university with nurses at the final part of their Masters degree. They were very beautiful and able girls, but they all declared their intention of working abroad as soon as they finished their degree.

While at a workshop in Bulgaria, Alex Papillaya joined the facilitators. He was the head of the department for family welfare at the University of Indonesia, a beautiful new university in a lovely setting outside Jakarta. Here we had workshops for multidisciplinary personnel, and separate ones for nurses. We had close contact with the nursing faculty and the workshops were run very efficiently. We also travelled to other towns in Indonesia, and to other islands. Two places stand out among the others in my memory. One was the fascinating city of Yogyakarta, seat of the Sultan who was also the Governor. We enjoyed the Sultan's Palace and its lovely grounds, and were awestruck by the massive Buddhist temple of Borobudur at one side of the city, and the no less beautiful Hindu temple at Prambanam. It was difficult to take in so much beauty and culture in such a short space of time and place. The Prambanam temple was our last stop, and we sat near the ruins and watched a brilliant sunset slip down behind the towers of the temple. Then we came down to earth in the dark as we searched for the right car park in which to locate our car and sleepy driver.

Another visit was in Sumatra where we took a long, winding drive up a mountain and through rain forest, to a heavily populated village We stayed in the beautiful house of the governor, while we visited some projects and had a review meeting to discuss ongoing and completed projects. Indonesia is such a beautiful country that it is not difficult to fall in love with it. It is my good fortune to go over usually once a year for a workshop, and site visits. The coordinator, Alex Papillaya, always finds something new of special interest and rare beauty to show us at the end of a workshop.

China is another huge country with a wonderful history and culture. As we drove back to our hotel in one of the large cities, the lights, huge shopping malls, MacDonalds and other fast food restaurants made us feel it could have been in any similar city in the west. I was glad to have seen this fascinating country in the early 1980s, when hotels were not too comfortable, the Friendship stores our shopping mecca, streets were full of bicycles, and the Chinese culture and mystery were all around us. We had very successful nursing workshops in the Faculty of Nursing at the Peking University Medical College (PUMC), the first university in the country to have a nursing degree course, and it is a joy to return each year. Some of the other early workshops were in the cities of the south west, Chengdhu, Nanning and Kumming. The last named is the one which remains in my memory because of the weather. It is named the city of Eternal Spring, but on the morning we were about to depart for the airport, we awoke to a curious quiet. There was a thick blanket of snow everywhere, the first in anyone's memory. Everything was at a standstill, including the airport. After a very inactive twenty-four hours, we were told we could head for the airport, but on arrival our hopes were dashed at the sight of buildings overflowing with people and very little activity. Some ten hours later our flight was called, but after embarking we sat for another three hours. Suddenly the patient Chinese became angry, and after the air hostess failed to calm them, the captain came down to talk. We were interested spectators, and so was a TV cameraman who happened to be aboard and decided to take advantage of a news story. Then we were asked to get off and identify our luggage, and got back again for another wait. And then, like something out of *Doctor Zhivago*, we saw a long stream of muffled figures carrying large cases, tramping along the snow-covered ground heading for our plane. They climbed on and, regardless of regulations, dumped their luggage as near to their seats as possible. Finally we took off, all of us listening with some concern while the heavily-laden plane trundled down the runway and, with a great effort, heaved itself into the air at the airport perimeter. We arrived in Beijing around 3a.m. cold and tired, to a vast and empty airport, and fell into taxis, which took us to the world-renowned Beijing Palace Hotel. As I got into bed, I reflected on the high cost of the rooms and the fact that we would have only three hours in them before we moved on to our next commitment.

On the most recent occasion we were in China, we stopped for a workshop in Macau. I had visited Macau many years ago when in Hong Kong, and at the time was taken round the small hospital where Sun Yat Sen was a young doctor. I was amazed at the development of Macau generally, but the same statue of Sun Yat Sen was still at the door of the hospital. It was a much bigger and very new hospital and the nursing school was similarly transformed. The nurses were still the same delightful young people such as the ones I had met some thirty years ago. It was a very happy three days' workshop we held there. We had travelled to Macau from Beijing and, when boarding for the next flight to Nanning, were stopped and told we needed another visa. We had all independently made the same error. Knowing that Hong Kong and Macau were now part of China, we had obtained a single-entry visa, but discovered that we required a multi-visit visa to move back and forth between the two administrative regions and mainland China. There was consternation, as we were expected in the early evening and were starting a workshop the next morning. We approached the China Travel Service for help, and they not only took new photographs and filled in visa forms, but did so with broad smiles and pleasure in being helpful. We had the new visas in four hours, were able to get seats on a charter flight and arrived in Nanning that evening in time to fulfil our commitments.

While I write these words I am just organising my tickets to return to Ndola in Zambia for another nursing workshop. We are in the middle of a very cold snap with a short but very sharp blizzard last night which left snow and icy roads and it will be good to exchange our winter for some warmth and sun. The programme for the rest of the year is not yet finalised, and it tends to unroll as the months come along. I look forward particularly to meeting my colleagues from Eastern Europe again, and perhaps Alex in the beautiful land of Indonesia. Maybe there will be the pleasure of seeing our colleagues at the PUMC Faculty of Nursing in Beijing, and revisiting some of the other cities for workshops. There is much to look forward to, and much to reflect upon.

It is interesting to look back across the years and see the thread which runs through them. It seems logical and in some respects planned. Yet one knows that the planning relies on the circumstances at the time, and very little seems a clear-cut choice when moves are made. I've been very conscious of the part that a number of people have played in my life and especially when the way forward seemed unclear. Some, I think, would be surprised to know how important they were to me – a secondary school teacher, one of the sisters at the convent where I was educated, a special ward sister, the matron of the Prince of Wales's Hospital, a particular hospital chaplain, a local parish priest, an eminent preacher, a world famous nurse; the list could go on. I owe a great deal to all of them. There are also places which stand out, and the one I remember particularly is Lourdes in France. It is a place of pilgrimage, but for me it is a place of prayer and renewal, and one to which I often return and am never disappointed. But most of all I am indebted to my faith. It was passed on to me as an infant, nurtured through my schooldays and became part of my profession. Except during the turbulence of young adulthood, it has grown and strengthened over the years. And if the years ahead seem short in comparison with those which have gone by, I know I can look forward to the end of this life with the same confidence with which I have lived these past decades. While I am delighted to be able to go on with work, I am very conscious that the sands are running out, and it's almost time to unpack.

Index